Praise for *Power Quest: Book One—America's Obsession with the Paranormal*

"I knew early on, when he richly profiled the diabolical and influential occultist Houston Stewart Chamberlain, that Doug Woodard had hit a home-run with **Power Quest**. *This important book, which provides so much background for understanding why our society is disintegrating, is one I will keep on a nearby shelf so that I can refer to it often. And Chamberlain's profile is just a fraction of the amazing information Doug has unearthed. This is one of those rare times when readers will be happy they spent hard-earned money; I think the book is that good."*

—Jim Fletcher, author *Prophecy Matters*

"Woodward presents much more than a litany of cold, hard facts—however amazing the facts may be. He provides a startling serenade of stories that spellbinds the reader. How can we believe this author's assertions? The answer of course comes from recognizing the numerous sources which support his conclusions. This isn't just one man's opinion. It is a cavalcade of authorities all testifying to the same remarkable realities of America's psychic history and how it has influenced our culture and our politics."

—Douglas Hamp, author, *Corrupting the Image*

"Doug has demonstrated courage in confronting topics most Christian authors avoid. He has done a great job intertwining history, science, and the Bible."

—Dr. Preston Bailey, author *Spiritual Warfare*
Executive Director, Spiritual Warfare Center

*"Doug Woodward's new book **Power Quest**, should be required reading by anyone interested in how the occult, and what I would call the Luciferian agenda, has influenced our culture. Woodward has certainly done his homework and his book reveals the hidden satanic mysteries that, like a deadly deceitful web, continue to ensnare those who are unaware of its presence. Bravo!"*

—L. A. Marzulli, author *The Cosmic Chess Match* and "The Watchers" series of DVDs Author, Researcher, Lecturer

"It takes balance to look into the shadowy historical crypts of... occultism and the machinations of the spiritualist elite without losing your perspective. Doug is particularly talented at exposing their schemes and making logical connections that others, following the same quest, have overlooked." (From the Foreword)

—Gary Stearman, author *Time Travelers of the Bible,* Editor, *Prophecy in the News Magazine*

"What's most troubling is the continual reference to the influences of Fascism and Nazism in America during the 20th century. After World War II, the American government (mostly in the areas of intelligence and defense) sold our soul to the devils we know as Hitler's henchmen. In case after case during the 1950s and after, Germans who were too valuable to hang and too threatening for the Russians to amass for their purposes, altered the way America built its empire. Our innocence was dashed by the esoteric minds that Bormann exported throughout the New World. The question for America to consider is, 'We will continue down the occultist power quest Woodward says covertly guides our nation?'"

—Dr. Thomas Horn, author *Apollyon Rising: 2012,* Editor and Publisher, Defender Books

What in me is dark Illumine,
what is low raise and support;
That, to the height of this great argument,
I may assert Eternal Providence,
And justify the ways of God to men.

John Milton, *Paradise Lost*

POWER QUEST

BOOK ONE

AMERICA'S OBSESSION WITH THE PARANORMAL

S. Douglas Woodward

Other Books by S. Douglas Woodward

Are We Living in the Last Days?
The Apocalypse Debate in the 21st Century

Decoding Doomsday:
*The 2012 Prophecies, the Apocalypse, and the
Perilous Days Ahead*

Black Sun, Blood Moon
Can We Escape the Cataclysms of the Last Days?

Contributing author to the following books
published by Defender Books:

Pandemonium's Engine

God's Ghostbusters

www.faith-happens.com

POWER QUEST

Book One:
America's Obsession
with the Paranormal

How our 400 year-old Fascination with Mysticism and
the Supernatural Distorted our Political Principles,
Changed our Culture, Redirected our Hope for Meaning,
and Threatens our Nation's Future

S. Douglas Woodward

FAITH HAPPENS
WOODINVILLE, WA

POWER QUEST

Book One:
America's Obsession with the Paranormal

COPYRIGHT S. DOUGLAS WOODWARD © 2011

FAITH HAPPENS
WOODINVILLE, WA 98077

ISBN-13: 978-1460907429
ISBN-10: 1460907426

PRINTED IN THE UNITED STATES OF AMERICA

TABLE OF CONTENTS

TABLE OF FIGURES

This book is dedicated to my three moms:
Rae, Ree, and Jeanne

ACKNOWLEDGEMENTS

With any historical work, the author stands on the shoulders of the others who have come before. This book is no less dependent upon many minds wiser than mine. Fortunately for me, a number of them have been willing to review and comment on this effort. Their thoughts and recommendations have made this study far more meaningful and dare I say, on point.

Throughout the past four years, I have spent a considerable amount of time reading and researching at a level far beyond what I accomplished in the four decades before. During this time I've written four books, driven in part to such a hectic level of effort by the urgency I feel as a result what is happening in our world and in particular, the United States. Devoting so much time to researching and writing means that the first thank you belongs to my family and in particular my wife Donna, for enabling my opportunity to write. Granted, she and I both would rather spend time enjoying our family, our little dogs, and sharing entertaining diversions. But she is well aware that the stakes are high in these 'interesting times' (as the Chinese proverb says)—and it is 'all hands on deck'. Her efforts underlie mine. Whatever praise I earn she shares equally.

Throughout these four years, Gary Stearman, Bob Ulrich and the members of the *Prophecy in the News* family have been a tremendous source of support, suggestions, and joint marketing. Gary and Bob believe in me and my work and do their utmost to encourage others to discover my writing. Bob always has great ideas and deserves more credit in the success of PitN ministry than many might suppose. Thank you to both of them and to Linda Church, the wife of the late and very great J.R. Church.

As a result, and in particular, I need to thank Gary Stearman for his graciousness in writing the Foreword to this volume. Gary is a great writer and perhaps one of the brightest minds I've had the good fortune to know personally. Having worked with the executives at Microsoft and Oracle earlier in my career (the reader can fill in the blanks as to who that might include), Gary takes second place to no one in intelligence, wisdom, and communication ability. Plus, he is a pleasure to engage in conversations and theological discussion when we are blessed with that experience. It is a privilege to know him and a humbling experience for him to say such kind things as he shares in the Foreword.

Another person I need to thank for his support over the past two years is Tom Horn. Tom has published two of my books, has provided critical feedback, and invested time and money into my writing. He is both a mentor and friend. I continue to seek his counsel and appreciate the chance to work with him in the smart and creative projects he originates such as *Pandemonium's Engine* and *God's Ghostbusters*. I have been fortunate to enjoy his company (not often enough, however) and receive his coaching. Plus, his writing inspires me and continues to educate. He is a brave thinker and likewise, spends a good deal of time seeking to understand what is happening in our world. His books have been ground-breaking to the discussion of 'last days', adding much to the dialogue of biblical prophecy as well as spiritual warfare. To those that haven't discovered him, it is high time you do.

Through Tom's, Gary's, and Bob's introductions, I have had the blessings to meet and get to know the many friends and scholars who provided review, comment, and additionally, were gracious enough to share their thoughts as approbations for *Power Quest*. Thanks to L.A. Marzulli, Dr. Preston Bailey, Derek Gilbert, Douglas Hamp, Jim Fletcher, and Stacy Lynn Harp.

Also, two other friends have contributed considerably to this volume through lengthy discussions: Douglas Riggs and Rob Skiba. They are great thinkers and dedicated to their respective ministries. Doug has offered a considerable amount of insight into mind control, dissociative identity disorder, and how healing can be achieved by the loving, but arduous work performed by the spiritual counselor. Doug has my admiration for his difficult duties. Rob is worthy of calling out because of his innovative study on mythology. He and I have enjoyed discussing this topic and its implications on biblical history. I look forward to working closely with Doug and Rob in the future.

Thank you to Russ Dizdar for reviewing Chapter Six and confirming the details regarding his ministry (many insights which are both astounding and revelatory). His experience in spiritual warfare is a 'modern marvel' in the battle between darkness and light.

Special thanks to fellow author David Lowe. David and I have recently become friends. I highly recommend his books (see the bibliography for a list) and have had the enjoyable experience to discuss his works (and mine) together for several months now. David has an amazing grasp of biblical issues and an extraordinary logical mind. His analysis and assessment have been especially helpful.

Thank you to Lowell Tuttman. Lowell is a friend and an expert on Winston Churchill, owning many especially hard to find volumes on the subject of this English leader. Lowell has been able to confirm many of the points I share in Chapter Five. However, anything I have gotten wrong in Churchill's history is my responsibility.

Other thanks go to the various interviewers who have been willing to allow me to demonstrate my excessive verbosity at their expense on their radio programs. This would include Rob Skiba, Derek Gilbert, Stacy Lynn Harp, GeorgAnn Hughes, Dr. Stanley Monteith,

Noah Hutchings, and last but certainly not least, Kristen Spurgeon. These brothers and sisters work hard to get the word out to their listening audiences and deserve much credit for their efforts.

There are many scholarly sources cited throughout the book. While I don't know most of them (and some are long departed), I certainly recognize their great research and gifted writing. These scholars include Jim Marrs who is a well-known writer on conspiracies. While I don't agree with all of his conclusions, his research is invaluable. David Wilcock, who I disagree with on many counts, is a brilliant writer and helped me better appreciate the arguments for 'the Source Field' as he labels the reality others call God. I cannot agree that we should equate the 'Source Field' with God as I am an unwavering theist; however, I can appreciate his great intellect and writing skill. Likewise, Joseph P. Farrell deserves mention here. His many works are fascinating and meticulously measured in their presentation. For readers who seek more details (and proof!) I recommend his books. A word of caution: his subjects and material may be difficult for some, while for others many of his insights will seem far-fetched. Yet, he is an indisputable scholar with a Ph.D. from Oxford. Also, while Farrell doesn't advertise his Christian theological standing (he is professor of Patristics—the 'Church Fathers'—and Apologetics, California Graduate School of Theology), his Christian point of view is apparent. I deeply appreciate his books and have drawn liberally from the incredible research there.

Despite my reliance upon these great scholars and sources I've mentioned above, the conclusions drawn in this study belong to me. As such, for them I am solely responsible.

S. Douglas Woodward
Woodinville, Washington
December, 2011

FOREWORD BY GARY STEARMAN

Author, Editor and Television Host of *Prophecy in the News*

I was privileged to review the manuscript of Doug Woodward's *Power Quest, Book One*, before it went to press, and I can assure you that it contains a great deal of valuable – in many cases, indispensable – information. His observations will allow you to make sense of the current political, economic and religious commotion that plagues the daily news cycle. This book is about what *really* makes history tick at the spiritual level.

It has always been true that there are clandestine operations behind the appealing political faces of power. Today, we look back and marvel at the rise and fall of Roman imperialism, the thrones of the Holy Roman Empire, of Marxist communism, National Socialism and numerous contemporary revolutionary coups. We tend to analyze them in terms of their socioeconomic development, as carefully delineated by accepted historical sources. Sadly, most scholars obscure more than they reveal.

Capturing the true essence of this world isn't easy. But Doug is a different kind of historian. With a documentarian's heart, he probes a little deeper, tying together myriad malevolent subversions of centuries past with well-known historical events. In the process, he brings us up to the present, demonstrating that today's international events are based upon something so sinister that at first, it seems unbelievable.

We tend to think that economics, culture, geography and the like, are based upon rational interactions. But in fact, they are undermined by a powerful history of spiritualism. Behind the scenes, shrouded in mystery, are the men whose beliefs are tied to the dark side... the authorities named in the Bible. We fight against, *"... principalities, against powers, against the rulers of the darkness of this world, against spiritual wickedness in high places." (Ephesians 6:12)* Doug has a special understanding of how these forces operate.

But let's pause for a moment. To help you understand his writing, I'd like to tell you a little about the man, himself. When you meet him for the first time, you'll quickly take note of his good-humored outlook and buoyant physical presence. He's quick to laugh and share his latest funny encounter. With gusto, he'll tell you about a recent encounter in crazy traffic, or at a meeting with friends. One way or another, you're sure to be treated to a rollicking and educational anecdote. Doug's good-natured manner is infectious, and he invites pleasant conversation as a natural part of his life. He bubbles over with conviviality.

As a friend and fellow student of Scripture, I always think of him as delightful company. His wonderful sense of humor, sharpness of wit and uncommon spiritual perception draw others to him just to see what he has to say. His thoughts bear the marks of a life that has been a rare combination of challenge and testing as well as leadership and executive success in the corporate world.

In past conversations with him, I have discovered we have much in common; we feed ideas back and forth in affable wordplay that blossoms into truly exciting revelation. He is a Bible-believing Christian who views the world through the lens of biblical truth, yet he avoids crimping the truth into his own restrictive field of view.

Still, his perspective as a well-grounded Christian always centers him in the worldview of prophetic truth. He understands that this present environment is in the process of passing away, and that we're living in the end times. He invites you to think.

The history of Western Civilization is usually condensed into a series of victorious high points. Orthodox Christianity and monarchies maintained the stable march toward increasing democracy. All this is set upon a foundation of Greco-Roman philosophy, literature and language. The thirteenth-century Magna Carta set the trend toward increasing human liberty. This development continued into the eighteenth-century Declaration of Independence and the U.S. Constitution. The smooth upward flow of economics, invention and wealth gave the world the appearance of being on the verge of a kingdom of peace! Then came the wars and revolutions of the twentieth century and the instability of the twenty-first. And once again, the end of peace and prosperity seems imminent. What's happening?

This book will tell you what's happening. As you read it, you'll find the convoluted details, twists and turns of a dark historical trail. It tracks the evil-spirited lives of men who have strived to consolidate the mahogany and marble vaults of tyrannical authority, turning them at last into what they believed would be an unconquerable power.

It takes balance to look into the shadowy historical crypts of their occultism and the machinations of the spiritualist elite without losing your perspective. Doug is particularly talented at exposing their schemes and making logical connections that others, following the same quest, have overlooked.

In the wrong hands, the journey that you will take through this book could be overpoweringly negative. But it's balanced by Doug's unique understanding and positive outlook. His passionate curiosity about the pathway of life means that he is never satisfied with the obvious. There are vignettes that float along the surface, or sparkle in the shallows. Doug looks past these and plumbs the depths, looking where others may have glanced, but never lingered to see what was really there. Nevertheless, he always returns to the sane and stable world of the Lord's leading.

His writing exhibits all these characteristics … and more. It's one thing to be a student of life and literature; it's quite another to have the gift of sharing your insights with others.

His mind for detail and his vision are unique; others have attempted to clarify the aspects of history linked to behind-the-scenes power, but they have muddied the waters. You may have read about secret societies and cults in the past, and were left wondering how they really worked, or how they were able to exert enough power to change the course of history. As you read this book, you'll have a wonderful "aha!" experience, as you see how it all fits together.

Doug has a natural desire to communicate, and it comes through every sentence of his books. When he digs out a nugget of truth, he's quick to share it and then, to connect it with other observations that give it weight and depth. Interconnections that bring disparate facts together into cogent observation are his stock in trade. Never satisfied just to write clearly, he forms logic chains that lead his readers ever onward to conclusions that they might never have reached on their own.

In short, Doug writes like an academic, but makes the complex so simple that one can easily follow his thoughts. His vision is transformed into rare insight. Get ready for a good read. You are about to receive a wealth of new ideas.

Gary Stearman
Oklahoma City, Oklahoma
November, 2011

DOES AMERICA STILL DESERVE OUR ADORATION?

In a time of universal deceit, speaking the truth is a revolutionary act.

George Orwell, (1903-1950)

Fascism is on the march again... unchecked corporate power has, to a significant degree, stultified the democratic process, and fascist groups in Europe and the United States feed upon this malaise.

Martin Lee, *The Beast Reawakens*, 1997

Despite the difference, the American church, like that of Nazi Germany, is in danger of wrapping the cross of Christ in some alien flag.

Pastor Erwin Lutzer, *Hitler's Cross*, 1995

In a 1940 speech, President Franklin Delano Roosevelt described the reality of a 'new order'—the 'New World Order' that is—as promised by the fascist regimes of Germany and Japan, with these ominous words:

> The history of recent years proves that the shootings and the chains and the concentration camps are not simply the transient tools but the very altars of modern dictatorships. They may talk of a 'new order' in the world, but what they have in mind is only a revival of the oldest and the worst tyranny. In that there is no liberty, no religion, [and] no hope. The proposed 'new order' is the very opposite of a United States of Europe or a United States of Asia. It is not a government based upon the consent of the governed. It is not a union of ordinary self-respecting men and women to protect themselves and their freedom and their dignity from oppression. It is an unholy alliance of power and self to dominate and to enslave the human race.

Political labels and ideological claims are often misleading—sometimes intentionally so. Championing 'a new world order', as the basis for cooperation among nations—especially multi-national organizations established 'in the service of mankind'—may have little to do with the real incentives behind such intentions. Just as FDR warned the American public in the quotation cited above—we can't necessarily believe what those in power say concerning their ideology. What's even more troublesome: those engaged in politics and the media in whom we often place our trust, may mis-interpret what they believe—not realizing what they profess is ac-tually the exact opposite of the ideology they claim to hold dear.

In politics, the dirtiest name one can call another is 'fascist'. Yet, this philosophy-cum-derogatory-remark is completely accurate for many top business and government leaders in America today. Why would I say that? It is rather simple: the more powerful someone becomes in business and politics, the more likely the indi-vidual tends toward Fascism in their thinking and action. Once we appreciate the many benefits Fascism provides extremely large businesses and those who run them, we can understand (though not excuse) such intentions—and why this moniker may apply to them.

However, this depiction shouldn't imply a status as universal truth. That is to say, we can rightly conceive of a successful businessman or politician free from any such taint. No doubt the majority who fall into this category are not consciously fascists. Nor are they nec-essary advocating the same. Nevertheless, it is highly likely that for many in our land today this accusation hits the mark. It truly de-pends on whether we distinguish what the word *Fascism* means.

Essentially, Fascism should be defined as *a governing ideology in which the State and corporate powers conspire together to 'rig' the games of government and business in favor of the wealthy.* In the process, the 'People' lose their voice, becoming victims of corporate greed and governmental excess. It should be no surprise that mega-corporations benefit from laws enacted to protect their market opportunity and preserve their wealth. Likewise, politicians benefit from corporate favors, donations, boondoggles, and the strengthening of their political stature. There exists a natural symbiosis between business and government. While government intends to facilitate as well as regulate business, all too often its actions favor those who lobby it most—resulting in more 'facilitation' and less 'regulation'—primarily, because the former pays better.

But getting back to the 'name calling'… Why does the label 'fascist' feel so dreadful when pinned to someone? No doubt part of the disgust owes to Fascism's implementation by history's worst of the bad guys: Adolf Hitler and Benito Mussolini. By their actions these twentieth century dictators personally portray the evil to which Fascism inevitably stoops when realized in a totalitarian regime. And yet, when we carefully review the essential definition of Fascism, we see it isn't necessarily connected to tyranny or to the evil specter of these ignoble figures. In and of itself, Fascism purposes an exercise of political power. Consequently, the form it takes in a particular culture *may be very different from one instance to the next.* I argue Fascism is rampant in America today—but it looks very different in our 'here and now' from how it was realized in Italy, Germany, or Spain a century ago.

In Germany during the ascendancy of Fascism (and in America too), it was easy to *equate the wealthy with the powerful.* More often than not, this correlation holds true. Today the combination of wealth and power belongs to the mega-corporation which most conservative members in our society uncritically venerate. On the other hand, liberal groups challenge the largest American business enterprises as power players taking unfair advantage. Be it Enron, WorldCom or more recently, Wall Street bankers whose intent to defraud their very own investors was highly publicized, we know corporate power reigns through its ability to dominate if not intimate the 'government machine'—which ultimately and inevitably legislates the corporation's agenda into law. *To the extent that the 'corporation' in America achieves this control, it is to that extent America has become a fascist nation.* When the government 'bails out' dying businesses because they are 'too big to fail', the populace should ponder just how distinct the two actually are.* It is in this context that critics ascribe the aspersion 'socialist' to the policies of the current Democrat administration. Of course history reminds us the former Republican President George W. Bush (43) and his treasury secretary (Henry Paulson) led the charge down this perilous path in 2008. Both Democrats and Republicans appoint Wall Street leadership to police their own investment and commercial banking industry. Perhaps it isn't as bad as charging the fox to guard the hen house; but it shouldn't be surprising when the banker-cum-regulator spares the rod. This isn't about which party is right or wrong. This is just the way America works. It is America that is wrong to sanction such activity.

Therefore, American Capitalism, at its highest level, no longer operates purely through 'free markets' which promise 'efficiency'. Alan Greenspan, the former head of 'the Fed', admits that 'free markets' don't regulate themselves as he once believed (failure to perform profitably over the 'long term' is an insufficient 'check' on bad judgment). There must be more rules and rule enforcement. Conse-

---

* Being too big to fail may be a worthy rationale for the action the federal government takes from time to time. But if our government salvages businesses that demonstrated flagrant disregard for their customers and then exacts no penalties for these pernicious actions, 'too big to fail' portends a misleading excuse proving my thesis. Government has ceased to protect the interests of the People.

quently, the government should become more involved—before Wall Street drives the car (we call our economy) off the end of the pier. It is not enough to post a sign which warns "trouble lies ahead." Our car now sits in traffic at a crossroads where the bankers who drive it (our economy) must allow the regulators to navigate. However, despite what happened on Wall Street during the past ten years (investment banks promoting 'derivative' securities based on bundled 'junk mortgages'), the government has done little more than reprimand the bankers for crashing the car 'into the Hudson'. Instead of taking punitive action against them and by promising unlimited capital (opening the Fed 'window' virtually to 'all-comers'— investment banks, insurance companies, mega-lenders) the Federal Reserve reinforces the horrendous behavior: funds are available at near-free interest rates to salvage these finance companies which operated without regard for the longer term consequences of their activities. In effect, the US government purchased a bigger, faster model for Wall Street drivers, removing the most important speed control: the risk of going out of business. This is the most egregious example of government-business collusion, which should be properly labeled, Fascism. While most officials and economists believed this step was essential to save the economy in 2008-9, it overlooks the situation which allowed the abuse (bankers operating without true independent supervision), and the questionable banking mechanism which provided the solution (an independent banking system, the Fed, owned by international banking families), which can create money by fiat enjoying the interest earned from the virtual money it brings into existence. Who are the real risk-takers in this scenario? Of course, it is U.S. taxpayers who serve as guarantors should the car crash again.

Can anything be done? Should anything be attempted? The backbone of our economic system: this independently owned banking system known as the Federal Reserve System generally works for the good of most people although a few ultra-rich families get richer. However, at this stage of the game, it is most unlikely that anything can be done politically to change the situation. History suggests that those who fight against it may lose their lives trying.[*]

This is not to denigrate our version of Capitalism from every angle. From a practical perspective, of all political systems *Capitalism has proven throughout history to create the greatest opportunity for the most people.* Despite its foibles, American Capitalism in particular provides a great success story. Certainly American Capitalism isn't free of abuses, with its many documented cases of public utilities and manufacturers polluting water supplies, farmers overlooking the rights of migrant workers, and infamous real estate scams galore. George H.W. Bush (41) asserted that Capitalism must find a 'kinder and gentler' form. This is particularly so when the 'checks and balances' stop working. And many in America today believe that state of imbalance is the state our State is in.

Obviously, I wouldn't make this argument, let alone write a book about it, if I didn't feel that the 'cooperation' between the American government and the largest enterprises in America slants toward 'big businesses'. Being a businessman myself, a former Microsoft and Oracle executive, as well as a Partner at the world's largest accounting firm, Ernst & Young LLP, I am a consistent (and somewhat successful) advocate for 'making a profit'. However, I am also an American who cherishes liberty, religious freedom, and the celebration of our forebears who established this land through great sac-

---

[*] This is certainly one of the oft-argued rationales behind the assassination of President Kennedy—he tried to curtail the power of the Federal Reserve by creating US Treasury notes—in which the US Treasury, not the Federal Reserve was the guarantor.

rifices and amazing feats of courage. Too much government interference too frequently applied to rectify our problems is a sign that we have become too eager to allow the government to save us. While government is meant to serve us, when we continually allow it to encroach on more and more aspects of our lives, we pay a price called *servitude*—allowing the government to direct what we do.

Unwittingly, by opening this door we allow government control to grow ever stronger. If we consider all the other areas in which we've trusted the government to call the shots, we shouldn't be surprised when we wake up one morning and conclude we know far too little about what is going on. Our lack of attentiveness enables all manner of tyranny to fester while we lie asleep.

Evangelical Erwin W. Lutzer, the Senior Pastor of the Moody Church in Chicago, wrote in his book, *Hitler's Cross*, "We must support our government, but we must be ready to criticize it or even defy it when necessary. Patriotism is commendable when it is for a just cause. Every nation has the right to defend itself, the right to expect the government to do what is best for its citizens. However, if the German church has taught us the dangers of blind obedience to government, we must eschew the mindless philosophy, "My country, right or wrong'."[*] As one socially conscious Christian commentator said back in the heyday of the Viet Nam anti-war protests, "Can you imagine the Kings of Israel telling the prophets Isaiah, Jeremiah or Zechariah, 'Israel: Love it or leave it'"?

Like Lutzer, I freely admit to my Christian religious commitment; specifically, possessing an evangelical and thus 'conservative' point of view on theological matters. Writing from this evangelical Chris-

---

[*] Erwin W. Lutzer, *Hitler's Cross*, Chicago, Moody Press, 1995, p. 204.

tian perspective, the reader would likely suspect my conservative theology would naturally result in my adherence to a conservative political philosophy as well. This expectation is a reasonable one: typically these two aspects of our thinking reinforce one another. However, in recent years, I've become much more attuned to the fact this connection between theology and politics isn't compulsory.

Consider the reverse: Isn't it obvious that just because someone's political philosophy is conservative; it doesn't automatically make them theologically conservative? Political conservatism has little to do with whether our theology adheres to *biblical orthodoxy*. Moreover, for sincere evangelicals, we must remember that being faithful to the Word of God requires *independence from humanly-derived ideology of any kind lest our creeds become idolatrous.* We must work hard to keep our thinking free from the lazy tendency to follow the pack on intellectual matters, especially theological ones. Christians must be as the 'noble Bereans' mentioned in the Book of Acts who searched the Scriptures daily to see "whether these things [be] so."[*] Additionally, Lutzer makes a very pertinent comment at this point, "The experience of the church in Nazi Germany reminds us that Christ must always stand alone; He must be worshiped not as One who stands alongside the governmental leaders of this world but as standing above them, as King of kings and Lord of lords."[†]

Given I hold to this admonition, what are those ideas about which must we remain vigilant? Unfortunately the answer to that question isn't simple or succinct. Our duties are many: we must listen care-

---

[*] *"These [the Bereans] were more noble than those in Thessalonica, in that they received the word with all readiness of mind, and searched the scriptures daily, whether those things were so."* (Acts 17:11)

[†] Lutzer, op. cit., p. 13.

fully to what our television news programs tell us… what our politicians promote as "the fact of the matter"… what the public relations programs of multi-national corporations advertise… even what lessons we were taught in school years ago. As the familiar aphorism advises, we must take every assertion 'with a grain of salt'. This is especially so when major media outlets broadcast political positions promoted from the mouths of present-day politicians, or promoted by Hollywood stars speaking on behalf of corporate America. In essence, we can be certain of one and only one thing: *truth is the most endangered of endangered species.* We must remain on guard and filter carefully what we hear and read. A true democracy demands nothing less of its citizens.

However, allow me to clarify that the point of view expressed in this book isn't meant to appeal solely to Christians.

Anyone who shares the view that the American government was constituted to be "of the people, by the people, and for the people" should find most of what I've committed to writing in the pages that follow not just intellectually arousing but existentially alarming. Indeed, the reader should find it useful no matter what he or she believes about religion. To be precise: I regard myself as thoroughly republican—but not in the sense of being a 'card-carrying member' of the Republican Party. My 'republican perspective' refers to the political philosophy and stance of historical American champions of republicanism like Thomas Jefferson and Abraham Lincoln. In other words, *individual liberty matters.*

Originally, our government was obligated to protect those freedoms above all else. To quote Henry David Thoreau: "Government gov-

erns best that governs least."[*] We are to take responsibility for ourselves. Study hard; work hard. Don't expect something for nothing.
Such are the values I was taught growing up in the Bible belt. My
father was an artillery-man in General Patton's Third Army during
World War II (who I'm happy to report as of this writing is still lu-
cid and lively at 92), and my late mother who was 'über-active' in
her much beloved United Methodist Church.[†]

The other key assumption I freely admit as fundamental to this book
will no doubt find far fewer supporters: *I believe in a cosmos created by the God of the Bible and in line with the Bible's explanation
and description.* In my opinion, the Bible's portrayal of the universe
(both seen and unseen) provides a compelling way to understand the
'cause and effect' of what happens in our world. As it regards this
book, this biblical cosmology yields more insight when it comes to
exposing 'what happens behind the scenes'. This proves to be true
since my primary thesis contends that the *paranormal* powerfully
influences today's America more than ever before—its culture, its
politics, and its population—a dynamic which changes lives for the
better or for the worse.

As I will document, this influence is not absolute nor is it *only* in
regards to contemporary America. Since the time of its first colony,
America has been influenced dramatically by *supernaturalism* (a
belief in that biblical cosmos I mentioned) but especially *spiritual-*

---

[*] Of course, it needs to be quickly admitted that such a government depends
upon an ethical and moral population. Once many in the populace fail this test, the
government necessarily must increase its control.

[†] I grew up in the Methodist Church and have many wonderful friends who I
met and worshipped with for years. However, this is not where my 'evangelical'
perspective was nourished. Rather, it was in college through my participation in
the organizations *Young Life* and *Campus Crusade for Christ.*

ism, which is a religious approach dominated by occult perspectives. Ghosts and goblins are notorious mainstays of this point of view. But spiritualism is also *a way to think about reality.* It contends we are subject to powerful forces we don't see and most of which we don't understand. Furthermore, *spiritualism affirms the efficacy and propriety of magic.* It claims we can manipulate the forces which exist in the cosmos, even when they are 'sinister forces' as noted author on the occult, Peter Levenda labels them.[*] The book is entitled, *Power Quest,* in part for this reason. Occultism encourages individuals to exercise power over nature (and other humans)—even if it means conjuring spirits from 'the other side' to aid them in seeking their agenda. *Occultism promises power to the practitioner.*

In concluding this Preface, America comprises a melting pot of many ideologies, many races, and most certainly, many religions. Initially settled by outcasts of European society and eventually integrated to a partial extent with Native Americans who had their own distinctive spiritualist belief systems, American thinking boasts a hodgepodge of romantic, colorful, and at times irrefutably odd ways of thinking. The story of how these various points of view came to shape what we think about the world provides what I find a most fascinating subject—hence, my submittal here. Hopefully my enthusiasm can be shared by the reader; the recital of many seldom disclosed facts regarding our 'paranormal' history will enliven the book and entertain those willing to consider these words.

---

[*] Even though in his book, Levenda doesn't feel compelled to offer an explanation for why they exist or what the extent of their powers may be. Of course, the Bible offers a particular explanation although there are varied interpretations of what the biblical account offers. Manichaeism is a popular view professed by many today. In this view, there is a God of good and a god of evil. It is, however, not the orthodox perspective.

But my ultimate goal is much more than entertainment. I strive to warn of what is all-but-set to transpire in America in the very near future. My concern: there are numerous disquieting trends evidenced by not-well-known historical facts concerning the widespread post-war infiltration and influence of Nazism in America. Coupled with this ominous threat springs the increasing growth of influential spiritualist dogmas. While the implications of these ideologies are worrisome enough; when combined with the prevalent fascist sentiments which exist in our land today (that seemingly possess a natural affinity to reinforce one another), the situation foretells a great struggle lies ahead for our nation. It was this combination of Fascism and spiritualism in early twentieth century Germany that led to the evil changing the face of our world. This evil union, already awakened in America during the past fifty years, threatens to dominate us once more: economically, politically, and even spiritually.

For these reasons, I propose the war for liberty in America will commence its next battle soon. The republic we love stands in jeopardy. Whether or not the reader agrees with my religious sentiments—I hope the mandate to take political action remains apparent to the reader after studying the facts I present regarding what has happened in our nation; especially, during the past half-century.

What I share in the pages ahead may frighten some. No doubt others will scoff at the details of what I report or predict is soon to transpire. Nevertheless, many will be compelled to consider the meaning of these prophesied outcomes in regards to their personal lives, political commitments, and their impact on the American way of life we all, regardless of religious affiliation, hold so dear. For we live in a country that, despite its shortcomings, remains the world's greatest and most congenial for personal freedom. Our landscapes showcase more beauty and our people prove more caring. We are privileged to live here. Yet in our patriotic fervor, we must not miss one very critical point: *our republic is not the same as it once was.*

Lee Greenwood's song celebrates, "I'm proud to be an American, where at least I know I'm free." I love patriotic music and get goose bumps very much like my father, the World War II vet. Mr. Greenwood's song is surely one of the best in this respect. But it may gloss over the point I'm making. *We no longer realize how much less freedom we have.* And like the cold-blooded frog slowly boiling to death in the hot water of the saucepan (since the temperature changes so gradually); we don't realize how much hot water we are in. Using another common analogy, we are being lulled to sleep by the sounds of the patriotic songs we enjoy singing, accompanied by the ongoing beat of everyday living, while often shuddering from our foreboding fears of terrorism—stimulating our desire for stronger security (even at the expense of liberty). As Francis Schaeffer, noted evangelical intellectual concluded at the end of his important and distinctive ministry in the 1980s: we are motivated by our demand for "personal peace and affluence," troubled above all else by anything which threatens to upset our selfish serenity.

Consequently, the time has come to consider how we have arrived at this crossroads and what will happen to America over the next two decades. This requires learning some important seldom-known facts from history which I promise to make interesting. Administering this necessary 'medicinal' analysis should do us good since most of us, especially those who tend toward conservatism such as myself, have little perspective on just how dangerous our prognosis has become—let alone, how much worse it could be if we don't stand up and oppose the downward spiral of an overly controlling government melded to an occult spirituality as incarnated in our American culture and political situation. While most of the 'facts' proving this influence are deferred until Book Two,

Book One provides the necessary historical underpinning to explain why the paranormal and the occult have taken hold in our culture and our political system.

So please consider this work (submitted in two parts) my attempt to inform and awaken the reader concerning what's at stake, how we've gotten to this point, why our republic is vulnerable, and what this foreshadows regarding our future *both personally and politically.*

In the days which lie ahead, nothing stands more crucial to our livelihood, our spirituality, and our liberty.

POWER QUEST

BOOK ONE:

AMERICA'S OBSESSION
WITH THE PARANORMAL

INTRODUCTION

Government is not reason; it is not eloquent; it is force. Like fire, it is a
dangerous servant and a fearful master.

George Washington

Our scientific power has outrun our spiritual power.
We have guided missiles and misguided men.

Martin Luther King, Jr.

Their final objective toward which all their deceit is directed is to cap-
ture political power so that, using the power of the state and the power of
the market simultaneously, they may keep the common man
in eternal subjection.

Henry A. Wallace (33rd U.S. Vice-President, 1941-1945)

Explaining the Dynamics of History

The appetite for power is insatiable in humankind. With power comes control. With power comes notoriety. With power in hand, we can achieve our most passionate and innermost desires. Humanity regards the wielding of personal and political power as the preeminent force transforming the world around us into the world we want it to be. Unfortunately, as the history of the world teaches, the fruit of such 'supremacy seeking' energizes evil much more often than it generates good.

From one perspective, explaining the history of the world pivots upon the topic of *who had power and who didn't.* The story of dominating empires features emperors of Egypt, Babylon, Greece, Rome, or China (to name but a few) who achieved and exploited power. Listed amongst the most influential men of history are dictators who gained supremacy over peoples and vast areas of geography. When we think of 'great men' (not necessarily noble), we eulogize Nebuchadnezzar, Alexander the Great, Julius Caesar, and Genghis Khan among a short-list of the world's most powerful persons. Closer to our own times, and perhaps a faint signal of the future promise of equality between men and women (still pending in most quarters), England's high water mark was achieved under a woman, Queen Elizabeth I. However, we must recall that her greatness lay not in her charity but in her 1588 defeat of the Spanish Armada expanding English control throughout the Old World (while simultaneously laying the groundwork for the New).

When we consider modern political struggle, many academics today still regard *the Marxist theory of class struggle* as the most fundamental explanation of what drives and directs history. "The [written] history of all hitherto existing society is the history of class struggle" [brackets in original].[1] By class, Marx and Engels didn't mean upper, middle, and lower classes; rather they were speaking of who controlled *the means of production.*[*] *Production ownership* establishes power. Whoever controls this asset has the ability to establish whether the *proletariat* (labor) and/or the *bourgeoisie* (capitalist) live well or merely survive.

In contrast, twenty-first century advocates of Capitalism label the communist doctrine the greatest myth of modern times. It seems outrageous to champion its validity inasmuch as Marx and Engels proposed that once labor dominated the State (and through it, the means of production), the State would own everything for the good

---

[*] Means of production refers to physical, non-human inputs used in production—the factories, machines, and tools used to produce wealth" (See en.wikipedia.org / wiki/ Means_of_production).

of all concerned. Eventually, the struggle between the classes would dissipate and *the State itself would simply disappear.*

Of course, given our observations today (how socialist states universally outgrow their organic means for sustaining themselves), the communist myth morphs from an overly optimistic philosophy to the tragic comedy we've seen played out on the world stage for the past ninety years. Believing evil to be vested in social structures rather than the human heart, Communism built its ideology upon the *rejection* of the Judeo-Christian premise that humankind is depraved (inherently predisposed toward selfishness, immorality, and oftentimes blatant wickedness). How ironic the Marxists founded their political philosophy upon an unswerving assumption of the goodness of humankind! Such not-so-benevolent dictators like Joseph Stalin and Mao Tse-tung could only feed their people by first annihilating over 60 million of their citizens (perhaps 20 million in Stalin's case and 40 million in Mao's China). Communist states, with few exceptions, found killing the 'surplus population' essential to keep the government up and running.[2]

But before Marx and Engels coined their notion of reality's guiding principle, another German, one of the greatest minds of history, Georg Wilhelm Friedrich Hegel, developed what he called the 'Master-Slave' dialectic. Hegel's *dialectic* (a process in which two-opposing forces or ideas rub against one another in the historical process until a synthesis is achieved)[*] comprised a core element

---

[*]The Encarta Dictionary in Word 2010 states **dialectic** is "the tension that exists between two conflicting or interacting forces, elements, or ideas." Hegel's and Marx's dialectic method consisted of "two apparently opposed ideas, the thesis and antithesis, become combined in a unified whole, the synthesis."

in Western thought's development, specifically the notion of *consciousness* of both individuals and humankind generally.

Here too, akin to Marx, the issue surfaces of whether *reality* actually corresponds to the conceptual framework proffered by the philosopher to explain it.[3] For a true 'synthesis' to occur, individuals and cultures must feel they are *neither master nor slave*—that they have overcome the 'dialectic'. They must trust they no longer belong to one or the other opposing forces. Given our world is still composed of the 'haves and the have-nots' (not just in terms of material goods but in regards to exerting political influence), and since institutions like the United Nations give voice to the nations who 'have-not,' suggesting the 'have-nots' can overcome the dialectic amounts to wishful thinking. Furthermore, from the perspective of the Bible, overcoming poverty denies what Jesus famously said, *"For ye have the poor [and dispossessed] with you always"* (Mark 14:7).[*] Jesus wasn't critical of charity to the poor; rather, His saying underscored humankind cannot achieve utopia apart from the Kingdom of God.

However, the Hegelian dialectic influenced numerous notable philosophers in different ways. Certainly, Søren Kierkegaard fathered the philosophy known as *Existentialism* out of his hatred for Hegel's 'system'. He saw Hegel trivializing faith. To Kierkegaard, Hegel juxtaposed Christianity as one 'thesis' in the dialectic while atheism served as the opposing 'antithesis'. According to Hegel's theory, ultimately both would be overcome within the historical process[4], as together they progressed toward 'synthesis' (which we might suppose to be *deism*). Finding no room for individual faith (which Kierkegaard poetically labeled 'passionate inwardness'); Kierke-

---

[*] Of course, Jesus was not saying that the status quo was inevitable or acceptable. He came to preach His gospel to the poor and to proclaim justice.

gaard championed a 'risky' faith (the famous 'leap of faith'). By this phrase, he meant a faith which 'risks everything' in the name of serving God—that we might find meaning in an otherwise irrational (pointless) life. We might characterize the conflict this way: from Kierkegaard's perspective, Hegel portrayed Christianity as a 'black and white documentary'—while S.K.[*] saw it as a dramatic adventure in 'living color.' For evangelicals, it is understandable if we sympathize with Kierkegaard's point of view—especially given our eagerness to depict our relationship with and to God as 'personal.'[5]

Figure 1 - Friedrich Nietzsche

Likewise, Friedrich Nietzsche forced the Hegelian Master-Slave dialectic a different direction. He welded it to explain the origin of morality and a path for morality's future. For Nietzsche, *this dialectic explains the religious history of humankind.* Nietzsche believed that both Christian and democratic morality was a 'slave morality' suffused with weakness as a result of Judaic, biblical teaching. Nietzsche staunchly advocated 'master morality'. Nietzsche contended humankind must strive to adopt master morality since the God of the Bible had been proven irrelevant (at least to Europeans at the close of the nineteenth century—the meaning of his assertion that "God is dead"). Of course, his 'master morality' consists of attributes like *superiority, nobility, and dominance.*

---

[*] S.K. is a popular way to abbreviate the name Søren Kierkegaard.

In contrast, according to Nietzsche the weakness of Christian morality stems from its overemphasis upon guilt. For Nietzsche, we must realize that "There are no moral phenomena at all, only moral interpretations of phenomena."[6] In other words, there is no reason to assume that *good versus evil* results from an inherent moral 'attribute' or property of the cosmos—certainly, *not from the existence of the God of the Bible*. Morality isn't built into reality—it results from the human condition; moreover, it is an invention of humanity. According to Nietzsche, from the Jews (certainly lumping Jesus into the race he ridiculed), comes the 'slave morality' which supports charity, turning the other cheek, humility, and the like. For Nietzsche, such 'slave' notions unfortunately influenced their overlords[*] over time and demanded they relinquish the qualities of masters—such as authority, greed, and control. Furthermore, Nietzsche laments how the *heroic* morality of Greece and Rome was conquered by the *slave* morality of Christianity. To him, the essential struggles of these cultures amounted to the heroic (Roman) mentality subordinating itself to the slave (Judaic) sentiment. Likewise, Nietzsche faulted our democratic ideology in America because it upheld *equality and freedom*. To him, *the democratic movement* amounted to the "collective degeneration of man."[7] With these words, we easily see how his notion of 'master morality' lent itself perfectly to the German employment of Fascism.

As I've discussed in other essays,[8] Nietzsche's hoped for transformation of society began with the arrival of *Übermensch*—the 'superman' who will overcome the death of God and build the basis for

---

[*] Christians might consider this attitude *repentance*. As Paul said to the Galatians counter to all 'dialectics': "*There is neither Jew nor Greek, there is neither bond nor free, there is neither male nor female: for ye are all one in Christ Jesus.*" (Galatians 3:28) Jesus Christ brings the ultimate synthesis to humanity.

a new ethic modeled after this 'master' morality. This new 'demi-god'* will be free from outmoded and 'unnatural' religions as well as moral prohibitions (he uses the word we translate 'organic' to justify the Übermensch fulfilling his every desire). In his own words,

Hegel "Spirit (Geist) Dialectic"
The master-slave dialectic explains 'Gôt' (Geist/spirit) working through world history

Kierkegaard "Leap of Faith"
Rejects Hegel's system to explain the Christian God or true Christian faith

Marx "Materialist Dialectic"
"Flips Hegel on his head" Matter not spirit works in world history thru class struggle

Nietzsche "Übermensch"
Repudiation of Christianity as 'slave mentality'—the key to a new world

Adolf Hitler's Aryan Race
The implementation of Nietzsche's vision of the Übermensch

Figure 2 - From Hegel to Hitler

---

* A demigod is a human being that is either treated like a god, or supposedly consists of both human and divine 'DNA' and is half god and half human.

"The word Übermensch [designates] a type of supreme achievement, as opposed to 'modern' men, 'good' men, Christians, and other nihilists[*]... When I whispered into the ears of some people that they were better off looking for a Cesare Borgia than a Parsifal they did not believe their ears."[9] In order to feel the full effect of Nietzsche's counter-intuitive advice, other historical facts are in order.

Cesare Borgia was the conniving son of Rodrigo Borgia (Pope Alexander VI, a contemporary of Christopher Columbus) who abused his power during his father's reign as pope. The series on *Showtime*, *The Borgias*, chronicles the horrendous exploits of this family which served as the model for Mario Puzo's *Godfather* saga and Francis Ford Coppola's cinema trilogy based by the same name. *Parsifal* was the German appellation for Percival (given to him by Richard Wagner, Nietzsche's one time best friend, in Wagner's epic opera by the same name).[†] Percival was the virtuous knight of King Arthur who sought after the Holy Grail by purifying himself and doing chivalrous deeds. Consequently, Nietzsche's implications are clear: *It is better to have a powerful scoundrel run the country than a pious prince.* Percival represents the hero; the Übermensch the anti-hero.

His sage advice would soon be realized with the arrival of Adolf Hitler. It was Hitler who leveraged the ideology of Nietzsche's Übermensch to help support his concept of a German master race—the *Aryan* race—coupled with Nietzsche's implicit anti-Semitism and hatred for Christianity. It is also instructive that Nietzsche wrote the books entitled, *The Antichrist* and *Thus Sprauch Zarathus-*

---

[*] 'Nihilist' derives from the Latin '*nihil*' meaning 'nothing.' Encarta's dictionary defines it: "a belief that life is pointless and human values are worthless" as well as "the belief that there is no objective basis for truth."
[†] And which is based on Wolfram von Eschenbach's *Parzifal*, a thirteenth century epic poem concerning the search for the Holy Grail.

tra (*So Spoke Zoroaster*) to provide a mythic format to expound his notions of Übermensch, the death of God, and the detrimental effects of Christianity on human society. As it turns out, Nietzsche's notion of the Übermensch is actually a well-crafted philosophical word-icon of what the Bible terms, "the man of sin" or "the son of perdition" who will base his actions on *lawlessness* (i.e., that law has no absolute basis). According to the Apostle Paul, it is indeed the defining characteristic of the Antichrist (II Thessalonians 2:3). But before I offer any more remarks concerning the Bible's predicted world ruler (most of which won't be divulged until Book Two), a quick review of civics is in order—at least as it relates to political power and how it affects the 'common man'.

The True Powers behind Human Government

Law undergirds power in human culture. Totalitarian dictators or democratic presidents ultimately justify their power based upon laws upheld within their domains. Of course, tyrants use the law as window-dressing to rationalize their personal ambition. Fascist governments, such as Hitler's Germany, argued the people exist for the benefit of the State. The 'collective' is more important than the 'individual.' While the communist governments of the twentieth century asserted that the State should primarily serve the interests of 'the common man' (aka, the laborers or proletariat) and not just those with money (aka, the bourgeoisie or capitalist owners), the actual implementation of Communism in such governments was *indistinguishable from Fascism.* 'The People' were little more than pawns being played by one of several groups striving to take control of their respective countries. Individual rights were always secondary to the needs of the State (and those powerful individuals supporting it) to achieve control and to keep the State in place.[10] We should always remember: protecting the status quo is an underlying motive for any government.[*]

A republic, in stark contrast, sets forth the principle that free individuals form the basis upon which any government should be built. Additionally, those individuals acknowledge that efficiency in government is better achieved by representatives, duly elected by the people, to make decisions on how their government should operate. Pure democracy ('one person, one vote') was feared by the framers of the American constitution because 'majority rule' can, in certain situations, become 'mob rule'. Therefore, the Founding Fathers believed the smartest and the best educated should be entrusted with the mission of establishing how our country should be governed. By free elections, *the People* would express their will and elect representatives to craft the necessary laws (paraphrasing a portion of the Preamble of the Constitution here) "establishing justice, ensuring domestic tranquility, providing for the common defense, and promoting the general welfare" of the populace and thereby ordaining a "more perfect union." That is why our constitution is based on the view government is derived from 'the consent of the governed.' As Lincoln said in his Gettysburg Address (1863), our government is intended to be "of the people, by the people, and for the people."

Unfortunately, just as in any other form of governance, there are individuals and groups which seek to dominate, forming a 'régime' to establish their agenda, maximize their opportunity to exercise power, and obtain what they deem to be in their best interests.

---

[*] And we should also keep in mind the true definition of conservative and liberal: Being 'conservative' means conserving what is—while liberal means liberating society or ideology from the status quo. Either approach can be good or bad.

In some cases, seeking such *hegemony** is driven by *ideology†* (to put in place a government consistent with the 'religion' of those seeking control); in some cases it is motivated purely by *greed* (obviously to obtain and keep material wealth); and in other cases, it is motivated by *prestige* (satisfying the desire for visible superiority over others). More often than not, as mentioned above in regards to Communism, espousing political ideology too often becomes a cover for those seeking power, and along with it profit and prestige.‡ When we think of a notable political family, such as the Kennedys or the Bushes, we find it increasingly difficult to believe in our heart of hearts that the real reason such families sought dynastic status was to ensure 'the little guy got a fair shake'. We protest, "Their motive wasn't about serving humankind." At best, our cynicism affords such sentiment little more than a wistful rationalization. At worst, we fear the true story ultimately concerns one powerful family hoping to dominate another powerful family in the public realm for financial gain (and most likely, at the People's expense).

More to the point: The most relevant governmental 'format' to contemplate in today's political situation across all national boundaries is *plutarchy* (derived from the Greek words *ploutos* [wealth] and *kratos* [rule]—literally meaning "the rule of the wealthy"). As we

---

* *Hegemony* is defined by Dictionary.com as "leadership or predominant influence exercised by one nation over others, as in a confederation." Synonyms would be 'control' or 'domination'.

† *Ideology*, just to be clear, is defined by the Encarta dictionary as a "set of beliefs, values, and opinions that shapes the way a person or a group such as a social class thinks, acts, and understands the world."

‡ No doubt, at the root of everyone's mistrust in politicians rests our assumption that 99% of those seeking elected office attempt to acquire profit or prestige through political office; such ambition we chalk up as their chosen means to gain political power in order to accomplish their personal, self-serving goals.

move into the second decade of the twenty-first century, the opinion of most supposes the structural difference between the governments in China, Russia, Europe, and even the United States has become inconsequential. At the end of the day, a group of wealthy individuals pull the strings. Power rests in 'an elite.' The elite may or may not be true aristocrats who possess 'royal blood'. They are akin to the 'landed gentry' of the Middle Ages. Furthermore, these fortunate ones possess great wealth and reckon themselves 'enlightened'. Typically, such elite hide from public view—yet most who express these concerns surmise they *'hide in plain sight'*. While we still acknowledge an *aristocracy* in Europe; America substitutes the notion of *dynasty*. With either label, they distinguish themselves from the rest of us not only by wealth, but by their ability to influence.

In the last two decades, there has been an increased awareness of a select number of politicians and corporate leaders (but mostly families of great status, on either side of the Atlantic) comprising, as it were—a *shadow government.* Even the most sophisticated acknowledge this to be so. Benjamin Disraeli in his book *Coningsby* wrote, ""The world is governed by very different personages from what is imagined by those who are not behind the scenes."

While fingers are often pointed at the *Trilateral Commission* (TLC) and the *Council on Foreign Relations (CFR),*[11] numerous writers who have taken up the subject refer to the *Bilderberger's,* a group of rich elite who first met in the Bilderberger's Hotel in May of 1954. According to a report by the BBC summarized as follows in Wikipedia, "The Bilderberg Group, Bilderberg conference, or Bilderberg Club is an annual, unofficial, invitation-only conference of approximately 120 to 140 [the article cited says 150] guests from North America and Western Europe, most of whom are people of influence [labeled 'elite' in the BBC article]. About one-third is from government and politics, and two-thirds from finance, industry, labour [labor], education and communications. Meetings are closed to the public and often feature future political leaders shortly before they become household names."[12] For instance, it is common knowledge that Bill Clinton and Tony Blair were showcased at the Bilderberger meeting before they appeared on their respective national political scenes. The endorsement of the Bilderbergers was strongly implied.

Figure 3 – Hotel De Bilderberg, Arnhem, Netherlands

On the surface, the idea of corporate wealth [read: multi-national corporations] influencing world governments *hardly seems conspiratorial.* It is common fare in cable news reports to cite lobbyists from various corporations or associations established by an industry seeking influence with law-makers.* The relevant issue is, "How

---

* For instance, Steve Largent, school mate of my wife in high school and famous football star of the Seattle Seahawks, after a failed run for Oklahoma governor, was hired by an association of cellular phone companies several years ago to

organized are the 'richest of the rich' to ensure that the wealthy stay in power?" "Does their organization include 'fixing' elections so that who they want to win is guaranteed?" The author supposes that if the rich didn't find ways to cooperate and insure their interests are well-represented, they would be short-sighted and perhaps naïve. Who would seriously argue *the 'fabulously wealthy' do **not** represent a 'ruling class' today?* Isn't this the way of the world? We might debate just how capable particular wealthy individuals or groups are to 'fix' elections to ensure their goals are met. However, it is hardly worth the debate to argue whether the rich elite dialogue (and most likely conspire) to maximize their influence. To deny that they do comprises *naiveté par excellance!*

Even 'the most trusted man in America' believed this was true. The famous anchor of the *CBS News*, Walter Cronkite (hardly a conservative Republican) shortly before his death was asked if he believed America was 'managed' by the wealthy, specifically, "Is there a ruling class?" Cronkite responded: "I am afraid there is. I don't think it serves the democracy well, but that is true, I think there is. The ruling class is the rich who really command our industry, our commerce, our finance. And those people are able to so manipulate our democracy that they really control the democracy, I feel." [13]

Chuck Collins, director of the *Program on Inequality and the Common Good for the Institute for Policy Studies*, is quoted by Jim Marrs in his most recent book, *The Trillion-Dollar Conspiracy*, as saying the following: "In our view, extreme inequalities contributed

---

lobby on behalf of the cellular industry. My brother Phil often lobbies on behalf of the Oklahoma Pharmacists Association. I see 'lobbying' on behalf of industries and professions of all kinds remains both legal and appropriate. It is incumbent upon the politician to maintain independence and make good judgments based upon such input and broader factors of which the politician is aware.

to the [current] economic collapse... This [fact] matters because *wealth is power*—the power to shape the culture, to distort elections, and shape government policy. A *plutocracy* is a 'rule by wealth'— and more and more the priorities of the society are shaped by *the interests of organized wealth.*" [14] [Emphasis added]

However, a plutarchy becomes especially sinister when it forces the downtrodden to stay deprived—eliminating their rights to 'life, liberty, and the pursuit of happiness'. If the general population discovers that the game isn't being played on a level playing field, *the People*—once enlightened—may find the courage to revolt.

This has certainly been the worry of the Chinese government for no less than the past thirty years. It has also been the primary reason the 'elite' at the helm in China allowed Capitalism to be introduced into the otherwise centrally-planned economy. By allowing more wealth to be created by individuals and *assets to be owned by persons* rather than the State, the boil of revolt could be effectively lanced. So far, this plan seems to be working.

G. William Domhoff, a professor in psychology and sociology at the University of California, Santa Cruz, provides a mountain of statistics in a 1960s bestseller, *Who Rules America?* Domhoff supports the position that a tiny minority of families own a majority of wealth in the United States and in the world. Plus, this wealth enables them to dominate our politics. Domhoff states (summarizing his findings) that 1% of the families own 34.3% of the wealth of the country. The next 19% (the managerial class) own 50.3%, leaving 80% of the people in American owning only 15%. His data is compelling enough to make some Republicans turn Democrat—well, at least perhaps those that are sitting on the fence![15] Furthermore, whatever the disparity in the 1960s, we know it grows far worse today. The middle class of America seems destined to be a vanishing breed.

Marrs summarizes Domhoff's work as "a strong argument that *wealth indeed equals power.* Such power comes with the ability to donate to political parties, engage lobbyists, and provide grants to experts to think up new policies beneficial to the wealthy… Wealth in the form of stock ownership can be used to control whole corporations, which today have inordinate influence in society, media, and government."[16] [Emphasis added]

The Deeper Conspiracy in Conspiracy Theories

However, the fear of conspiracy goes deeper than mere economics. Indeed, the rub for most conspiracy theorists surfaces when the rich elite who pull the strings (whether they operate behind a parliamentary system, a fascist organization, or a socialist schema), secretly promote an *ardent ideology driving the agenda* for government— while they keep the populace in the dark, unaware that an ideology, *perhaps even a spiritual belief system,* is the dominant motivation. I suspect the reader may believe this possibility too bizarre to be seriously considered. But is it?

For those familiar with the television series, *The X-Files*, perhaps these readers may recall the "committee of the wealthy" who managed the relationship with one of two competing groups of aliens planning to return to our world in a 'hostile takeover'. As we learned in the first *X-files* movie, the aliens didn't merely seek to harvest minerals from the earth; they sought to invade the bodies of humans re-introducing their population to earth; their plan was to use our bodies as little more than 'vitamin packs' to nourish the growth of their horrific selves inside human skins. We learned that the committee of the wealthy (headed by the so-called "well-dressed man") did a deal with these alien 'devils'. The committee agreed to some manner of co-existence as a desperate measure to save a remnant of humanity (although we learn it was only the committee and their families!) Despite the stellar work of Mulder and Scully, their plan progressed until the second group of aliens, enemies to the first, intervened—quashing the strategy by annihilating the committee and their families, after all had gathered at an air force base hanger awaiting evacuation through the agency of their alien allies.

While this 'out-of-this-world' scenario certainly appears to be complete science fiction, there exists a more widely-held and less 'over-the-top' conspiracy: *The intrigue of a coming global government centuries in the making.* Many believe (and provide a compelling case) that the world's wealthy elite have plotted for centuries to form a one-world government. The common term for these conspirators today is 'globalists'. In jeopardy is the sovereignty for any and all of the nearly 200 nation states existing around the world.[*] To many intellectuals such as Zbigniew Brzezinski, President Carter's National Security secretary, deems such sovereignty outdated and increases the danger of world war.[17] For other secret societies, like the Freemasons (and their more devote elder brothers, the Rosicrucians), organizing humanity into a single people world-wide fulfills the original plan of Nimrod at the Tower of Babel. 'Together we can become one people, whose aspirations reach into the heavens'.[18] (Thus, religious affirmations may lie at the heart of this endeavor.)

Jim Marrs, an award winning journalist and author of many books (and previously cited), is the most well-known researcher laying out the evidence of the globalist agenda. His book, *Rule by Secrecy,* connects the dots arguing that political power is generational—powerful families form dynasties with blood lines or 'genealogies'

---

[*] Note: As a data point, 193 members make up the United Nations in 2011.

traced for centuries—be they royal or not—which share goals that comprise family legacies. He proposes that these plans take decades if not centuries to be implemented. Furthermore, this generational power is connected to ideologies transcending the mere issue of making money. To Marrs, what these various families *hold to be true, their beliefs* drive political actions for generation after generation.

In *The Trillion Dollar Conspiracy,* Marrs identifies how political power crosses decades while extolling consistent political philosophies. At the end of the day, once families have obtained power and influence, they plot to keep it—even if it means committing what some would consider treasonous acts to their country of origin. In essence, their personal agendas transcend nation states and apparently, *outdated nationalist sentiments.* Marrs distills this from the history of interplay between several especially rich and famous Americans through their financing of Nazi Germany:

> When these same globalists became fearful of worldwide Communism they needed separate national or economic blocs to play off against each other for the tensions necessary for maximum profit and control) [consider the Hegelian dialectic we discussed earlier], they supported National Socialism in Germany. German army intelligence agent Adolf Hitler was funded to provide a bulwark against the Communist tide by enlarging his National Socialist German Workers Party (Nazis), in turn sowing the seeds of World War II. Three prominent Americans who were instrumental in funding the Nazis were National City Bank (now Citicorp) chairman John J. McCloy; Schroeder Bank attorneys Allen Dulles and his brother, John Foster Dulles; and Prescott Bush [father of George H.W. Bush], a director of Union Banking Corporation and the Hamburg America shipping line. It is interesting to note that, following World War II, McCloy became the high commissioner of occupied German; John Foster Dulles became President Eisenhower's secretary of state; Allen Dulles became the longest-serving CIA director; and Bush, as a senator from Connecticut, was instrumental in forming the CIA...[19]   Af-

ter World War II, the globalist agenda was advanced by the creation of the United Nations. An earlier attempt to create a transnational organization, the League of Nations, *failed because the U.S. Senate thought that ratification would end American sovereignty.* [Emphasis added]

To make the same point, but updating the political landscape to current day, Marrs quotes President George H.W. Bush's ('41') assistant secretary of housing, Catherine Austin Fitts. Fitts relates her experience of presenting a paper to a 2001 investment conference in London composed of journalists covering the move of governments to turn over program administration and financing to private concerns (aka, 'privatization'). Observing the various topics and speakers she comments:

As the pieces fit together, we shared a horrifying epiphany: the banks, corporations and investors acting in each global region were the exact same players. They were a relatively small group that reappeared again and again in Russia, Eastern Europe, and Asia accompanied by the same well-known accounting firms and law firms. Clearly, there was a global financial *coup d'état* * underway. [Emphasis in original][20]

Marrs concludes these comments by stating his thesis outright: "These globalists, who have manipulated world history for decades, if not centuries, are working a plan to turn the once-free and prosperous Republic of the United States into a socialist state populated by dumbed-down and destitute zombies by draining dry the nation's money supply. It is truly a trillion-dollar conspiracy."[21] As we will see, when Marrs says 'socialist state' he is actually saying a 'nation-

---

* A *coup d'état*, is "a sudden and decisive action in politics, especially one resulting in a change of government illegally or by force." (Dictionary.com)

al socialist state', meaning it leans to the far right, not far left as if it was only one-step short of Communism.

The Real Power in Government: Who Holds It?

Whether calling this progression the 'Fourth Reich' is overstating the case or not, the issue of globalism and the power of wealthy families who dominate what happens in our world *isn't really my ultimate focus in this study*. At some level I believe the evidence already proves the pursuits of powerful globalists are inconsistent with American principles of government. However, *a different matter needs to be underscored and brought to the attention of the American public.* While the wealthy indirectly rules the masses through pre-approved candidates (as the previously presented material indicates), instead, we must aim a spotlight toward their 'stage location' to bring to light the ideology of such wealthy elite—whether these elite are made rich by generational inheritance or 'world-class' success in corporate business (either 'old money' or 'new money'). We must ask, "What is their motivation?" In other words, we should study carefully what they believe. I argue their affirmations about politics, their agenda to remain in power, and in some cases *even their assumptions about the cosmos*, threaten America and our liberty.

To portray this issue properly, first we must appreciate that the populace has become increasingly cynical about the American government's ability to manage the country. In 2011, we are much more likely to agree that political ideologies of 'liberal' and 'conservative' (much less 'socialist' or 'capitalist') are no longer meaningful ways to label competing political 'players' and their plans. Most Americans draw the conclusion it doesn't seem to matter which Party has control—nothing gets done. We wonder why this is the case.

Perhaps we should question whether this governmental gridlock really results from the lack of either party enjoying a plurality in both houses of Congress. Could the malaise in our government be due to the lack of authority our representatives possess, especially after they learn how little influence they enjoy in setting direction for our nation? Could it be true that politicians realize (after serving in Washington for several years), what they accomplish has little effect on our nation's destiny; that the final result is fixed, and they do little more than rearrange the deck chairs on the Titanic? This is not to question their sincerity or their commitment to service. My challenge supposes there looms a prevailing despair which encourages loyalty to party politics over 'doing the People's business', since changing the fate of America resides outside their control. In the final analysis, politicians can only advance their careers within the Party—they can't change what happens to our country. The opportunity to 'make a difference' rests with non-elected power players.

In America, an increasing number suspect that behind both Republicans and Democrats are principals (i.e., personalities) manipulating both. For instance, the Council on Foreign Relations and the Trilateral Commission certainly include members of both parties. In some ways, whether politicians declare themselves liberal or conservative matters very little.[22] When we study the broad brush strokes painting the political picture in the world today, we readily see how, in the grand scheme of things, these differences are secondary. Instead, the real question today should be, "What forces are at work dominating the direction the *world* is heading?" This is a global question. Perhaps we should really say it is *a globalist question.* The point being: Americans should care less whether our leaders are Republican or Democrat. Instead, we should care earnestly whether our representatives are committed 'nationalists' or 'globalists'—whether they favor the elite ruling the world—or, whether they still believe our government should derive its power from the consent of the governed. Do the People still matter? Will the politician in question stake their career on what's best for the People? Do Americans come first? Almost to the man (or woman), our politicians are entirely silent on this subject, *even though it stands ultimately as the most important issue regarding governance in our time.*[23]

We should recall from our earliest training in American history that our Founding Fathers rejected monarchical and church dominance in government. Clearly, kings and priests were not elected officials. There *should be* separation of Church and State. The People, acting by majority, should determine who governs them. This was the core founding guideline of the United States.[*] Having said that, this constitutional principle doesn't mean Americans fail to yearn for kings and queens to make a fuss over (consider 'Camelot and the Kennedy's' or the love America displayed for Princess Diana of England). Nor does it mean that the ancient monarchy of Europe has had no impact on American politics. Toward the conclusion of Book Two, I will argue it does. Nonetheless, the essence of my argument remains steady: the People are to be in charge through their elected officials, not the rich and powerful through special favoritism granted by patronized politicians. That comprises the political aspect of my argument.

---

[*] In other words, we reject the premise of the Old World. There is no such thing as 'the divine right of kings' nor is there a place for the ecclesiastical hierarchy to dictate affairs of State. While the policy of 'separation of church and state' remains the excuse for limiting the place of Christian sentiments in schools, as a principle for protecting the rights of individuals to be governed by elected officials, it stands as the most essential element of our republic.

However, what lies at the heart of my concern goes well beyond political philosophy. It deals with spiritual commitments made by individuals in our society and the great families of the world who lay claim to power with the help of forces beyond the media and political influence.

The Paranormal Power Quest

Instead of the explicit danger of globalism, my ultimate concern regards something much more titillating and controversial. Essentially, as I hinted above, it lies with the spiritual allegiances and affirmations made by the rich and powerful in our world. The question can be phrased as follows: "What happens to a country *when its leaders seek power from occult (hidden) or unnatural sources?*

To which 'unnatural power sources' am I referring? Let me be clear: I speak of powers that lie beyond the *empirical*[*] world (what we can encounter through our five senses). To be even more specific, allow me to ask and answer a more intriguing question: "What happens when humanity lays hold of technologies that transcend powers we find in the 'everyday world' (such as the media, money, and political influence)?" My answer: pursuing such powers, a *power quest* if you will, inevitably guides such governments into unfathomable evil. Totalitarianism becomes inevitable. Moreover, the reach of the government goes even deeper than controlling freedom of speech, the right to own guns, or the right to assembly.

---

[*] Empirical is defined in the Encarta Dictionary as "based on or characterized by observation and experiment instead of theory" and empiricism as a "philosophy derived as knowledge from experience, particularly from sensory observation, and not derived from the application of logic."

I contend this decrease in freedom is happening in America today. Even though this is the nation I love and much prefer to live in, the facts tell us our country has been moving increasingly this direction since the end of World War II. It gained momentum with the death of John. F. Kennedy. However, the driving forces are more than out-of-control greed and the maneuverings of the military-industrial complex. Our country has been led down this darkened pathway by English supernaturalism, German occultism, and American 'spiritualist' ideologies (such as *Theosophy*) from the nineteenth and early twentieth centuries. I argue this *power quest*—far more detrimental if not debilitating to American democracy—continues at work today. And far too few Americans, even evangelicals in America who may fancy themselves politically attuned, have little idea just how far down this *spiritualist trail* America has already traversed—and the political implications it promises over the longer-term.

The fact that globalism comprises a good portion of this itinerary is important only in that there exists little offsetting force to limit the damage which will result (here I'm employing the Hegelian dialectic in a practical sense). Nothing stands in the way of a self-conscious and directed 'nationalist' political platform, with spiritual sensitivity to the hidden (occult) agenda held by some members in government (and more importantly, the powerful who stand behind the curtains influencing our government). Consequently, no active and organized political counter-point opposes the globalist agenda. But even more importantly, no conscious effort exists to rebuff and restrain (if not rebuke) the power source behind *this globalist power quest.* Any attempt to counter it, exposes such a person to public ridicule or charges that such a one is mixing politics and religion in the public square. Surely this is a 'politically *incorrect*' course of action! Nevertheless, let the chips fall where they may.

Back to the disclosure of the 'power source': I argue this pernicious force resides amidst the *supernatural** or *paranormal*. As we will see in Chapter Two, our failure to recognize it for what it is, stems in part from our misunderstanding of the distinction between the realms of *the supernatural and the natural*. This force hides behind the cloak provided by the continued advance of *modern physics*. Because of many new vistas in this 'precise' science, we find it more difficult today to distinguish what is *normal* from what is *paranormal*. We will bother ourselves to study these astonishing new scientific insights because they *inspire spiritualism*—that is, a spiritualist sees them as *proof* his or her view is correct. Hence, despite the intellectual difficulty to grasp all of the principles of the 'new physics', it remains a highly relevant and key subject in our study.

To reiterate, my argument asserts that any regime which embraces an 'other-worldly' or occult (and I argue necessarily pagan and fearful) ideology inconsistent with a Judeo-Christian worldview or cosmology,† will radically alter the 'standard operating procedures' of said administration in regards to human rights, personal liberty, and justice. In short, the rule of law upon which western society is based can and will be threatened if such a widespread ideology *based upon historical (read: pagan) supernaturalism* becomes (or more likely, *continues to be*) a dominating influence amongst those who govern. Like witches casting spells on their victims, governments that employ technologies that are (or border) on the paranormal, inevitably

---

* The **supernatural** consists of anything besides what one holds to be natural, exists outside natural law, and beyond the observable universe.

†According to Dictionary.com: "**Cosmology** is the branch of philosophy dealing with the origin and general structure of the universe, with its parts, elements, and laws, and especially with such of its characteristics as space, time, causality, and freedom."

lead to exploitation of the governed. Although claimed that all actions are taken to secure the nation from enemies foreign or domestic, manipulation of personal liberties often goes unchecked when its justification ultimately lies in the principles of that ideology.

In effect, *a pagan supernaturalism should be judged another **religion** from which the 'governed' should not be subjected.* It is, however (due to the way its promoters define it), an *inconspicuous religion* masquerading as a secular philosophy. As a result, it slips through the filter our constitution established regarding the separation of 'Church from State'. And as I have argued elsewhere (along with others, such as Dan Brown, author of *The Lost Symbol),* the signs of such paganism are writ large in our national symbols and stand out clearly in the very design of our nation's capital.

So is it preposterous that a quiet, spiritually-based (and perhaps clandestine) *coup d'état* could happen in our country? Is it possible that for all intents and purposes, *it has already happened* and there is no turning back from its implications? Or is this scare just the same view promoted by overly zealous, nationalistically-minded conspiracy theorists that see communists or socialists behind every bush?

In the pages ahead, I hope to document just how much the ideals of pagan supernaturalism have *already* influenced America and why, in the years to come, America *could* become the launch pad for the charismatic leader the Bible calls Antichrist, who according to the prophet Daniel, embodies the 'god of forces'.[24] In Daniel we read, *"But in his estate shall he honor the God of forces: and a god whom his father's knew not shall he honor with gold, and silver, and with precious stones, and pleasant things"* (Daniel 11:38).[25]

No doubt, my most vocal supporters will be those who take such biblical prophecies seriously. For the Bible's story and implied cosmology contend an ongoing conspiracy (millennia old) rages amongst sinister forces rejecting God's plan for the world and the place of humankind in it. As a result, these *sinister forces* become one of the most important factors in what transpires within the political realm. I contend spiritualism reigns on many levels. Indeed, *spiritualism* remains a dynamic power in the today's world. This is true whether it presents itself with the stereotypical unsophisticated occult trappings; or whether it appears cultured and erudite (minus the overt footprint of the devil of course), representing higher consciousness and world-peace as its calling card.

To some readers, my perspective may seem ridiculous and completely lacking in substance. But I argue, *wait until we place it in the context of recent history.* In the opening chapter, we will study the reality behind what motivated Nazi Germany during the twentieth century, a foreshadowing of a government system based upon an invasion of supernaturalism. My contention (and my fear) is that *what happened in Germany can and will happen in our world again.*

Specifically, America may be the target of history repeating itself. While academic historians have consistently dismissed or downplayed the supernatural aspects of Nazism, many of today's authors who represent history in their works reveal that the tide is turning. Through more recent discoveries and research, we now know that the *worldview* of the Nazis, their *weltanschauung*[*], was indeed based upon a *magical* understanding of *a pagan cosmology.* Hitler, Himmler, and many of the leaders of the Third Reich were far more than mere occult devotees. They were full-fledged black magicians with the most fantastic of creeds. They sought to amass occult power

---

[*]According to the Merriam-Webster dictionary, "*weltanschauung* is a comprehensive conception or apprehension of the world especially from a specific standpoint."

to govern their people and to rule the world. It was the center of their motivation and their guiding principle. It was not a peripheral issue. Therefore, the issue isn't "has any government ever sought paranormal power to govern its people?" It clearly has. The question is, "Will it happen again?" More subtly, "What shape or form will it take if it does?" If it occurs in America, could we recognize it before it becomes too late to oppose it?

Accordingly, I contend the issue of power that dominates politics in our future will be at the most fundamental level, a *spiritual contest.* And the players behind the scenes go far beyond the Rockefellers, Morgans, Warburgs, and the Rothschilds. It is not that these families (along with the Bushes and selected monarchies in Europe) aren't the primary semi-visible movers and shakers. They certainly seem to be. However, we will examine that there are other, much deeper ultra-dimensional forces playing a part in what occurs in our world. And despite popular notions to the contrary, these powers aren't drinking to our health and good fortune.

The Basics of Bible Cosmology—The Lie of Satan

"In the beginning" the Bible teaches that Satan tempted Eve with the prospect of knowing good and evil. But knowledge in and of itself wasn't the real temptation—*the quest for power was behind his suggestion.* "You shall be as gods" said the talking snake in the Garden. Knowing the difference between good and evil (what the apple represented), was merely the hors d'oeuvre. The captivating goal transcending the temptation was achieving *a dominant position to secure one's station or one's place at the table*—to carry the food analogy perhaps a bit too far. The most essential aspect of

Satan's assertion was, "You shall not die." The core element in the Judeo-Christian theodicy[*] is what Satan promised humankind: they would be *as the gods* and more importantly, *they would be immortal.* (In the final chapter of this book we will assert, immortality is indeed the final arbitrator of significance—the 'snake' had put his finger on the most sensitive issue.) Many Christian scholars believe Satan's promise to be what the New Testament calls, "The Lie."[†] Others believe this to be the driving motivation behind humanity's willingness to consider *Satan*, rather than God, as the savior of humankind, another topic into which we will soon delve.

Francis Bacon said, "Knowledge is power" and in this context, hardly could truer words be spoken. The 'snake' disputed the Word of the Lord and suggested that humankind would be better off obtaining its own power and becoming 'as the gods'. "Better to control your own destiny" he argued. His offer hints Adam and Eve might have already been entertaining such thoughts. So if we concluded the gardeners of Eden made a snap decision simply because they wanted to crunch an apple, our conclusion would be way off target. In the final analysis, the temptation certainly wasn't a bite of fruit nor was it a craving for any food at all. The issue was whether obtaining power and being "like God", through independent action, was the better way to go. Were they capable of becoming like God?

In one sense, the story of the Bible can be streamlined to a single issue (as it relates to what evangelicals call experiencing a 'personal

---

[*] A theodicy is an explanation of why evil exists in the world despite an unswerving conviction that God is good and created the world to be good.

[†] "*For this reason God sends them a powerful delusion so that they will believe* **the lie**" (II Thessalonians 2:11, New International Version). The Greek word is *pseudos,* from which we derive the prefix, *pseudo,* meaning *false or fabricated, i.e., not authentic.*

relationship with God'): "Are we willing to rely upon the Word of God (and His power) to guide and safeguard our lives; or would we rather demand (in the famous words of a national hamburger chain) that we 'have it our way'?" In other words, "Do we wish to trust in God and His plan; or instead, bank on ourselves?" Satan's temptation both then and now suggests we 'go our own way' and by so doing, unwittingly, follow his fabricated (inauthentic) and self-seeking passageway to ruin.

As a nation clearly teetering on becoming far less than we once were, similar questions must be asked regarding the destiny and purpose of our culture and society: "Just how much do we believe the words on the coins we mint, 'In God We Trust'? Do we believe that our fate rests in the hands of God and whether we obey His laws? Or would we rather tap into other sources of power and rely upon those 'powers' to establish our security and prosperity?" Are we capable of doing without God? Would we be better off if we did?

Despite the popular view held by our culture—that we are now by-and-large *totally secular and scientific in mindset*—the facts argue otherwise. America has always been a haunt for the supernatural. Today's overt interest in vampires, ghost hunting, and Wicca is just the latest outbreak in what has been a never-ending epidemic in our popular culture. That it often entraps many of our brightest intellectuals makes the mystery all the more menacing.

In summary, the shadow leadership of our nation (and elsewhere in the world) engages in a *power quest* to achieve global dominance through the aid of forces it mistakenly believes to be beneficent— forces which our leadership should instead emphatically repudiate. In effect, we don't realize (although many do), the wealthy and powerful who pull the strings have become the 'sorcerer's apprentices'. Unbeknownst to them, they thrive merely one degree of separation apart from the diabolical force empowering the very sorcerer himself.   It is to disclose this situation, to pull back the curtains if you will, to which this author pledges his efforts in the pages ahead.

NOTES

[1] Marx and Engels, *The Communist Manifesto*, 1948.

[2] "In his book *Red Holocaust*, Steven Rosefielde argues that Communism's internal contradictions "caused to be killed" approximately 60 million people and perhaps tens of millions more, and that this "Red Holocaust" – the peacetime mass killings and other related crimes against humanity perpetrated by Communist leaders such as Joseph Stalin, Kim Il Sung, Mao Tse-tung, Ho Chi Minh and Pol Pot—should be the centerpiece of any net assessment of Communism. He states that the aforementioned leaders are "collectively guilty of holocaust-scale felonious homicides." Rosefielde (2009) *Red Holocaust* pp. 1, 7. (See Wikipedia.org/wiki/Mass_killings_under_Communism).

[3] We are reminded of Francis Bacon's contention that nothing was so absurd that some philosopher at some time hadn't already said it!

[4] The historical process in Hegel comprises an early example of 'idealism' in which 'mind' guides what happens in the world. For Hegel, 'mind' is God, just as for Alfred N. Whitehead, 'process' is God. Teilhard de Chardin also falls into this group as do many New Age thinkers who draw upon these ideologies. The point: God progresses through time—He is 'becoming'. Orthodoxy supposes this axiom would admit an imperfection in God's being.

[5] Evangelicals, as Francis Schaeffer noted rather harshly in regard to S.K. (See his two books, *The God Who is There* and *Escape from Reason*), do regard our faith as 'personal' but not irrational, as S.K. ever so adamantly insisted that it was. However, in fairness to S.K., the 'rational' was the Hegelian system that he abhorred, which supposed God was only a great mind and an historical process, without the quality of personhood that orthodoxy adamantly professes.

[6] Nietzsche, Friedrich. *Beyond Good and Evil*. London: Penguin Books. (1973) p. 96

[7] Ibid, p. 127.

[8] See my essay, "The Übermensch and the Antichrist", in *Pandemonium's Engine*, published by Defender Books, Crane, Mo., (2011).

[9] Nietzsche, Friedrich, *Ecce Homo*, from the Chapter, "Why I Write Such Good Books." This self-analysis was written in 1888 and published in 1908 *Ecce Homo* either means, "How one becomes what one is" or as is translated with Pontius Pilate's words to the Jewish crowd regarding the presentation of

Jesus, "Behold the man!" My bet, given Nietzsche's hatred for Christianity is the latter, in something of a sick pun.

[10] Additionally, we should underscore that Fascism implies collusion between the State and mega-corporations (popularly translated into German that would be "über-businesses!")

[11] One a political think tank composed of major political players, academicians and staff (CFR) and the other an association of politicians and business persons from the world's democracies in Europe, Japan and North America hoping to coordinate their respective agendas (TLC).

[12] See http://www.bbc.co.uk/news/magazine-13682082, and http://en.wikipedia. org/wiki/ Bilderberg_Group#cite_note-BBC_News_Magazine_2011-0.

[13] Marrs, Jim, *The Trillion-Dollar Conspiracy*, New York: Harper Books, p. 16.

[14] Ibid., p. 42.

[15] Domhoff's suggestion is that it is not historically true in America, but had become a current fact (this book was published as I said in the 1960s). Of course, 50 years later, the statistics argue conclusively that it is even truer today than it was then.

[16] Ibid, p. 45, 46. My point of course is not to denigrate the capitalist motive to operate independent of the government and to generate profit. The question is how that profit is used and whether it is unfairly abused to ensure that the middle class has little say in what happens with their government.

[17] See his book, *Between Two Ages.*

[18] This metaphorical interpretation does not rule out a very literal interpretation of what Nimrod may have sought on the plain of Shinar.

[19] George H. W. Bush (son of Prescott, and 41st President of the United States) was likely a CIA operative in the 1950s and was at the center of the CIA's involvement in the plot to assassinate Kennedy according to author, Russ Baker in his book, *Family of Secrets*, Bloomsbury Press, New York, 2009. If true, this adds to other evidence that one of the most important dynamics in American politics during the twentieth century was the family squabble of the Kennedy's versus the Bushes which may have culminated in murder.

[20] Ibid. p. 16.

[21] Ibid, p. 18.

[22] This is not to deny the great polarization amongst politicians and the people of our country. The extremes of both sides get the most press. The country seems 'split down the middle', 50/50. But the great majority of Americas are 'centrist' and it is for this reason that Presidents always find themselves forced to 'govern from the middle.'

[23] Given what we will document in Book Two about John F. Kennedy and possible reasons for his assassination, it is likely that every politician on the national scene is well aware of how dangerous this discussion can be to one's personal longevity as a politician... or more directly his or her mortality.

[24] The standard scenario of end-times experts is that the Antichrist will arise in Europe and head up a ten-nation confederation there. I don't wish to contradict this point of view. However, it is conceivable that America, because it is a colony of Europe being populated heavily by Europeans could still lead this confederacy. There is little doubt that America's closest political alliances are with the English, the French, and the Germans... all of which are likely vital to the final ten-nation confederation headed by Antichrist. Today, if the Antichrist were to appear and lead military powers that lie beyond the ability of any to oppose ("Who can make war with the Beast?"), he would have to be an American president. Only time will tell whether that shift in power will in fact transfer from America to Europe or whether the biblical fulfillment of Daniel's and John's prophecy of 'the coming prince' (Daniel 9:24-27; Revelation 13) rests with America. *This book proposes that possibility*—hence, the call for Americans to resist his coming.

[25] My interpretation of this verse: the Antichrist will have Jewish blood and therefore 'his fathers' who honored Jehovah did not honor the god of forces, which the Bible calls 'angels, powers, and principalities.' (See Ephesians 6:12, Colossians 1:16). His forebears honored a personal God, Jehovah. The reference to jewels may also suggest that the Antichrist and fiscal power are tied together too.

CHAPTER ONE:

THE ASCENDANCY OF SPIRITUALISM IN TWENTIETH CENTURY EUROPE

For what we do presage is not in grosse,
For we are brethren of the Rosie Crosse;
We have the Mason Word and second sight,
Things for to come we can foretell aright.

Henry Adamson, *The Muses' Threnodie**, Perth, 1638

It is apparent that the SS itself is the visible extension of the Thule Ge-sellschaft into the Third Reich. Or, to put it differently, via the National Socialist Party, an occult secret society had seized the reigns of authority in one of the world's great powers, and could thus direct the entire ener-gies of that state into the overt and covert pursuit of its agendas.

Joseph P. Farrell, *The SS Brotherhood of the Bell*, 2006

Magic Men in Modern Times

To understand the spiritual force which quietly and secretly motivates political dominance in America, we must first understand how it manifested in Europe. There its sinister power fanned the flames of hatred, racism, and violence igniting the globe into two worldwide, catastrophic wars. Neither was the 'war to end all wars' as the first was initially hailed. Indeed, the essential premise of this study reckons this same force continues to circulate today and will eventually spark another world war, with the focus on the Middle East engaging America as its most formidable player.

---

* '*Threnodie*' spelled in modern English, *threnody*, is a lament for the dead in the form of a song, poem, or speech.

At the beginning of the twentieth century, mysticism and magic had already captured the imaginations (if not the souls) of many rich and intellectual. As Nietzsche proclaimed in Germany, God was dead. However, spiritual philosophies disassociated from theism persisted like a bad habit. Although this perspective flies in the face of conventional wisdom from our 'post-modern' point of view, these affirmations of faith in the paranormal weren't from the simpleminded or illiterate. The new faith in the supernatural was embraced by the rich, the intelligent, and the elite. Mind you, the crème de la crème weren't merely adopting a new strain of pantheism—they had progressed far beyond that in their esoteric aspirations. They were engaging *in magic*—not just any old magic—they were into black magic and seeking to become its esteemed practitioners, even if they would be viewed as such only by those who held the same malevolent views.

One of the most intriguing books written during the past 50 years is a work by two Frenchmen, Louis Pauwels and Jacques Bergier entitled *The Morning of the Magicians* (subtitled, *Secret Societies, Conspiracies, and Vanished Civilizations*). Published in 1960, the insights gathered in this volume still provoke new vistas into the mechanisms of history and in particular, Hitler and the Third Reich.

This French tandem chronicles the origins of formative influence on Nazism. As we will see, many of the extreme notions that Hitler and Himmler inflicted upon the world actually originated from the English (and from others in America). Indeed, while the pagan legends of gods were well dispersed throughout Europe; it was in England (and all of the United Kingdom) that the ground was especially well-tilled for growing a healthy crop of paranormal partisans. It is perplexing how supernaturalism was made widespread in English literary groups and secret societies by the middle of the nineteenth century when one would have supposed the Enlightenment of the eighteenth century was still dominating culture.

Pauwels and Bergier comment, "The Golden Dawn, founded in 1887, was an offshoot of the English Rosicrucian Society created twenty years earlier by Robert Wentworth Little, and consisted largely of leading Freemasons. The latter society had about 144 members [a number specifically sought by its founder for occult numerological reasons], including [Lord Edward] Bulwer-Lytton, author of *The Last Days of Pompeii*."[1] Of Bulwer-Lytton, we will have more to say in a moment. But take note of the cross-over memberships of those involved in occult groups. The Rosicrucian Society[2] mentioned here had quietly existed for almost 300 years in England. It was founded many believe by Francis Bacon but certainly by one or more of the many notable members of the so-called 'Invisible College' (Christopher Wren, Robert Boyle, and Bacon to drop only a few of the relevant names). This group would emerge after Oliver Cromwell's 'protectorate' (once his puritan politics were no more than a memory) and eventually form the Royal Society (the cadre of the most supremely eloquent and erudite in England). We discover from Pauwels and Bergier's remarks that Freemasons were present too (who we might consider, at least for now, 'Rosicrucians Light').

As many have documented[3] Freemasonry existed in the United Kingdom (beginning in Scotland) in the 15th century and may have begun as early as the first decade of the 14th with the escape of the Knights Templar from the rage of Philip IV ('the Fair') of France, as part of his roundup of the ill-fated Templars on Friday, October 13th, 1307. Besides destroying the first truly international banking organization, Philip forced those Templars underground (or more accurately off the soil of France altogether). Their theorized trek to Scotland enabled many to escape burning at the stake (such as their Grand Master Jacques DeMolay, 1240-1314) or dying a miserable death in a French prison. Although disputed by most academicians (who make a habit of dispelling widely held popular legends, many times incorrectly), it nevertheless remains a pervasive point of view in alternate history inasmuch as the most well-known historians within the Rosicrucians and the Freemasons point to the Knights Templar as their forebears.[4]

But before we get caught in the quagmire of passing judgment on the veracity of Templar influence in Freemasonry; we should return to the Order of the Golden Dawn, recognizing it to be far more than a civic club or an institution pursuing charitable objectives:

> The Golden Dawn, with a smaller membership, was formed for the practice of ceremonial magic and the acquisition of initiatory knowledge and powers. Its leaders were [William] Woodman, [Samuel] Mathers, and Wynn Westcott... It was in contact with similar German societies, some of whose members were later associated with Rudolf Steiner's famous anthroposophical movement and other influential sects during the pre-Nazi period. Later on it came under the leadership of Aleister Crowley, an altogether extraordinary man who was certainly one of the greatest exponents of the neo-paganism whose development in Germany we have noted.
>
> S. L. Mathers, after the death of Woodman and the resignation of Westcott, was the Grand Master of the Golden Dawn, which he directed for some time from Paris, where he had just married Henri Bergson's sister.
>
> Mathers was succeeded in his office by the celebrated poet W.B. Yeats, who was later to become a Nobel Prize winner.
>
> Yeats took the name *Frere Demon est Deus Inversus* (Brother Devil is God Reversed). He used to preside over the meetings dressed in a kilt, wearing a black mask and a golden dagger in his belt.
>
> Arthur Machen [who we will discuss below] took the name of *Filus Aquarti* [his intended name is a bit unclear, my translation: Water Boy]. The Golden Dawn had one woman member: Florence Parr, Director of the Abby Theater and an intimate friend of Bernard Shaw. Other members included: Algernon Blackwood, Bram Stoker (the author of *Dracula*), Saw Rohmer, Peck, the

Astronomer Royal of Scotland, the celebrated engineer Allan Bennett, and Sir Gerald Kelly, President of the Royal Academy. It seems that on these exceptional people the Golden Dawn exercised a lasting influence, and they themselves admitted that their outlook on the world was changed, while the activities they indulged in never failed to prove both efficacious and uplifting.[5]

Arthur Machen is of particular interest to us not because of his few but intriguing literary achievements; rather, because he was a deep occultist and had a following of other notable, intellectual, and elite friends.[6] Toward the end of his life we learn he was in desperate financial straits; however, several friends and followers rushed to his aid. Pauwels and Bergier comment: "In 1943 [George] Bernard Shaw (he was then eighty years old), Max Beerbohm, and T. S. Eliot formed a committee to raise funds, which would save him [Machen] from ending his life in a workhouse. He was able to end his days in peace, in a little house in Buckinghamshire, where he died in 1947."[7]

I could go on, but the point is made that a considerable number of the elite and intellectual believed in the 'fantastic'. The list of giant literary figures alone is a "Who's Who"—Shaw, Eliot, and Yeats. Therefore, we should conclude (rightly I might emphasize) that at the turn of the century (twentieth century to be clear), many of the rich and powerful were up to their top hats in the occult as practitioners of magic and avid fans of those who wrote about and promoted the paranormal. It seems the enlightenment of the eighteenth century had waned in favor of the occult during the nineteenth.

Indeed, looking back from our historical perch today, we commonly assume such enlightened individuals would be skeptics, inclined toward scientific methods, and eschew anything remotely mystical. If anything, as we've just shown, *the trend of the day was the very opposite.* Equally puzzling, this startling trend didn't appear solely in the confines of our Mother Country.

When we turn to the emergence of German secret societies, it is important we recognize the connection to their English counterparts through shared 'intellectual history' (or more precisely 'occult history'). Despite the far more sinister and ultimately destructive Teutonic incarnations, their heritage and core ideology were energetically held in common on both sides of the English Channel.

Indeed, the most important linkage between the English and the Germans, from a literary perspective at least, was with the lesser known author and Freemason, Edward Bulwer-Lytton (1803-1873). Bulwer-Lytton was the originator of oft-repeated phrases such "The pen is mightier than the sword", "Pursuing the Almighty Dollar", and "It was a dark and stormy night." Yet, it was a different group of his most fanciful words that propelled the Third Reich forward.

Figure 4 - Lord Edward Bulwer-Lytton

Rising Supernaturalism in Pre-Hitler Germany

The story of German supernatural secret societies that ultimately led to the genesis of National Socialism (Nazis) was "founded, literally, on Bulwer-Lytton's novel *The Coming Race*."[8] Bulwer-Lytton's most famous novel, as mentioned earlier, was *The Last Days of*

Pompeii. But his *Coming Race* gave rise to the ideology self-identified as *The Vril*, a 'force' invented by Bulwer-Lytton in his novel. "The book describes a race of men psychically far in advance of ours. They have acquired powers over themselves and over things that make them almost godlike. For the moment they are in hiding. They live in caves in the center of the Earth. Soon they will emerge to reign over us."[9] Pauwels and Bergier comment that Bulwer-Lytton's 'fiction' intended to describe the future: "He set out to emphasize the realities of the spiritual world, and more especially, the infernal world. He considered himself an Initiate.[10] Through his romantic works of fiction he expressed the conviction that there are beings endowed with *superhuman powers*. These beings will supplant us and bring about a formidable *mutation* in the elect of the human race."[11] [Emphasis added] Bulwer-Lytton intended life should imitate art. Of course, he wouldn't be disappointed.

These esoteric concepts inspired a Berlin group called the Luminous Lodge, or *The Vril Society*. The story of Nazism begins with the Vril:

> The Vril is the enormous energy of which we only use a minute proportion in our daily life, the nerve center of our potential divinity. Whoever becomes master of the Vril will be the master of himself, of others round him, and of the world. [To them] this should be the only object of our desires, and all our efforts should be directed to that end. All the rest belongs to official psychology, morality, and religions and is worthless. The world will change: the Lords will emerge from the center of the Earth. Unless we have made an alliance with them and become Lords ourselves, we shall find ourselves among the slaves, on the dung heap that will nourish the roots of the New Cities that will arise.[12]

We see how the earlier discussion of Übermensch (in the Introduction) progresses toward an even more menacing path. No longer is the Übermensch a philosophical construct—a means to create a new foundation for morals and ethics. The Übermensch becomes a messiah figure, an 'Antichrist' if you will (a name Nietzsche would have endorsed as a worthy appellation for his iconic creation). In fact, this idea would become a 'binding' concept linking the various groups committed to such occult views. In essence: *the supernatural begat the superman.* Pauwels and Bergier provide this warning:

> We must also beware of the notion of the "unknown Superman." It is found in all the "black" mystical writings both in the West and in the East. Whether they live under the Earth or *came from other planets,* whether in the form of giants like those which are said to lie encased in cloth of gold in the crypts of Tibetan monasteries, or of shapeless and terrifying beings such as [H.P.] Lovecraft describes [an American author of horror, fantasy and science fiction, 1890-1937], do these "Unknown Superman," evoked in pagan and satanic rites, actually exist? When Machen speaks of the World of Evil, "full of caverns and crepuscular beings dwelling therein," he is referring, as an adept of the Golden Dawn, to that other world in which man comes into contact with the "Unknown Supermen." It seems certain that Hitler shared this belief, and even claimed to have been in touch with these "supermen."[13] [Emphasis added]

In fact, Pauwels and Bergier quote Herman Rauschning (1882-1982) who related these recollections: [14] "'The new man is living amongst us now! He is here!' exclaimed Hitler, triumphantly. "Isn't that enough for you? I will tell you a secret. I have seen the new man. He is intrepid and cruel. I was afraid of him.' In uttering these words, added Rauschning, 'Hitler was trembling in a kind of ecstasy.'"[15] The Vril according to Bulwer-Lytton was an energy source that those who lived underground wielded to their advantage. It is similar to the concept of "The Force" in George Lucas' *Star Wars.*

How enthralling that in both cases a fictional work introduced a spiritual concept many came to believe depicted the essential substance of spirit. Yet, we should be even more astounded how humankind, even while laying claim to both enlightenment and skepticism, incurably affirmed belief that 'reality' builds upon a spiritual base!

The Hyperboreans and the Thulists

However, the *Thule Society* which was much more important in establishing Nazi Germany. The name *Thule* came from a Nordic legend about a land far to the north of Germany, called Hyperborea.[16] Thule was its capital. Initially, before it became a Nordic notion, the legend had been handed down from the Greeks. Research suggests it arose from the earliest records of Pythias (now lost), one of their earliest historians (c. 330 BC). Pythias believed that the land of Hyperborea was actually England, the home of the Celts. Considering the distant and dangerous journey to this Island Kingdom one thousand years before Christ, it is easily seen why England would be held to be far to the north of Greece.[17] Later Greek historians doubted Pythias' account and offered other conjectures (corresponding to their expanding knowledge of geography). However, in Germany, the legend of Thule and Hyperborea was considered sacred and a satisfying explanation for the origin of the Aryan peoples—those connected to the 'Secret Doctrine'—most notably, *the lost continent of Atlantis.*

At the heart of the Thule Society was one Dietrich Eckart. Eckart shared an initiation with Hitler into 'higher consciousness' through the drug *mescaline*—it having been newly developed early in the twentieth century. Imprisoned together after the turmoil involving battles with the Bolsheviks early in the 1920's, these 'German workers' discovered they had much in common (inasmuch as both had lived ne'er-do-well lives to that point). But it would be Eckart who would eventually initiate Adolf Hitler into the sexual magic of the Englishman *Aleister Crowley.* We should note in passing that besides his participation in the Golden Dawn, Crowley would become the founder of the *Ordo Templi Orientis* (OTO) founded in 1904.[18] The OTO would continue to be a factor in the development of the occult in America as we will discuss later in this book.

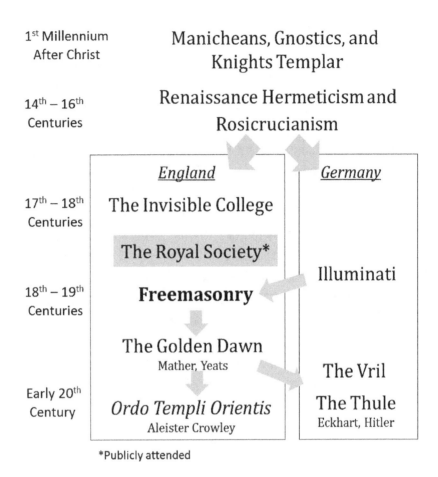

1st Millennium
After Christ

14th – 16th
Centuries

17th – 18th
Centuries

18th – 19th
Centuries

Early 20th
Century

Manicheans, Gnostics, and
Knights Templar

Renaissance Hermeticism and
Rosicrucianism

England   *Germany*

The Invisible College

The Royal Society*

Freemasonry

Illuminati

The Golden Dawn
Mather, Yeats

The Vril

Ordo Templi Orientis
Aleister Crowley

The Thule
Eckhart, Hitler

*Publicly attended

Figure 5 – Evolution of Key Secret Societies

Another voice who contributes significant 'in-between the lines' information is a mystic named Trevor Ravenscroft and author of several captivating books. Ravenscroft himself was heavily influenced by Gnosticism (more specifically, Manichean Christianity) having been a student of Walter Johannes Stein—himself a student of Rudolf Steiner. Steiner was the Founder of Anthroposophy[19] in Germany, also during the same period as The Vril. Of Steiner too, we will have more to disclose later. But for now, we can depict Steiner and Stein as purveyors of the "good side of the Force" to use filmmaker Lucas' construction.[20] Ravenscroft provided the memoirs of Walter Johannes Stein in his fascinating book *The Spear of Destiny*. In this work, we learn Stein was a personal acquaintance of Adolf Hitler when Hitler was a young man. After Stein fled Germany prior to the beginning of the War (WWII) fearing what was to come, he would later become a clandestine consultant to Winston Churchill supplying insights into Hitler's psyche, in part using his paranormal abilities as well as his personal acquaintance of Hitler, helping to predict the German Fuehrer's next move.

Ravenscroft offered many insights into the importance of the *Thule Gesellschaft* and its role in the formation of the German Workers Party (soon to be known as the National Socialists):

> Only a small nucleus, ordered to attend by [Dietrich] Eckart himself [who Hitler considered the father of the Nazi party], had graduated to a deeper knowledge of occultism through participation in many different orders, lodges, movements and societies more or less closely associated with the nineteenth-century renaissance of Oriental philosophy and ritual magic. It was this compact inner circle within the Thule *Gesellschaft*, the existence of which was unknown to the general membership, which was awaiting the imminent appearance of a German Messiah.[21]

> Dietrich Eckart was not among the earliest members of the Thule Group and he only joined it to use the movement for his own purposes. He had already made the acquaintance of the so-called Count Heinrich von Sebottendorf, who founded the Thule Gesellschaft as an offshoot of an anti-Semitic Lodge of the ancient *Germanenorden*. It did not take Eckart long to discover that this 'nobleman's' real name was Rudolf Glauer, or that he had been born the son of an engine-driver from Dresden. Rudolf Glauer claimed he had been officially adopted under Turkish Law by Heinrich von Sebottendorf and had right to the title of Count. Eckart made no attempt to expose him for he did not wish to undermine the reputation and power the Group was beginning to establish in Bavaria.[22]

Glauer had spent 13 years of his life in Turkey where he studied Sufi meditation and read Oriental philosophy. During this experience he was heavily influenced by Madame Helena Petrovna Blavatsky's ponderous *Secret Doctrine*. Ravenscroft comments:

Figure 6 – Cover,
The Spear of Destiny

Glauer himself was entirely lacking in spiritual faculty. He simply transposed Blavatsky's grotesque descriptions of the magical conditions prevailing in the vanished civilization of 'Atlantis' to give a pre-historical background to the mythological world of the Edda in which Gods, giants, men and beasts were engaged in a bloodcurdling struggle for survival. In respinning the age-old legends of Niflheim, Muspellsheim and Midgard, he introduced Theosophical ideas about the magical relationship between cosmos, earth and man. He predicted that the latent powers and faculties slumbering in the blood of the Aryan race would unfold in the twentieth century when 'Supermen' would reappear on earth to awaken the German people to the glories of their ancient heritage and lead them in the conquest of the world.

The original conception of the modern Thulists was extremely crude and naïve. The more sophisticated versions of the legend of Thule only gradually developed in the hands of Dietrich Eckart and General Karl Haushofer, and were later further refined and extended under the direction of Reichsführer SS Heinrich Himmler, who terrorized a large section of the German academic world into lending a professional hand at perpetuating the myth of German racial superiority.[23]

Ravenscroft reveals Hitler loved the Teutonic myths from his youth and gained his idea of the 'Fatherland' from these. "In Vienna he had even written bloodthirsty dramas about the epic heroes of the Edda whose deeds he believed were living on in the German blood in his veins. Now through his new associates in the Thule Group he was plunged into the world of cosmology and magic which had inspired the twentieth-century rebirth of Thule."[24]

But beyond adopting the cosmology of a supernatural universe, Hitler's character and perspectives were influenced by "the inner core within the Thule Group [that] were [sic] all Satanists who practiced Black Magic. That is to say, they were solely concerned with raising their consciousness by means of rituals to an awareness of evil and *non-human Intelligences in the Universe* and with achieving a means of communication with these Intelligences."[25] [Emphasis added]. Such *intelligences* will, as we shall see, become a common theme throughout the twentieth and into the twenty-first centuries. It is intriguing that even at this early point in time (1920s) the Vril mediums such as Maria Orsic would communicate how *these intelligences were from worlds beyond earth.* The star system from which they supposedly communicated was our nearby neighboring star *Alderbaran* (65 million light years from earth).[26]

The German Mystical Mindset

Ravenscroft admonishes Westerners to step up to the necessary challenge and come to terms with the insanity of Hitler that could and did reach these extreme bounds. Our incredulity, he believes, stems from our dissimilar attitude to what Germans hold to be the connections between 'heaven and earth'—or as Hermes Trismegistus[27] proclaimed, "As above, so below." Ravenscroft cites numerous passages from Johann Wolfgang von Goethe (1749-1832), specifically from his *Faust*, to point out the different mindset in Germany from the rest of Europe. One such passage is quoted below: [28]

> *How each the whole its substance gives,*
> *Each in the other works and lives!*
> *See heavenly forces rising and descending*
> *Their golden urns reciprocally lending:*
> *On wings that winnow sweet blessing*
> *From heaven through the earth they're pressing*
> *To fill the All with harmonies caressing...*

The then-contemporary German mind had a much more mystical appreciation for occult mysteries than did the English counterpart. However, this didn't mean that all Englishmen were purely naturalists as we've already documented. Ravenscroft distinguishes the English occult temperament from the German *zeitgeist*[*] with these words:

> Despite the fact that the most significant early growth in the reappearance of ancient magic in the modern age took place here in England [Ravenscroft being an Englishman], it is the Western mind that finds it almost insuperably difficult to accept the existence of any kind of magic as a reality. Perhaps this is so because the basic concept behind all magical practice is a belief in a correspondence between the Universe and Man, that is, between Macrocosm and Microcosm. The Western mind grounded in materialism finds such thinking totally unscientific and, in the case of the older generation anyway, the average Englishman, like Shakespeare's Hamlet, can get no further than a belief in the existence of 'ghosts'.[29]

Pauwels and Bergier echo essentially the same sentiment regarding the majority in the Western world today that fail to grasp the German view:

---

[*] *Zeitgeist*, a German concept of a 'world spirit'—perhaps 'animated'—that encapsulates ideas prevalent in a culture, particularly as expressed in literature, philosophy, and religion

It was not, in reality a mere temporary coalition of basic enemies that went to war with Germany, but a whole world—a single, united world that believes in progress, justice, equality, and science. One world having the same vision of the Cosmos, the same understanding of Universal laws, and one that assigns to man the same place, neither too exalted not too humble, in the Universe. One world that believes in reason and the reality of things, a world, in a word, which was to have disappeared altogether to leave room for another of which Hitler felt himself to be the prophet.[30]

And they conclude: "They [the Nazis] thought they were preparing the way for a demigod [the Übermensch] who would command the elements. They believed in a cycle of fire. They would conquer the ice, on Earth and in Heaven, as their soldiers died of exposure in performing their natural functions. They had fantastic ideas about the evolution of the species, and thought that far-reaching mutations would take place."[31]

Entering the 'interwar' period between World War I and II, we can surmise Germany was searching for its roots and ultimately its soul to find answers to explain its defeat in 'the Great War' (World War I); additionally, it was probing for a path to follow thenceforth. Yet, the message it found and the trail it chose went down the ancient *pagan* pathway—not the neo-orthodoxy (new orthodoxy) of Christian theologians Karl Barth and Dietrich Bonheoffer,[32] who were German contemporaries to Hitler and could have supplied the needed answers to the riddle of German destiny. Instead of the 'slave morality of Christ', Germany chose the 'master morality' of Rome. In contrast, better echoing the ideal implicit within the American 'spirit', Jesus had said, ""*Enter through the narrow gate; for the gate is wide and the way is broad that leads to destruction, and there are many who enter through it*" (Matthew 7:13, New American Standard Version). And as American poet Robert Frost conveyed, the pathway chosen makes all the difference.

Yet knowing how way leads on to way,
I doubted if I should ever come back.
I shall be telling this with a sigh
Somewhere ages and ages hence:
Two roads diverged in a wood, and I—
I took the one less traveled by,
And that has made all the difference. [33]

The Other Chamberlain

One of the most memorable villains from the American point of view at the start of the Second World War was Sir Neville Chamberlain (1869-1940). As Prime Minister of England, it was he who led a contingent of English and French to negotiate away Bohemia (Czechoslovakia, specifically the *Sudetenland*) to Hitler in hopes that peace would be maintained in Europe. Hitler desired *Lebensraum*—a "living space" to serve as a region of colonization for Germany.[34]

Figure 7 - Houston Stewart Chamberlain

Since the British and French imperialism of earlier centuries had supplied these peoples with profitable colonies, Germany felt it should have colonies too; although Germans proposed they carve out colonies from Eastern Europe and Russia. Chamberlain returned back to England announcing "Peace in our times" perhaps from a pacifist mentality borne as a first-hand witness of the millions killed in World War I (this 'peace' was known as the Munich Agreement of 1938). However, the peace negotiated was short-lived (without any input from the Bohemians of course—the arrogance of the English was in full force at that time). Consequently, Chamberlain's name shall forever be associated with one of the most maligned terms in politics: *appeasement.*

However, while Sir Neville is the most remembered Chamberlain from the period before the Second World War, it is his nephew, Houston Stewart Chamberlain (1855-1927), which actually deserves notoriety for being the more influential of the two. As we will learn, the story of Houston Stewart Chamberlain is another hard fact *linking the German quest for paranormal power with a similar disposition among the English elite.* Brought up in Paris, the son of an English Admiral, he was schooled there under the tutelage of a highly regarded Prussian instructor. With passion, he took to the great works of the German poets and philosophers such as Goethe, Hegel, Wagner, and

Figure 8 - Richard Wagner

no doubt Nietzsche. Chamberlain had a German mind and spirit even though English blood ran through his veins.

We learn from Ravenscroft that Chamberlain was enamored with Nietzsche's friend and composer Richard Wagner, but more for his ruminations on race and the future of humankind than his music. In fact, he was so enthusiastic about Wagner that he moved from England to Germany to be near him even though he didn't know him at the time. Before too many years went by, Chamberlain was elevated as a spiritual mentor to the Kaiser at the Palace in Potsdam. "His position there was more securely established and yet more dangerous than Rasputin's hold over the Romanov Court."[35]

Chamberlain's most famous work was entitled, *The Foundations of the Nineteenth Century* (1899). The book was an apologetic for the importance and influence of the Teutonic peoples on the western world. While Chamberlain argued that all Europeans derived from the Aryan race, he simultaneously provided a historical argument for anti-Semitism.

At the head of the Aryan peoples were the Teutonic race. To Chamberlain, Germany should be viewed as the purist of the European descendants of this 'Indo-European' race and all Europeans should even speak the German language. He viewed the meeting of Wilhelm of Prussia, Otto Bismarck and General Helmuth Karl von Moltke on the soil of the defeated French in 1871 as a "world-historic moment" when the German Master Race was born. This uniting of the German peoples was the dawn of "The Second Reich" (lasting until Germany's 1918 defeat ending World War I).[36]

By the time of his death in 1927, Chamberlain was paralyzed. His spirits were raised by a visit to his bedside at Bayreuth, Germany by two notable rising stars in German politics: Adolf Hitler and Joseph Goebbels. Chamberlain wrote Hitler an effusive thank you note which provides (almost) all we need to know about his true sentiments regarding Nazi Germany:

> Most respected and dear Hitler: It is hardly surprising that a man like [you] can give peace to a poor suffering spirit! Especially when he is dedicated to the service of the fatherland. My faith in Germandom has not wavered for a moment, though my hopes were—I confess—at a low ebb. With one stroke you have transformed the state of my soul. That Germany, in the hour of her greatest need, brings forth a Hitler—that is proof of her vitality... that the magnificent [Erich von] Ludendorff [the well-respected German general controlling the armed forces during the period between the wars] openly supports you and your movement: What wonderful confirmation! I can now go untroubled to sleep... May God protect you![37]

But Chamberlain's background and motivations are best explained when we look to Ravenscroft's 'inside information' from Walter Stein regarding this eccentric 'German lurking in British clothing' who history declares *to be Nietzsche's unexpected successor and the leading philosopher for German superiority*, being the author of Nazi ideology. Ravenscroft comments concerning Chamberlain's *Foundations* and its contribution to the Nazi identity with these words:

> With a stupendous erudition which mesmerized the German intellectuals, he contrived to synthesize the opposing doctrines of Richard Wagner and Friedrich Nietzsche. To the delight of the Junker families and the elite of the Officer Corps, he developed and expanded Wagner's doctrine of the Aryan Master Race. According to Chamberlain there was no need for the tragedy of the "Twilight of the Gods" [Wagner's Opera about the death of the Gods at the end of the world, an unsuspected influence upon Tolkien's *Lord of the Rings*] brought about by the pollution of inferior races. With one stroke of the pen, he eradicated the whole idea that a noble race needed to decline and decay with the force of a natural law. For it was at this point in the extension of Wagner's thinking that he cunningly incorporated Nietzsche's belief that a "Higher Race" could be bred. [38]

Indeed, the staggering facts disclosing Chamberlain's malevolent muses provide a foreshadowing of the presence and agenda of forces we will encounter throughout our study.

It seems that when Chamberlain became the spiritual leader of the Kaiser, his General—Helmuth von Moltke, a follower of Rudolf Steiner—became suspicious. For von Moltke, it was upsetting that an Englishmen had such privileged access to the German Kaiser. However, Ravenscroft explains why von Moltke's suspicions reached much further than the mere matter of possible covert operations in play through a citizen of a national rival. Drawing upon the clairvoyant awareness of Steiner,

General von Moltke knew a great deal about Chamberlain of which the Kaiser and his entourage at that time had no idea. He knew, for instance, that he wrote most of his works in a condition of trance in which hierarchies of evil spirits manifested themselves before his gaze. And that he never knew when or where his very soul would be seized by demons who drove him on into the feverish continuation of his work, leaving him later

like an exhausted shell, frequently in the near hysteria or on the point of collapse. Agents of the Abwehr keeping a close watch on Chamberlain had even reported seeing him fleeing from such invisible demons![39]

This stunning information is confirmed in principle at least by the famous historian of the Third Reich, William L. Shirer in his famous and highly regarded, *The Rise and Fall of the Third Reich* (1960). Shirer discloses:

Figure 9 - Rudolf Steiner

Houston Steward Chamberlain was given to seeing demons who, by his own account, drove him relentlessly to seek new fields of study and get on with his prodigious writings... Once, in 1896, when he was returning from Italy, the presence of a demon became so forceful that he got off the train at Gardone, shut himself up in a hotel room for eight days and, abandoning some work in music that he had contemplated wrote feverishly on a biological thesis until he had the germ of the theme that would dominate all his later works: *race and history*... Since he felt himself goaded on by demons, his books were written in the grip of a terrible fever, a veritable trance, a state of self-induced intoxication, so that, as he says in his biography, *Lebenswege*, he was often unable to recognize them as his own work, because they surpassed his expectations.[40]

Conclusion: What's Old is New Again

So it is that one of the greatest secrets of World War II is how the English literary (and occult) elite set the fuse to the firebomb that exploded throughout Nazi Germany. This seldom understood historical fact is superseded only by the more fantastic information (I deem now to be adequately documented for most readers) that the energy driving the Third Reich was contained in the sincere and passionate belief in powers (or forces) from beyond the sensible world. That is to say, National Socialism originated in ancient European myths, first from the Greeks, but colored by Germany's Teutonic heritage. Out of despair and frustration, the German leadership grew to believe the destruction they experienced at the close of the Second Reich (1918) could be overcome; however, their victory would only be achieved by throwing off the mores of Christian sentiments and returning to the paganism of Germany's past.

To cite Nietzsche's premise once more, Germans must become masters, not slaves. The abhorrent 'slave morality' must be vanquished. Germany's fate now lay in the creation of the Übermensch and the race of supermen. Surely technology would play a key part. However, like the fire of Prometheus, technology itself might best be captured directly from these gods now awakened by Eckart, Hitler, Himmler, and their ilk after two millenniums of fitful slumber.

Devilish fantasies developed in fictional stories of modern literary figures (Bulwer-Lytton) and a rewriting of European history disclosing factors most important to German reawakening (Chamberlain)— both contributed by Englishmen as we've underscored—added to the mythical Nordic stories, provided an ideology heavily reliant upon the supernatural and the occult. Germany would now seek power. But the power it would pursue would not be merely through its building the world's best war machines with traditional technologies. Decisive victory would be achieved only by harnessing forces from beyond the normal world of empirical experience and putting those powers to work in service of the Third Reich. As we will see, the exact nature of those forces would be 'fantastic' to say the least.

To clarify, it is not that such forces would be *plainly paranormal*—the truth is much more nuanced—these would be forces fundamentally distinct from those inherent in the worldview held by 'secular man'. In essence, these powers would emanate from a new view of *nature made to appear supernatural* and from a *supernature deemed capable of manipulation for military and governing purposes.*

Causality—the action of cause and effect—the basis for all true science (although much aligned in the prior hundred years by skeptics such as David Hume), *would be reinstated as a trusted way of looking at the world.* Additionally, the science of the Third Reich would allow other-worldly entities to become addressable agents responsive to the German hierarchy in order to influence the natural domain. In short, specters and saints—the demonic as well as the divine—indeed all manner of spiritual forces or entities, would have a *scientific* place in the new reality occult sages were formulating.

Consequently, we will study the contribution of the new and alternative *strange* physics, as the basis not only for scientific purposes, but as inspiration for the elite families of the world who seek to alter political power structures, not only before World War II in the European theater, but afterwards throughout the western world. We will see the influence of ideologies claiming support of this 'physics' and its principles most notably in America, the haven of the world's most popular and strident forms of spiritualism.

However, I will curtail my analysis at this point, lest I get ahead of the story.

NOTES

[1] Pauwels and Bergier, *The Morning of the Magicians*, Rochester, Vermont: Destiny Books, p. 189.

[2] "According to historian David Stevenson, it [Rosicrucianism] was also influential to Freemasonry as it was emerging in Scotland. In later centuries, many esoteric societies have claimed to derive their doctrines, in whole or in part, from the original Rosicrucians. Several modern societies, which date the beginning of the Order to earlier centuries, have been formed for the study of Rosicrucianism and allied subjects." See en.wikipedia.org /wiki/Rosicrucian.

[3] *The Knights Templar Revealed* by Butler and Defoe, and *Rule by Secrecy* by Jim Marrs, and in fictional accounts supposedly based on true history such as *The Da Vinci Code* by Dan Brown.

[4] See my book, *Decoding Doomsday*, for a more thorough sketch of the Templars and how they would up in Scotland. This would include Albert Pike and Manly P. Hall.

[5] Ibid. pp. 189-190.

[6] In his own right, Machen was a highly skilled author writing a meditation on the Grail called *The Great Return* in 1915 and a criticism of the modern world's explicit 'naturalism' in light of religious experience *entitled The Secret Glory* in 1922.

[7] Pauwels and Bergier, op. cit., p. 186.

[8] Ibid. p. 192.

[9] Ibid. p. 192.

[10] An initiate is (from the Encarta Dictionary), someone "knowing the secrets of a group, organization, or religion. Wentworth Little founded the English Rosicrucian Society in 1867. "Little was in contact with the German Rosicrucians. He recruited his followers, to the number of 144, from the ranks of the higher-ranking Freemasons. One of his disciples was Bulwer-Lytton." Ibid. p. 193.

[11] Ibid. p. 193.

[12] Ibid. p. 192.

[13] Ibid. p. 193.

[14] Rauschning's account in Conversations with Hitler and Hitler Speaks some experts now question. See http://www.ihr.org/jhr/ v06/ v06p499_Weber.html. However, this discussion in Wikipedia includes this important quotation from the famous historian Hugh Trevor-Roper that underscores its likely truthfulness: "The non-revisionist historian Hugh Trevor-Roper's initial view that the conversations recorded in Hitler Speaks were authentic also wavered as a result of the Hänel research. Whilst, in the introductory essay he wrote for *Hitler's Table Talk* in 1953 he had said:

"Hitler's own *Table Talk* in the crucial years of the *Machtergreifung* (1932-34), as briefly recorded by Hermann Rauschning, so startled the world (which could not even in 1939 credit him with either such ruthlessness or such ambitions) that it was for long regarded as spurious. It is now, I think, accepted. If any still doubt its genuineness, they will hardly do so after reading the volume now published. For here is the official, authentic record of Hitler's *Table-Talk* almost exactly ten years after the conversations recorded by Rauschning". From *Table Talk*, 1973 "Introduction" p.xiv.

[15] Pauwels and Bergier, op. cit., p. 195.

[16] It is interesting that Nietzsche addressed his followers as 'fellow Hyperboreans'.

[17] See http://en.wikipedia.org/wiki/Thule for a lively account of Thule's origins.

[18] Ravenscroft, Trevor, *The Spear of Destiny*, York Beach, ME, 1973, p. 164. Ravenscroft comments that Thule was also a group of assassins that committed hundreds of murders during the years 1919-1923. Many others were 'missing'. He conjectures, "And it was from among these missing persons, most of whom were either Jews or Communists, that we must look to find the 'sacrificial victims' who were murdered in the rites of 'Astrological Magic' carried out by Dietrich Eckart and the innermost circle of the Thule Gesellschaft" (p. 170).

[19] Steiner's *Anthroposophy* was a more sophisticated form of *Theosophy*. Switching the preface from 'Theo' to' Anthro' was also a more honest attempt to appropriately name this form of mysticism. *Theo* represents a personal but transcendent God whereas *anthro* relates to humanity as in 'anthropology'.

[20] But not the God of the Bible, I'm afraid.

[21] Ravenscroft, Trevor, op. cit., pp. 157-158.

[22] Ibid. pp. 158-159.

[23] Ibid. p. 159.

[24] Ibid. p. 160.

[25] Ibid. p. 161.

[26] Is this just another interesting coincidence or did George Lucas know a great deal about the Vril? Lucas' invented the name Alderaan, the second planet in the Alderaan system, the home of Princess Leia (Organa) in the *Star Wars* epic.

[27] A personage that may have only been legendary; however, 'Christian' writers "including Lactantius, Augustine, Giordano Bruno, Marsilio Ficino, Campanella and Giovanni Pico della Mirandola considered Hermes Trismegistus to be a wise pagan prophet who foresaw the coming of Christianity" (hence, his origin was pre-Christian and most likely in Hellenist Egypt). See

http://en.wikipedia.org/wiki/Hermes_Trismegistus. His writings were lost to Europe until brought to Italy by a priest serving as a book buyer for the collector Cosmi de' Medici (circa 1420). His works, found by the priest in Macedonia, helped spur the renaissance. Sometimes great moves in history begin with small insignificant things—like a monk on the back of a donkey buying books.

[28] Ibid. p. 162.

[29] Ibid. p. 161.

[30] Pauwels and Bergier, op. cit., p. 240.

[31] Ibid. p. 242.

[32] Barth, Bonheoffer, and Bultmann were three German theologians living in Germany during the first half of the twentieth century. Barth published an important theological treatise, *The Epistle to the Romans*, in 1921, which would encourage a reformation of sorts among many theologians in Europe. His view was much closer to the evangelical perspective than the liberal, emphasizing the transcendence of God, the deity of Christ, and a serious treatment of the Scriptures (although he did believe the Bible had the capacity to contain error). Bonheoffer of course was a martyr for Christianity. Hitler had him put to death just prior to the end of the war for his participation in a plot to assassinate Hitler. Bonheoffer's theology was even closer to orthodoxy including a strong commitment to a 'supernatural' basis for Christian belief (in a biblical sense – See *Revolt against Heaven*, Kenneth Hamilton, 1970, for a fair and bold treatment of Bonheoffer's views). Rudolf Bultmann (1884-1976) is a more difficult theologian for evangelicals to accept given his emphasis upon 'demythologizing' the New Testament to arrive at its true meaning. The point however, is that there were great German Christian minds at the time prior to the war, but they had no impact upon Nazism. Even noted theologian Paul Tillich, a staunch 'liberal,' recognized the demonic when he met Hitler and took his family to Switzerland where he lived out the war.

[33] From *The Road Less Chosen* by Robert Frost.

[34] "The official German history of World War II was to conclude that the conquest of *Lebensraum* was for Hitler and the rest of the National Socialists the most important German foreign policy goal. At his first meeting with all of the leading generals and admirals of the *Reich* on February 3, 1933, Hitler spoke of 'conquest of *Lebensraum* in the East and its ruthless Germanization' as his ultimate foreign policy objectives. For Hitler, the land which would provide sufficient *Lebensraum* for Germany was the Soviet Union, which for Hitler was both a nation that possessed vast and rich agricultural land and was inhabited by what Hitler saw as Slavic *Untermenschen* (sub-humans) ruled over by what he regarded as a gang of blood-thirsty, but grossly incompetent Jewish revolutionaries. These people were not Germanizable in his

eyes; only the soil was. Total extermination was not required only because Eastern Europe was regarded as having people of Aryan/Nordic descent, particularly among their leaders." (See en.wikipedia.org/wiki/ Lebensraum).

[35] Ravenscroft, op. cit., p. 117.

[36] The First Reich, just to complete the set, began during the Holy Roman Empire when Otto I of Germany was crowned Emperor in 962 until 1806 when Francis II, Emperor, abdicated during the Napoleonic Wars.

[37] Stackelberg, R., S.A. Winkle (2002). *The Nazi Germany Sourcebook: An Anthology of* Texts, Routeledge. pp. 84–85, quoted from Wikipedia.

[38] Ravenscroft, op. cit., p. 116. Again in this statement, we meet the concept of mutations that will produce a 'super race' or the Übermensch.

[39] Ibid. p. 119.

[40] From *The Rise and Fall of the Third Reich* by William L. Shirer, quoted by Ravenscroft, op. cit., p. 114.

CHAPTER TWO:

THE EMERGING COSMOLOGY—PHYSICS, ALCHEMY, AND THE NEW REALITY

There's nothing religious in any of these matters,
In the superstitions or in the prophecies
Or in anything that people call the occult—
Above all there is a way to look at nature
And a way to interpret nature
Which is completely legitimate.

Guillaume Apollinaire (1890-1918)

The Humbug * *is not the man who dives into mystery*
but the one who refuses to come out of it.

G.K. Chesterton (1874-1936)

Scientific Regard for the Supernatural

Conventional thinking assumes 'every cause has an effect' which specifies that whatever happens can be explained without recourse to the supernatural or the miraculous. The 'average person on the street' today, supposes most scientists continue to subscribe to this 'enlightenment way of thinking'. However, old conceptions of reality which dismissed esoteric phenomena (a point of view so dominant among the intelligentsia for more than 300 years) are now being questioned by serious thinkers. This is so despite skeptics like Richard Dawkins of the so-called *'Brights Movement'* who represent a diminishing number of noisy atheistic naturalists, in select scientific and secular circles, which reject the God of the Bible (or even the deistic/gnostic 'Supreme Being' of

---

* Something "silly or makes no sense; something… meant to deceive or cheat people." (Encarta Dictionary)

Freemasonry). Nevertheless, when one scans the panorama of various philosophies in play today, there are in fact *far fewer skeptics.* When it comes to the willingness of most philosophers and intellectuals to, shall we say 'expect the unexpected', many smart people find reasons to believe in the mystical. Mystery, if not mysticism has found a place in the twenty-first century among many scientific scholars, especially those entrenched in exotic technology. It turns out that *the 'newer' brute facts of physics encourage a scientific form of spiritualism*—however paradoxical we assess such a notion to be.

Pauwels and Bergier note: "Physics unveils a world which operates on several levels at the same time and has many doors opening on to infinity. The exact sciences [physics or astronomy] border on the fantastic. The humane sciences [such as psychology or sociology] are still hedged about with positivist[*] superstitions. The notion... of evolution dominates scientific thinking." Although their view was penned in 1960, their observation arguably has been proven correct. Not only is their 50-year-old opinion an accurate assessment of the various sciences of their day, but a valid prediction of the contemporary situation. And yet, we should realize there have always been voices challenging the skeptics of naturalism[†].

Under-publicized if you will, are numerous respected declarations throughout the past 300 years that present 'the minority report'— questioning whether such skeptical certitude about nature and normality is justified. Goethe,[1] a poetic voice during the Age of Enlightenment, offered a strongly worded, contrarian opinion: "We walk in mysteries. We are surrounded by an atmosphere about

---

[*] *Positivism* is the "theory that knowledge can be acquired only through direct observation and experimentation, and not through metaphysics or theology" according to the Encarta Dictionary.

[†] *Naturalism* is the view that all effects are the result of natural causes—the paranormal has no place in reality whatsoever.

which we still know nothing at all. We do not know what stirs in it and how it is connected with our intelligence. This much is certain, under particular conditions the antennae of our souls are able to reach out beyond their physical limitations."[2]

Today, this advocacy for the 'abnormal' grows even stronger. The esoteric steadily encroaches upon the fortress of skepticism built over the past three centuries during *naturalism's* hegemony. Not since *before* the Enlightenment with the *Neo-Platonists of the Renaissance* has the supernatural made such broad headway amongst intellectuals in Western society.

These Neo-Platonists of the Renaissance period were particularly important in seeking to develop a cosmology that blended mysticism and magic into Christianity, creating a supernatural cosmology similar to Gnosticism in ancient times and Shamanism today (a subject we will take up in a later chapter). Pico della Marandola was noted for his attempt to develop a Christian form of Cabbala. Giordano Bruno was excommunicated by Catholic and Protestant churches alike for his occult beliefs. Heinrich Cornelius Agrippa wrote *De Occulta Philosophia Libri Tres.*[3]

A brief synopsis in *Wikipedia* states, "Agrippa argued for a synthetic vision of magic whereby the natural world combined with the celestial and the divine through Neo-platonic participation, such that ordinarily licit* natural magic was in fact validated by a kind of demonic magic sourced ultimately from God. By this means Agrippa proposed a magic that could resolve all epistemological problems raised by skepticism in a total validation of Christian faith."[4]

Bruno, Marandola, and Agrippa were thoroughly "Renaissance Men" living in the sixteenth and seventeenth centuries. No doubt,

---

* *Licit* in this context conveys something allowed by God's law.

they were 'illuminated' men that would have remained committed to a mystical view of reality even if, hypothetically speaking, they would have encountered the 'enlightened' skeptics of the eighteenth and nineteenth centuries who found no reason whatsoever to believe in such 'mumbo jumbo'.[5] So while the majority of intellectuals following Bruno, Marandola, and Agrippa dismiss any sense of the supernatural (thereby eliminating the chance for the miracles of Christianity), they opted to 'throw out the baby with the bath water'. Except for the contrarians noted, doubt and skepticism would hold serve from thenceforth to our own day.

Likewise, mainstream Christian theology would evolve in Europe into a *faith without miracles* except in selected evangelical pockets. America's mainline denominations too, in the twentieth century would disparage the supernatural and depart from the true faith. Consequently, with the 'about face' of physics later in the twentieth century and now in the twenty-first—seemingly eager to embrace a much more mystical point of view—it is all the more astounding that the 'new found faith' springs forth from the 'exact sciences' and not from mainstream theology which remains hopelessly lost in 'demythologizing' theological content. Christian theology does little more in our day than stumble around in search of a reason to affirm some type of God-concept along with justifying the value of faith in Him—or more accurately, *it*. The author laments that just when the game is going down to the wire, mainstream Christianity is hopelessly feckless, unable to enter the fray as an 'impact player'. Having spent most of my Christian life in such churches (with good people but bad theology), my frustration on this point is profound.

The New Reality

Pauwels and Bergier's primary purpose in writing *The Morning of the Magicians* was to build a case for "fantastic reality"—a cosmology explaining the universe which overcomes the limitations of the positivist approach; whereby it incorporates the new physics, modern mathematics, and opens the door to the realization that *the natural and supernatural may not be so distinct.* In short, *many aspects of this 'supernature' aren't supernatural at all*—there need be no recourse to supposed actions of other-worldly beings to explain the behavior of physical objects.

However, by itself, this perspective has *nothing* to do with whether or not God created the heavens and the earth; and yet, it has everything to do with our ability to fully comprehend how (from this author's vantage point) God[*] created (and sustains) His Universe. In other words, the issue is we simply don't understand physics and mathematics well enough to plumb the wisdom or methods of our Creator.[†]

As part of their closing argument, Pauwels and Bergier tell a story of a Serbian genius, Roger Boscovitch (*Ruđer Josip Bošković*, 1711-1787) who was two centuries ahead of his time in these 'precise sciences'. In relating his story they make the point that the human mind is capable of far greater insightful leaps than we might suppose. Indeed, someone like Boscovitch was way too advanced for his peers. The challenge for Boscovitch was not so much that his peers doubted he could obtain genuine breakthroughs. At fault was that without societal support, such revolutionary insights (which contradicted contemporary conventional wisdom of his times) would not be acceptable to the science of that day and thus of necessity lie dormant (on the shelf, as it were) for centuries before others would arise smart enough to fathom such concepts. It turns out this is precisely the case

---

[*] This God could be the God of the Bible, the 'Supreme Being' of Freemasonry, or a pantheistic notion. I am not arguing here that God necessarily has to be the creator *Yahweh* although my personal belief is that He is.

[†] Of course, we who are evangelicals identify God as incarnated in Jesus Christ.

with Roger Boscovitch and his cosmologic model of the universe. A brief recital here of his story will be helpful to our study.

By the time he was 29, Boscovitch was already a teacher of mathematics in Rome and a science advisor to the Pope. On June 26, 1760 at 49 he was elected a Fellow of the Royal Society in England, publishing on that occasion a poem on the visible features of the sun and moon that had his colleagues exclaiming "This is Newton speaking through the mouth of Vergil [also spelled *Virgil*]." Only in the 1950s, at the behest of the Yugoslav Government [today's Serbia], had Boscovitch's *Theory of Natural Philosophy* (1758), began to be seriously reconsidered.

> It seems that Boscovitch was in advance, not only of the science of his time, but of our own [surpassing Einstein's theories which apparently cannot be integrated with the Quantum mechanics theory of Heisenberg]. He [Boscovitch] proposed a unitary theory of the Universe, a single general and unique equation governing mechanics, physics, chemistry, biology, and even psychology. According to this theory, matter, time, and space are not infinitely divisible but composed of points or grains... We find in his works the quanta, the wave mechanics, and the atom formed of nucleons. The scientific historian, L.L. Whyte, assures us that Boscovitch was at least two centuries ahead of his time, and that we shall only be able to understand him when the junction between relativity and quantum physics has finally been effected [sic]. It is estimated that in 1987 [Pauwels and Bergier wrote this prediction in 1960], on the two hundredth anniversary of his birth, his work, will be appreciated at its true value.[6]

Pauwels and Bergier proclaim victory for their thesis through the efficacy of *mathematics*—proof positive their hope (to restore among us an appreciation of the "fantastic reality" that is nature) is becoming more compelling with each day that passes, as mathematics continues to achieve new breakthroughs demonstrating their view to be correct. They summarize this proclamation with these words:

The language of modern mathematics is the only one, no doubt, that can give some account of certain results of analogical thinking. There exist in mathematical physics regions of the "Absolute Elsewhere" and of *"continus de mesure nulle,"* that is to *say measurements applied to Universes that are inconceivable and yet real.* We may wonder why it is that the poets have not yet turned to this science to catch an echo of the music of those spheres of *fantastic reality*—unless it be for fear of having to accept this evidence—that the magic art lives and flourishes outside their study walls.

The mathematical language which is proof of the existence of a Universe beyond the grasp of a normal waking consciousness is the only one that is in a state of constant ferment and activity.[7] [Emphasis mine]

To Pauwels and Bergier, the proof isn't in the pudding but lies in the recipe (more accurately, the *equation*) that explains why the *universe* behaves the way it does. As they say, mathematics continues to ferment relentlessly, eventually righting the wrongs in formerly mistaken methods of how we perceive reality.

What If Einstein was Wrong?

However, while new mathematical vistas may pave the way to overturn cherished beliefs about gravity, light, space, and time, as we study the writings of various physicists over the past century, we may soon conclude that what one scientist finds compelling another mistrusts. Despite the inconsistencies their two models (Einstein and Heisenberg), the 'standard theory' nevertheless perseveres. However, even the 'standard theory' is nowadays farther away from consensus. For instance we know that Nikola Tesla (1856-1943, see adjacent figure), a famous American scientist financed by J.P. Morgan, never agreed with Albert Einstein's model regarding the relativity of time and the possibility that space could be 'bent' by mass. Tesla perceived the physical phenomenon that Einstein was describing to be caused by undiscovered properties of time and space unknown to Einstein. Other standard axioms of physics (the well-celebrated laws of *thermodynamics*), such as the *indestructibility of matter*, the law of *conservation of energy* (energy can change forms but there is no loss of energy); even these 'laws' Tesla believed are subject to challenge—they are not immutable—they may even be outright wrong.

To be specific, what is now being considered is this: in our universe, *the mass of an object can fluctuate depending upon its surroundings*

as intersected by the properties of space or time at that place and moment. Additionally, *entropy* (aka heat loss, increase in randomness) is presumed but not consistently observed countering what most scientists would predict. As we will see below, time itself yields an *energy* that may serve as a *preservative* of sorts to processes; this energy may overcome entropy forestalling what is known as 'thermal death.' In short, our assumptions about reality (and therefore, Einsteinium physics) may have

Figure 10 – Nikola Tesla reading Roger Boscovitch's Book
Theoria Philosophiae Naturalis

focused on the wrong aspect of space-time. Therefore, even the supremely sacred laws of thermodynamics may be erroneous.

This really shouldn't surprise us. The final word in physics has not been spoken. The possibility for one cosmological model to trump another has been famously seen numerous times. We know Einstein's model explained certain deficiencies in Newton's laws of gravity (commonly expressed as stating that time and space are not absolute and fixed, but *relative and subject to fluctuation*). Likewise, Heisenberg theorized that matter was composed of 'quanta' (think of *particle* as a simple analogue) at its lowest level whose speed and location could not both be determined through measurement *without affecting the quanta* (reality appears like a wave or field instead of a 'particle'). Known as Heisenberg's 'uncertainty principle', physics has implied ever since that science is limited in its ability to measure reality (at the sub-atomic level) because science couldn't predict with exact certainly the properties of the quanta. Furthermore, with the cast-iron certainty of *Planck's constant* (there is a limit to how small a particle can get in our universe), and the measurement of the total mass in the Universe (we can in fact accurately calculate the number of atoms in the cosmos); we know that *the universe is not infinite on either end of the spectrum*. We live in a finite cosmos. It may be growing, but it had a definite beginning and it does not extend to 'eternity'. In the final analysis, what was presumed to be true about nature in 1900 was passé by 1910. What was true in 1910 was passé by 1925. And what we've believed ever since that point in time may be ready for capsizing today as well.

Science has searched feverously (beginning with Einstein and ever since) for what is called a 'unified field theory.' In simplest terms, the idea is that every attribute or property about space, time, matter, energy, (and the distinction of the various fundamental forces and particles) can be expressed and held to be true in every single point in the cosmos (reflect on your high school geometry and picture a specific coordinate point defined *dimensionally*—the old 'x-y' axis to be precise). The unified field theory seeks to explain both the usual and the unusual—everywhere, every time. "[So far] there is no accepted *unified field theory*, and thus [it] remains an open line of research. The term was coined by Einstein, who attempted to unify the general *theory of relativity* with *electromagnetism*, hoping to recover an approximation for quantum theory. A 'theory of everything' is closely related to unified field theory, but differs by not requiring the basis of nature to be *fields* [think of a magnetic field to get the idea], and also attempts to explain all physical constants of nature."[8] [Emphasis and comments added]

It is fascinating that this 'new physics' is not really new. Its life in the shadows was partially because, in the case of Roger Boscovitch, *the new reality* didn't achieve the notoriety to become the *standard* theory. At the very least, Boscovitch lacked a publicist. (Or more precisely, someone like Tesla who grasped the point that Boscovitch was making). But in the case of the next physicist we will study ('in the dock' as it were), his obscurity was *intentional*—stemming from a 'top secret' status his theories held in the Soviet Union.

Is It Time for the Aether?

According to historian, Joseph P. Farrell[*] in his book, *The Philosopher's Stone* (2006, subtitled, *Alchemy and the Secret Research for Exotic Matter*) the work of a particular Russian during the 1950s was a breakthrough in providing a predictive model *that is unified* not only explaining 'physics' but also plumbing the depths of 'human consciousness' too. This physicist was Nikolai Kozyrev (1908-1983).

Farrell points out that Nikolai Kozyrev's theories appear to coincide with Nikola Tesla's assertions (and we might add appear to support Roger Boscovitch's work as well—note the figure earlier

---

[*] Farrell is a professor of Patristics (the study of the Church Fathers) at California Graduate School of Theology. He has authored books on the East-West Schism in Christianity and books of alternative history and science. He received a M.A. degree at Oral Roberts University and doctorate at Pembroke College, Oxford.

where Tesla studies Boscovitch's book). The reason that Kozyrev is not a household name like Einstein stems from the Soviets who kept his studies classified *top secret*. Only in the past few years have his theories become public. A researcher, David Wilcock[9] (who we will quote in later portions of this book) is cited by Farrell as follows, "The awesome implications of his work and of all those who followed him, were almost entirely concealed by the former Soviet Union..." Farrell continues, "In other words, Kozyrev's work was so awesome and extraordinary in its implications, not only for the development of the foundation of theoretical physics, but also for its dangerous potential applications, that the Soviet leadership wisely classified it at the very highest levels."[10] Then Farrell cites Wilcock twice more in the following paragraph to tie the theories of Kozyrev and Tesla together:

> Tesla, Wilcock notes, stated in 1891 that the physical medium "behaves as a fluid to solid bodies, and as a solid to light and heat." Moreover, with "sufficiently high voltage and frequency" the medium itself could be accessed. This was, as Wilcock correctly notes, Tesla's "hint that free energy and anti-gravity technologies were possible." [Of course, free energy didn't please Tesla's patron, J.P. Morgan, owner of Standard Oil.] It is Tesla's assertion that the medium has fluid-like properties that ties his work directly with the work and thought of Dr. Kozyrev. [Comments added by this author]

What does Farrell mean by 'medium'? The 'medium' means that whatever 'it' is, 'it' is the most essential aspect of reality, the most basic building block, if you will. As such, this is the key 'scientific' (some would say, quasi-scientific) issue to grasp in this chapter. Therefore, the reader is encouraged to pay careful attention!

Throughout history, scientists and alchemists alike—from alchemists of ancient times like Trismegistus (ca. 300-150 BC) to Paracelsus (1493-1541), to the German Franz Anton Mesmer (1734-1815, from which we derive the word 'mesmerized'), to today's parapsychologists—have suggested that there is a discrete 'medium' that extends throughout the Universe which is actively involved in influencing mass and energy. It is often called, the 'aether'. The very foundation of *the dark art of alchemy is based upon this notion.* "Aether theories in early modern physics proposed the existence of a medium, the *aether* (also spelled *ether*, from the Greek word— αἰθήρ-*aether*—meaning "upper air" or "pure, fresh air"), a space-filling substance or field, thought to be necessary as a transmission medium for the propagation of electromagnetic waves [just as air is the medium to propagate sound]. The assorted *aether theories* embody the various conceptions of this *'medium'* and *'substance'.*" [11]

Figure 11- Nikolai Kozyrev

The notion of *the aether* has been hotly debated over the centuries as the reader would imagine. Most scientists believe that Einstein rejected it (assuming that it was not 'elegant'!). Robert Youngson's 1998 article in *Scientific Blunders asserted this point of view*: "By 1930, younger physicists would smile in a supercilious fashion at any reference to the aether. All scientists now that, in the words of the American homespun philosopher: 'There ain't no such critter.'" [12] However, David Wilcock challenges this traditional characterization of Einstein. By 1918, Einstein was swayed to believe in a 'medium'. We read:

[Any] part of space without matter and without electromagnetic fields seems to be completely empty... [But] according to the general theory of relativity, even space that is empty in this sense has physical properties. This... can be easily understood by speaking about an ether, whose state varies continuously from point to point. [Brackets in Wilcock's citation][13]

Despite what Youngson contends, other physicists are reintroducing it as it explains some phenomena that are now observable—for instance, *how particles can affect one another at rates millions of times faster than the speed of light!*

Kozyrev (and apparently Tesla) believed that *'time' itself was in fact this aether.* As Farrell says using the language of a physicist (actually quoting Kozyrev), "time is not a 'scalar'" (by which the physicist means that time is not simply a *hypothetical* point, line or vector as we would have conceived of in that geometry class I referred to a moment ago). Instead of a hypothetical *scalar*, time has substance and properties. Time *actively contributes* to what makes matter and energy what they are. Tesla's own words spell this out quite well:

During the succeeding two years (1893 and 1894) of intense concentration I was fortunate enough to make two far reaching discoveries. *The first was a dynamic theory of gravity,* which I have worked out in all details and hope to give to the world very soon. It explains the cause of this force and the motions of heavenly bodies under its influence so satisfactorily that it will put an end to the idle speculation and false conceptions, as that of curved space...

Only the existence of a field of force can account for the motions of the bodies as observed and its assumption dispense with space curvature. All literature on this subject is futile and destined to oblivion. *So are all attempts to explain the working of the universe without recognizing the existence of the ether and the indispensable function it plays in the phenomena.*

...I consider myself the original discoverer of this truth, which can be expressed by the statement: *There is no energy in matter other than that received from the environment.*

...It applies rigorously to molecules and atoms as well as to the largest heavenly bodies, and to all matter in the universe in any

phase of its existence from its very first formation to its ultimate disintegration. [14] [Emphasis in citation]

Such a notion regarding the essence of time is not only revolutionary; it begins to break down the wall between *nature* as we've known it, and *'supernature'* as we've felt obliged to characterize it—especially in theological discussions—to explain phenomena *beyond the observable world.*

In fact, several scientists suggest that time is what influences our universe to contain *spirals*—from the double-helix of DNA to the immense winding arms of galaxies. Why? Because time has a shape and it confers (imparts) that shape to matter if only to a slight extent. Time is like a whirlpool (*vortex* being the more proper physics term). Time can be *contorted* (energetically twisted out of shape). The issue of 'where we are' and 'when we are there' can only be explained by 'torsion physics'. We will discuss the concept of torsion more in a moment.

Furthermore, there is much else to say about how time is 'structured'. The shaping of time is in fact compared by Farrell to a *crystalline latticework.* Just in case the reader isn't familiar with the structure of crystals, I will put a different analogy to use.

The universe at its most basic, most fundamental level consists of an invisible skeleton-like structure to which 'everything' is attached. Think of scaffolding filling an immense cathedral under renovation. Consider the scaffolding closely connected at its joints with pipes of very tiny diameter and length such that the scaffolding is able to fill every nook and cranny of this edifice. Additionally, this delicate scaffolding is so densely placed about, you can't see through it.

Having digested these notions, now conceive of the scaffolding as present everywhere throughout the cathedral as described so far, but add *invisibility*—it's there, you know it, but you can't see it. Finally, think of the cathedral as the universe and the scaffolding as the 'aether' we call time which completely fills the cosmos. Like this scaffolding in the cathedral, time is spread throughout the cosmos with an invisible latticework to which all other particles attach.* This conception is actually quite fundamental to what time is and does. Granted, there is more to time than this underlying structure to reality—it has more properties, indeed it is 'active' and not 'passive' in affecting matter, i.e., anything that is must be 'attached' to it.   But first and foremost, it is *time* that provides the universe's discrete skeleton.†

For thirty-three years Kozyrev experimented to test and prove this theory.   These experiments were contentious like the aether he sought to depict.   We read: "What made them controversial was that Kozyrev viewed the spiraling patterns of nature and of life itself as a manifestation of time, and that as a consequence of this view, time itself was not a dimensionless 'coordinate point' or a 'scalar' as scientists and mathematicians would call it, but that time was itself a kind of physical force, and a very subtle one at that."[15]

One of the most provocative aspects of Kozyrev's theories, however, is another stunning hypothesis that explains the behavior of fusion reactions: Farrell tells us that hydrogen bombs, like stars in the universe, generate far more energy that they should according to mathematical calculations. Therefore, additional energy must be included from some unexpected source.

Kozyrev's 1947 doctoral thesis made the audacious claim that the explanation for why stars and hydrogen bombs generate so much extra energy goes beyond the mere process of fusion—these massive reactions *are leeching (sucking) energy from time itself!*   "In

---

* And I use the wording *'other' particles* intentionally because time itself may be another particle—an infinitesimally small—particle.
† Technically, what we find created is itself also a composition of time. Time is the raw material of Space-Time and the Matter and Energy that dwell within it.

other words, Kozyrev had concluded that the geometry of local celestial space is a determinant in the energy output of fusion reactions, and that the latter, depending upon that geometry, will 'gate' now more, now less, energy into the reaction itself as a function of that geometry."[16]

Foreshadowing (actually falling on the heels of) the assertions of alchemists, the amount of energy depends upon the precise *status of time at that moment.* That is, time can fluctuate in its properties. Our common personal experience of feeling time moving faster or slower could be because it actually varies! *We could say, time doesn't convey the same timing all the time.* The quotation cited earlier referencing Einstein infers the same thing: The aether varies "from point to point."

The word used frequently by physicists like Farrell in depicting the physical nature of this model, so much so that it becomes a defining label for the model is, *Torsion* * *theory*. Farrell explains:

> Torsion is a dynamic and changing phenomenon, and not merely a static field, for if the basic idea of torsion is that it is related to a rotating system, [and] then it will be apparent that the universe is composed of rotating systems within other rotating systems, producing a continuously changing system with a changing flow of time. And if in addition those spinning systems are in turn emitting energy, such as a star pouring out its electromagnetic radiation from the fusion reactions within it, then that dynamic changes yet again, and with the constantly changing "spiraling and pleated" field of time, time itself takes on dynamic properties.
>
> Such complex, interlocked systems of rotation may be thought of as "knots" of space-time that are so intensely concentrated that they

---

* Torsion is the distortion caused by applying torque in opposite directions to each end of an object—it is mechanical stress placed on an object by twisting it. A soda 'twisted back and forth' is an analogy that Farrell supplies to picture the nature of this process.

form the objects observed in the physical universe. As such, all systems are in fact "space-time machines," and since they "contain" space-time they are not ultimately "constrained" by it, but rather, interact constantly, and in some cases, instantaneously, with it.

And this means that physics had to modify its mathematical modeling of time and space significantly.[17]

Consequently, with such a radically different approach to explaining the 'natural' laws of the universe, "Kozyrev announced a wholesale assault on two of the foundations of modern physics and some of its hidden, and very counterintuitive, assumptions: Relativity and Quantum Mechanics."[18] That is to say, while Kozyrev offered alternative explanations for certain types of phenomena, he actually reinstated the common sense view that (1) time flows in one direction because it is in 'time's nature' to do so[*], and (2) science can measure a particle's speed and location' simultaneously without 'tampering' with the results (we don't 'force' any one of those properties to be contradicted just because we take a peek at it). Since more is involved in any such system which is being observed or measured—the 'uncertainty principle' is not sacrosanct. In other words, what Heisenberg supposed, that scientific measurements are being made by scientists in 'closed systems' (no other factors are involved to influence the measurements) turns out not to be a proper scientific way to think of these 'systems'—any and all such systems being measured are *open systems* with multiple influences, not the least of which is time itself, since time is *not* a constant.

Further explanations for why this is so, I will leave to the curious reader who wishes to explore Farrell's explanations of Kozyrev's theory in more detail.[19]

---

[*] Wilcock challenges this, asserting that time flows into any particular point from all directions, swirling into an atom, a pyramid, or a galaxy.

Consequently, is it 'about time again for the aether'? Or should I just ask 'is time this aether'? In asking this question, a challenge surfaces because such language arouses contempt from the scientific community. I will allow a Nobel Laureate to explain the situation through his analysis of why we shouldn't use the scandalous term, *aether*:

> It is ironic that Einstein's most creative work, the general theory of relativity, should boil down to conceptualizing space as a medium when his original premise [later, as we pointed out, he changed his mind] was that no such medium existed...
>
> The word 'ether' has extremely negative connotations in theoretical physics because of its past association with opposition to relativity. This is unfortunate because, stripped of these connotations; it rather nicely captures the way most physicists actually think about the vacuum. [*Vacuum* is the name most scientists would prefer in referring to this medium]. Relativity actually says nothing about the existence or nonexistence of matter pervading the universe, only that any such matter must have relativistic symmetry.
>
> It turns out that such matter exists. About the time relativity was becoming accepted, studies of radioactivity began showing that the empty vacuum of space had *spectroscopic structure similar to that of ordinary quantum solids and fluids* ['it' could be detected and measured—'it' existed]. Subsequent studies with large particle accelerators have now led us to understand that space is more like a piece of window glass than ideal Newtonian emptiness. It is filled with 'stuff' that is normally transparent but can be made visible by hitting it sufficiently hard to knock out a part. The modern concept of the vacuum of space, confirmed every day by experiment, is a relativistic ether. But we do not call it this *because it is taboo* [Emphasis and comments added].

Why so taboo? Because once the aether is allowed into the discussion with the characteristics we've described here, we can't help but draw the conclusion the universe is that "fantastic reality" Pauwels and Bergier proposed. *Doors swing open to spiritually-oriented phenomenon where they were formerly shut tight.* No longer does nature rule out the possibility that fantastic events can and do happen. The nature of such events, such as the leeching of energy from time in fusion reactions, (or the transmutation of mercury into gold as we are about to discuss) is no longer impossible for a scientist to conceive. For those willing to examine the facts, it becomes a matter of documented history with top-shelf science to back it up.

Farrell provides a number of intriguing examples of how understanding exotic particles and a different explanation of space-time dimensions radically changes the science of physics and how the world works. His primary case study has to do with one David Hudson, an Arizona farmer, who in the 1980s discovered that alchemy is a fact and not merely a figment of an over-active occult imagination.

David Hudson's Gold Strike

Hudson spent several years and a small fortune, ultimately being rewarded with the discovery that his land was perhaps the richest in the world containing gold, platinum, iridium, and other precious metals—all *hiding* in plain sight—since it wasn't existing in its 'natural' molecular manner. Through alchemical processes, initially administered quite by accident, Hudson struck it rich and in the process taught the world about 'monatomic particles', 'super deformity', 'high spin rates'; and what certain chemicals and specific chemical processes—administered with extreme care—*beget a synthetically derived gold* (all loosely resembling the ancient quest of the alchemist!) Hudson didn't synthesize just any old gold—mind you—but precious metals of all sorts with exotic properties to boot. His story is nothing less than, shall we say, mesmerizing.

"You have," [said Hudson's metallurgist to him] "four to six ounces per ton of palladium, twelve to fourteen ounces per ton of platinum, a hundred fifty ounces per ton of osmium, two hundred fifty ounces per ton of ruthenium, six hundred ounces per ton of iridium…"[20] In other words, Hudson hadn't just struck gold, he had the richest set of precious metal deposits anywhere. It was lucky for him he had enough working capital to finance the investigation necessary to 'prove his claim'. "Working on this problem from 1983 until 1989, Hudson had employed 'one PhD chemist, three master chemists, (and) two technicians,' all working fulltime." Consequently, Hudson's quest to solve various 'strange' properties of the minerals on his land wound up making him the richest alchemist in history— with the possible exception of the Egyptian Pharaohs who may have understood alchemical properties and manufactured gold as many have speculated.[21]

Hudson's materials were capable of changing properties and becoming one of several different precious metals based upon exposures to intense heat for precise periods of time. One experience Farrell relates regarding the transmuted metal: by striking it with a hammer, the material emitted gamma rays (the blows triggered brilliantly bright mini-explosions). This property of the material was confirmed by experiments going on simultaneously at General Electric (GE). "To his surprise, Hudson had learned that the GE engineers had experienced the same unusual 'explosions' as well"[22] when they were working on devising new ways to create fuel cells with rhodium. "When our material was sent to them, [the GE engineers], the rhodium, as received, was analyzed to not have any rhodium in it. Yet when they mounted it on carbon in their fuel cell technology and ran the fuel cell for several weeks, it worked and it did what only rhodium would do…"[23]

But the most astounding property of the materials Hudson and his technicians were working with was yet to be explained: the weight increases and decreases of the material, *as if mass was being lost into thin air!* In a manner of speaking, this was exactly what they discovered. Taking the material through various heating and cooling states, the weight changed radically. This is not scientifically explainable—at least not according to the rules of the 'old physics'. We read in Farrell's story quoting Hudson directly:

> We heated the material at one point two degrees per minute and cooled it at two degrees per minute. What we found is when you oxidize the material it weights 102%, when you hydro-reduce it, it weights 103%. So far so good. No problem. But when it [the material] turns snow white it only weights 56% of the beginning weight. Now that's impossible.
>
> If you put that on a silica test boat and you weighed it, it weights 56%. If you heat it to the point that it fuses into the glass, it turns black and all the weight returns. So the material hadn't volatized away. It was still there; it just couldn't be weighed any more. That's when everybody said this just isn't right; it can't be.
>
> Do you know that when we heated it and cooled it and heated it and cooled it and heated it and cooled it under helium or argon that when we cooled it, *it would weight three to four hundred percent of its beginning weight, and when we heated it, it would actually weigh less than nothing[?] If it wasn't in the pan, the pan would weigh more than the pan weighs when this stuff is in it.*[24] [Emphasis in original]

Just like in alchemy, as transmutations occur color changes are evident. What is most intriguing is that these color changes are consistent with the writings of the alchemists from the time of the Renaissance. In other words, their experience as documented wasn't religious fiction or wishful thinking brought on by their pecuniary enthusiasm. Hudson's team was seeing atomic transmutations of elements causing elemental alterations to occur.

As a quick aside for readers sensitive to Judeo-Christian issues, given the properties of precious metals when treated with certain chemicals and massive heat, several mysteries of the Bible may have found explanation. We know that Moses was an "Egyptian prince taught in all the ways of the Egyptians." (Acts 7:22)[25] Could it be that the Ark of the Covenant was influenced by alchemical knowledge learned by

Moses? Is this why the Ark was supposedly far lighter in weight than it should have been, having been constructed with gold veneers and a lid of solid gold? Could the exterior gold or possible internal contents containing this special gold—alchemically altered into what Hudson called "monatomic elements"—have been the explanation for why the Ark could apparently 'levitate'?

The notion of how the strange dimensionality of this new reality works was published in March, 1989 in *Physical Review* by one of America's most highly regarded physicists: Dr. Hal Puthoff (who we will meet again in Book Two regarding clairvoyance and his work with America's psychic spies at the Stanford Research Institute). Hudson ran across Puthoff's article which discussed a 'strange white powder' that is a perfect superconductor. Puthoff explained that when in this form, the material loses precisely four-ninths (4/9) of its weight, leaving five-ninths of its mass behind (5/9). It just so happens this fractional anomaly, once you do the simple math, equals the 56% (55.5555...) that Hudson and his team observed.

> During their discussions, Puthoff told Hudson that "when this material only weights 56% of its true mass, you do realize that this material is actually bending space-time [?]" Such a material, Hudson noted, was what Puthoff "called exotic matter in his papers." Hudson had, in other words, literally stumbled across some of the exotic matter that forms so much of the quest of modern theoretical physics—not to mention mediaeval alchemy—and it was there right beneath his feet in the soil of his farm, and it was not really all that exotic at all. It was ordinary chemical elements, but in some sort of state not hitherto known.

But that wasn't all that Puthoff told him...

> If the mysterious white powder was indeed losing 44% of its mass, then said, Puthoff, "theoretically it should be withdrawing from these three dimensions... it should not even be in these three dimensions."[26]

And with that mind-bender, we are ready for the next part of the story: uncovering how all of these 'exotic' notions of the new reality were in fact discovered much earlier than Hudson or even Kozyrev; they were working hypotheses of the notorious *Third Reich,* in its vain attempt to develop a weapon of war that would make Germany victorious. To that discussion we turn next.

The Third Reich and Its 'Take' on the New Physics

A book was published before World War II (1933 to be precise) by Baron Rudolf Von Sebottendorf, *Before Hitler Came*, which painted the occult picture of the Third Reich and so infuriated the Nazi's (perhaps for letting the cat out of the bag) that it was put on their index of prohibited publications. "Part of the reason may lie in the fact that, according to Von Sebottendorf, the influence of the *Thulegesellschaft* [Thule Society] on the Nazi Party's formation and ritual was pervasive... [but] a more important reason for the ban on the work, however, must surely lie in the lists of its members that it contains, not only of prominent figures in the future Nazi State..." but identifying the linkage to a former inmate in an insane asylum who went on to become Himmler's personal consultant on all things occult, *SS Brigadier General Karl Maria Wiligut.* "With recent scholarly publications, we are now also in a position to see the possible connection of alchemy to the SS' esoteric culture and its advanced physics projects via the various conceptions entertained by Wiligut, and passed on to Himmler."[27] Farrell even refers to Wiligut as equivalent to The Czar's 'Rasputin'. It is Wiligut's deep occult commitments and his teachings regarding alchemy that leads Farrell to agree that the relationship between secret societies in Germany did indeed run "directly to Hitler, and on that basis, such researchers [he mentions] often speculate that he [Hitler] was actually an initiate into one or more of these... esoteric societies and influences"[28] (e.g., *The Thule Society* and the *Order of the New Templars*).

However, Farrell states it was *Wiligut's connection to Himmler of which we can be absolutely certain.* "As such, it is less accurate to speak of an occult influence on the entire Nazi State, as it is to speak of an esoteric influence at the uppermost levels of the command structure of the SS. One is, so to speak, dealing with a Black Reich within the Reich, and at the uppermost reaches of the SS, with a very secret esoteric, and specifically *alchemical*, belief system." [29] [Emphasis added] Farrell continues, "While Wiligut's work to some extent paralleled that of the notorious SS *Ahnenerbedienst*, 'his work was essentially separate from that office. Wiligut worked *for Himmler personally*, whereas the *Ahnenerbe* was part of a much larger structure subject to more objective academic standards." Wiligut was "instrumental in the selection and design of Himmler's infamous SS "Order Castle" at Wewelsburg, in the actual design of the SS ring, and the creation of SS rituals... he issued a 'steady stream of reports on esoteric matters of theology, history, and cosmology... for the most part *directly to Himmler*."[30] [Emphasis in original] This connection and inspiration is important because it is Wiligut's alchemical influence on Himmler that motivated weapons research built upon a conception very similar to the 'new reality' we've outlined in the previous sections. Sounding almost like Pauwels and Bergier, Farrell states,

> In a certain sense, Himmler had willed into existence an entire government bureaucracy [*Ahnenerbe*] to do nothing but military studies of the esoteric, all under his personal control. This created an unusual if not unique first in modern history because for the first time in modern history a technologically and scientifically sophisticated great power was acknowledging, even if covertly, the existence of a very ancient Very High Civilization whose science it was intent upon recovering. Himmler had decreed, in effect, that the Third Reich was not only going to look

for a "paleoancient Very High Civilization," for "Atlantis," but more importantly, for its science. [Emphasis in original][31]

One of the most striking comments we have to document this fact is from Wiligut to Himmler (June 17, 1936) which lands him right in the midst of a controversial discussion today amongst those who speculate that the *history of the solar system* is far more mysterious than we realize (to be discussed in a later chapter in Book Two regarding NASA and its possible top-secret agenda).   It involves 'worlds colliding' and peoples from another world tampering with the human race for their own purposes. Wiligut asserts:

> Each of these evolutionary epochs which have occurred up to now were, according to the oral secret doctrine [an indirect reference to Madame Helena Petrovna Blavatsky's *Secret Doctrine*], brought about by an enormous world-wide catastrophe culminated by unifications of our earth with one of the heavenly bodies attracted into its orbits.
>
> ...In the process, the remnants of humanity which remained on the earth assimilated with those who came "from heaven" (stars) to the "earth." This assimilation brought about similar intelligences and thus established a new humanity which instituted new racial types.[32]

Farrell goes on to explain that while aspects of these very ancient tales (today popularized by the works of the late Zechariah Sitchin derived from his translations of the Sumerian cuneiform tablets), reveals not just a cosmic war, but a war which used weapons "on a cosmic scale" involving rotating physics, i.e., the *'vortical'* or torsion nature of time described earlier. Farrell concludes this portion of his story with these words, "In short, of all the esotericists and occultists within the milieu of Himmler's SS, it is Wiligut himself who represents the best possible esoteric influence and basis for some of the SS' subsequent projects to reconstruct the technology of that physics."[33] This war is a discussion that Farrell pursues in several of his other books which fall outside this study's scope.[34]

While we won't dive into that subject in this chapter, Farrell is refer-ring to the Nazi *Bell*, a famed 'wonder weapon' based upon its abil-ity to generate a torsion field that could leech massive energy from time. In effect, the Nazi Bell would surpass the power and *practical* use (if I may be allowed to call it that) of the atomic bomb by turn-ing time itself into a radiation free hyper-explosive. (The Bell could make the manipulation of *time* a 'weapon of war' by incorporating an 'alchemical process' of opposing hyper-rotating cylinders to steal energy from time and transform it into a mega-bomb.)

Farrell provides a number of direct quotes from Wiligut that speak of "the primal twist", a "Rotating Eye" (*Drehauge*)[35] when speak-ing of the flow of Matter-Energy-Spirit. "Gôt is eternal—as Time, Space, Energy and Matter in his circulating current."[36] Therefore, Farrell concludes:

> The physics jargon employed—"circulating current"—suggests that he has in mind precisely a physics metaphor or interpretation for the whole scheme, for a circulating current suggests precisely time as the fundamental component of his "primal twist"... By invoking a physics terminology with his reference to "circulating current," Wiligut is implying that this whole alchemical-theological theme is at root based in physics and not metaphys-ics[*]. Thus, as he avers, this "Gôt" is "beyond the concepts of good and evil." In a Europe already concussed with loss of faith and a confidence in Christian institutions and morality, such a statement could only have disastrous moral consequences, for the whole mistaken thematic identity of this physical process with the Christian Trinity and therefore with the whole edifice of

---

[*] *Metaphysics* is defined by the Encarta Dictionary as "the branch of philos-ophy concerned with the study of the nature of being and beings, existence, time and space, and causality." However, in this context Farrell is comparing *physics to nature* and *metaphysics to supernature*, inasmuch as *Meta* means 'beyond' or 'surpassing'. Adopting this distinction (incorporating the same meaning Farrell asserts), will be helpful in our discussion as well.

Christian morality inevitably led to a similar mistake in ethics: if they were based only in a physical process neither good nor evil, then there could be no ultimately good or evil action, only actions now more, now less, in harmony with the process itself. With Wiligut's "triune Stone" the way was open for the genocidal alchemical transmutation of man himself.[37]

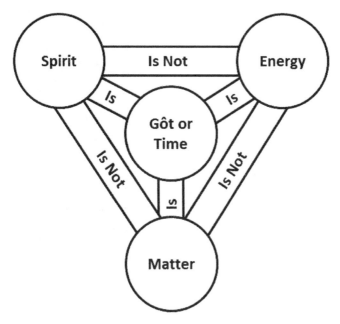

Figure 12 - Wiligut's Version of the Triune Stone

In other words, by associating God with 'time' (the 'new reality'), good and evil is discredited because there is no 'personal God' to sanction it. To Wiligut, God is impersonal. God doesn't transcend the natural universe, *albeit a mysterious nature.* Consequently, the Nazi aspirations to transform man into the Übermensch (or annihilate the Jews for failing to measure up to the capability of 'the new man' because of their inferior 'blood') are perfectly consistent with the reality of nature. According to Wiligut, *Gôt* resides in the natural or physical world—not the metaphysical (or supernatural) realm. Note: This alchemy—transmuting *a personal God into an impersonal force*—eradicates any element of morality from the cosmos.

The *triune Stone* mentioned is a pictogram Farrell presents not just for Wiligut but for St. Augustine and others to portray how various true or would-be scholars (like Wiligut) have understood the fundamental nature of God and His analogue in the world of matter, energy, space, and time. Wiligut's version is drawn by Farrell (and reproduced by me) in the figure adjacent.

Farrell indicates that there are other statements Wiligut makes that provide the ideological connection between his alchemical physics and the "highly classified secret weapons research project, *The Bell*; statements that indicate that, in part, these esoteric views might have formed part of the rationalization for the project, at least, as far as the unscientific leadership of the

Figure 13 - The Insignia of the Thule Society

SS was concerned."[38] Wiligut discussed research that was completed prior to 1933 involving the separation of two rotating fields—going in opposite directions—which was the basis for *The Bell* project. "Wiligut is implying by means of his reference to the swastika and the torsion-based physics it symbolized, that the fabric of space-time has a spin orientation."[39] Indeed, the contention is that *the symbol of the swastika itself reinforces this notion*! When we evaluate the swastika as illustrated in the 1919 insignia of the *Thule Society* (see figure above), the 'spin' nature of the emblem is strongly suggested.

Farrell provides compelling additional evidence for the alchemical connections of Wiligut, Himmler, and secret weapon research of the Nazis based upon the *torsion* conception of time. Interested readers are encouraged to investigate his evidence further.

Normal vs. Paranormal—Revising the Distinction

The point of this lesson in 'revised' physics and how it relates to the thesis of the book is simply this: what many formerly considered an example of magic—notably *identifying the philosopher's stone* (as we've learned from Joseph Farrell's exploration into comparing the ancient art of alchemy with the new insights of exotic particles), is now radiating (pun intended) astounding new insight into *the discoveries of revised atomic theory.* Alchemy, the ancient art of turning lead, mercury, or other non-precious metals into gold, has been proven to be much more than a magic trick of a showman or a genuine act of wizardry. It is authentic science.

It turns out to be the case that *the alchemist is a chemist after all*— we can now see the alchemist simply practices a very advanced and seldom understood form of this science. All talk of hocus pocus and personal transformation aside (core aspects of the alchemical folklore), along with understanding the nature of exotic particles in the genuinely 'natural' universe, underscores how postulating supernatural causes and effects for many phenomenon is actually just another way of saying *"we now seek to understand the science of the unusual"(but not the impossible).* The universe is very different than what we once thought. *Its behavior can be so strange it almost seems supernatural.* But upon closer inspection and a better conceptualization, this aspect of 'supernatural' is still natural—it's just our empirical understanding has progressed, taking into account natural laws we didn't comprehend before.

Consequently, this enlightened awareness doesn't disparage science in the least; and furthermore, it certainly doesn't dismiss science. If anything, it indicates that science stands as a valid and necessary human activity. The point to be made is this: science *must maintain humility.* As smart as we think we are, the final word hasn't been spoken. We still have much to learn. Speaking somewhat metaphorically here, the instruments we use through our scientific inquiries—and even more importantly, how we interpret their results—need to be considered cautiously and our axioms considered 'provisional' ; that is, they must always remain open for the possibility of further mid-course correction. The bottom line: we will continue traveling down the scientific road of discovery until time itself (for those adopting a Judeo-Christian perspective at least) comes to its conclusion. Many phenomena which might have caused us to think we were dealing with the supernatural—having no measurable traces of physical, chemical, or electromagnetic forces—may still be explained by an enhanced understanding of the universe and its 'natural' laws.

However, here we must assert a strongly-worded BUT. This improved understanding of the organic, albeit misunderstood forces of nature, doesn't imply that all that is *is nature*. In other words, *a distinct supernatural or paranormal may still exist.* For those of faith, *it does still exist.*

Certain phenomena for people of faith are still yet to be explained. An expanded 'nature' must be supplemented by powers, notably personal in character, that can't be reduced to impersonal 'forces' or 'fields'. We will tackle this assertion during our discussion of Christian cosmology in Chapter Seven.

Conclusion—Powers Beyond the New Supernatural

The Nazis delved into both sides of this new reality, or more precisely, an uncommon *understanding* of reality. The first portion of the new reality was nature transformed by a distinct understanding of space-time (and as we will discuss later, *time-space*) and how to manipulate the 'medium' (the aether) to create true weapons of mass destruction. But the underlying portion of reality, what Christians and Jews distinguish to be 'eternity', still remains distinct.

In this other aspect of the 'new reality' (later we will see it labeled time-space in distinction to space-time), we encounter and engage *personal* forces transpire; these forces could be, to use the words of 'spiritual warfare',[*] 'bound' or 'loosed' at the will of the magician (or the 'spiritual warrior'). To be clear on this point, these forces, be they *demonic* (or to use Jung's terms, *archetypal),* still exist in traditional Judeo-Christian cosmology *despite the new discoveries or ways of thinking about nature we've just discussed.* As Trevor Ravenscroft (and even Joseph P. Farrell to some extent) well documents, Hitler became a ritual magician through the tutoring of Dietrich Eckart. The 'mediums' of the Third Reich took actions based upon the powers that magicians purportedly possessed. They may have connected these forces with the ethereal 'Vril' of Bulwer-Lytton and the Vril Society. But there remains little doubt they also believed and interacted with *personal* forces of evil. These forces transcend the "fantastic reality" of Pauwels and Bergier. They imply the cosmology of the occult and the Bible. In this sense, the cosmos is a 'personal' reality inhabited by spiritual beings: demons, angels, and perhaps those that have passed on from this life into the next. But most importantly, the principal player remains *God.* Ironically, the Nazis concluded that God was an *impersonal* force—despite the fact they still knowingly engaged with *personal demons*! However, illogical this may seem, the facts state this plainly.

While pop spiritism often makes use of the 'new reality' *of the first type* (a fantastic reality) to substantiate its occult beliefs and its use of ritual magic, this doesn't logically mean that the spiritism to

---

[*] Spiritual warfare is a phrase that Christians use to reflect the process of challenging spiritual forces, which may be visible or audible during the confrontation. Exorcism is the most radical and notorious type of 'warfare'—but prayer, while less audacious, may nevertheless comprise a primary weapon of choice.

which they aspire *is an impersonal force,* despite the fact this is how they wish to characterize *the medium.* That false conclusion is where these advocates of ancient wisdom and the 'New Age' take an unfortunate detour leading to a dead-end.[40]

As we will discuss, occult enthusiasts may depict the new reality 'pantheistically'. Moreover, they often describe it as humankind's 'super-conscious' that transcends individual minds and resides in the 'supernatural world'—but this concept of consciousness, *according to them,* belies the power unique to humanity which we can and should master. In their estimation at least, through these means, we will become spiritually adept.

However, in the final analysis their instruction is quite deceptive. For while the new reality provides fantastic new explanations for why nature works the way it does, it offers no explanation for why there are genuine spiritual forces which still dwell beyond nature— no matter how fantastic—that can be influenced by the 'technical know-how' of the magician (or for that matter. the prayer of the godly). For as many authors in this genre indicate (including Farrell when mentioning the infamous 'aliens' who abduct humans), such 'extraterrestrial' origin is suspicious for many scientific reasons—but mostly because it challenges the truthfulness of the assertion the 'ETs' are other-worldly beneficent beings' essentially due to the evil behavior they exhibit. Indeed, it is this factor (that these forces *can be and are evil*), which argues so convincingly that the cosmology of the Bible is the most persuasive worldview offering explanation to why such evil exists. If authentic good and evil inhabit the universe (in other words, good and evil are real, they aren't just a sentimental verdict or metaphoric judgment), *impersonal forces* are no longer fit explanations for the essence of these powers. At its most fundamental level, going beyond neutrons, gravitons, and any other exotic particle, *reality is personal.*

As we turn to this *other realm of the new reality* and the power quest of individuals who seek to master it, the quest demonstrates a logical necessity: the metaphysical does exist and personal beings inhabit it. If so, as said above, the most fundamental reality must be *personal*—it must be real—and that which we call *good and evil* are truly present in the cosmos. Like alchemy was once believed to be, these attributes are much more than a figment of our spiritual imagination!

NOTES

[1] Johann Wolfgang von Goethe (1749–1832), mentioned earlier, was the genius of German literature and author of *Faust*.

[2] As quoted by Daniel Pinchbeck, *Breaking Open the Head: A Psychedelic Journey into the Heart of Contemporary Shamanism* (New York, NY: Broadway Books, 2002), 112.

[3] *Three Books Concerning Occult Philosophy*, Book 1 printed Paris, 1531; Books 1-3 in Cologne, 1533.

[4] See *http://en.wikipedia.org/wiki/Heinrich_Cornelius_Agrippa*.

[5] The memory of these Renaissance men should not be metaphorically burned at the stake for 'divination' even if all that is at risk is their reputation. Why? They were sincerely seeking a 'place' for faith and miracles. They hoped by citing occult examples and unifying the occult worldview with the Christian, they could make 'sense' of the biblical cosmology to which they were committed. It would offer 'proof' for the supernatural, and thus, the Bible. We should be sympathetic to their goal, although their thinking and approach falls outside the bounds of biblical orthodoxy. It is instructive that Jesus received vocal validation from demons that He was the Son of God—despite the cloak of human flesh. Jesus refused to accept their acknowledgement. He commanded they be quiet. The 'miracles' of the occult are not to be sought as evidence that the Bible is true—although they are evidence enough of the supernatural.

[6] Pauwels and Bergier, op. cit. p. 351. This prediction may be slightly too optimistic—his theories however, are consistent with other non-standard physicists as we will see in the next section.

[7] Ibid., pp. 322-323.

8 See http://en.wikipedia.org/wiki/Unified_theory. Further detail: "According to the current understanding of physics, forces are not transmitted directly between objects, but instead are described by intermediary entities called fields. All four of the known fundamental forces are mediated

by fields, which in the Standard Model of particle physics result from ex-change of gauge bosons. Specifically the four interactions to be unified are:

Strong interaction: the interaction responsible for holding quarks togeth-er to form neutrons and protons, and holding neutrons and protons together to form nuclei. The exchange particle that mediates this force is the gluon.

Electromagnetic interaction: the familiar interaction that acts on electri-cally charged particles. The photon is the exchange particle for this force.

Weak interaction: a repulsive short-range interaction responsible for some forms of radioactivity that acts on electrons, neutrinos, and quarks. It is governed by the W and Z bosons.

Gravitational interaction: a long-range attractive interaction that acts on *all* particles. The postulated exchange particle has been named the graviton.

Modern unified field theory attempts to bring these four interactions together into a single framework..."

[9] David Wilcock is a researcher and author, with a Bachelor's in Psycholo-gy, with numerous books and movies to his credit. David believes that he may be the reincarnation of Edgar Cayce and has written material to support this (which this author is simply sharing here, without passing judgment). He has also made a number of public predictions including the JFK Jr. death (the night before on radio) and the 911 disaster. See his credentials at his web site: http://divinecosmos.com/component/content/158?task=view.

[10] Farrell, Joseph P. *The Philosophers Stone, Alchemy and the Secret Re-search for Exotic Matter*, Port Townsend, WA. Feral House, 2009, pp. 151-152. Quoting David Wilcock, "The Breakthroughs of Dr. Nikolai A. Kozyrev," *The Divine Cosmos*, www.divinecosmos.com, pp. 1-2.

[11] See http://en.wikipedia.org/wiki/Aether_theories.

[12] Wilcock, David *The Source Field Investigations: The Hidden Science and Lost Civilizations behind the 2012 Prophecies*, New York: Dutton, 2011, p. 226; quoting Robert Youngson, *Scientific Blunders: A Brief history of how wrong scientists can sometimes be.* London: Constable & Robinson Publish-ing, 1998.

[13]Quoting from Albert Einstein, see http:///www.mathem.publro/proc /bsgp-10/0KOSTRO.PDF.

[14] Quoted from Farrell, Joseph P.'s book, *The Brotherhood of the Bell*, Kempton, Illinois, 2006, pp. 376-377; citing Tesla's words from O'Neill, John J., *Prodigal Genesis: The Life of Nikola Tesla* (Las Vegas: Brotherhood of Life, 1994), p. 250, emphasis added by Farrell.

[15] Ibid., p. 153.

[16] Ibid., p. 155.

[17] Ibid., p. 158.

[18] Ibid., p. 160.

[19] See Farrell's detail explanation on pages 161-165 of The Philosopher's Stone.

[20] Ibid., p. 95.

[21] According to the episode, "Aliens and Temples of Gold", airing of August 18, 2011, from the *Ancient Aliens* program on the *History Channel,* the Kings surrounding Egypt asked the Pharaoh to share some of his gold inasmuch as it was "as common as the dust in Egypt." Several authors interviewed speculated that the Pyramids themselves may have been involved in generating gold from ancient technologies pre-dating the flood of Noah. Another fascinating anecdote: According to the broadcast, at the time of Sir Isaac Newton, his explorations into alchemy and the possibility of manufacturing gold from cheaper metals led the English Crown to outlaw the practice of alchemy. The royals didn't want the price of gold to fall if it turned out that gold could be made from mercury or lead! Prices would have eroded if gold had begun to flood the market.

[22] Ibid., p. 95.

[23] Ibid., p. 95. When measured afterward, the rhodium was present.

[24] Ibid., pp. 96-97.

[25] "And Moses was learned in all the wisdom of the Egyptians, and was mighty in words and in deeds." Acts 7:22.

[26] Ibid., pp. 99-100

[27] Ibid., pp. 248-249.

[28] Ibid., p. 250.

[29] Ibid., p. 250.

[30] Ibid., pp. 252-253.

[31] Ibid., p. 254.

[32] Ibid., p. 257.

[33] Ibid., p. 258.

[34] See Farrell's catalogue of works at en.wikipedia.org/wiki/Joseph_P._Farrell.

[35] Cited by Farrell, ibid. p. 258, from *Flowers and Moynihan, The Secret King*, p. 70

[36] Cited by Farrell, ibid. p. 258, from *Flowers and Moynihan, The Secret King*, p. 79, from Karl Maria Wiligut, "The Nine Commandments of Gôt," signed manuscript.

[37] Ibid., pp. 262-263.

[38] Ibid., p. 263.

[39] Ibid., p. 264. The article by Wiligut referenced is entitled "Ancient Family Crest of the House of Wiligut" published in the magazine *Hagal* in 1933.

[40] And, if the book of Revelation be true, as Christians preach: a second death.

CHAPTER THREE:
A BRIEF HISTORY OF SPIRITUALISM
IN AMERICA

There are more things in heaven and earth, Horatio,
than are dreamt of in your philosophy.

William Shakespeare, *Hamlet*—Act 1, scene 5

The world is infested, just now, by a new sect of philosophers, who have
not yet suspected themselves of forming a sect, and who, consequently,
have adopted no name. They are the Believers in Everything Old.

Edgar Allan Poe, from "Fifty Suggestions"

It is no indulgence in hyperbole to suggest that the modern origins of
America are spiritual (or, at least, religious) in nature, and that America
has spent the last five hundred years trying—usually
unsuccessfully—to ignore that fact.

Peter Levenda, *Sinister Forces*

The Witch Doctor Next Door

In today's version of what Aldous Huxley called the 'perennial philosophy' (aka, pantheism), the core ideology within the self-identified *New Age Movement*,[1] there resounds loud accolades for *shamanism*.[2] Daniel Pinchbeck, author of two relevant books on the subject, *Breaking Open the Head*, and *2012: The Return of Quetzalcoatl*, promotes the importance of shamanism as rediscovered at the close of the twentieth century. He regards shamanism as one means (if not the primary means) to transform humanity's awareness in 2012. "The exploration and unbiased study of these mind-expanding molecules—an interrupted legacy of scientific and psychological research begun in the 1950s and shut down with hysterical force during the late 1960s—is the one way to unify these opposite approaches [brain-based *materialism* versus spirit-oriented *shamanism*] to the nature of reality. Perhaps it is the only way."[3] Pinchbeck, also a follower of the early twentieth century German white magician Rudolf Steiner mentioned in Chapter One, calls for the use of hallucinogenic drugs, such as mescaline or the more exotic *ayuhusca*, a ritual drink of South American occult practitioners, to help "break open the head." (Recall from Walter Stein's testimony, Hitler began his personal power quest in like manner.)

Another popular author of alternative history, Graham Hancock, echoes the same sentiment. In his 2007 book *Supernatural*, Hancock offers this definition of *shamanism:* "Shamanism is not confined to specific socio-economic settings or stages of development. It is fundamentally the ability that all of us share, some with and some without the help of hallucinogens, to enter altered states of consciousness and to travel out of body in non-physical realms— there to *encounter supernatural entities and gain useful knowledge and healing powers from them*." [Emphasis added] [4] The important element to catch in Hancock's statement is how we should encounter mentoring entities, which is more ominous than experiencing only a feeling of euphoria. Hancock praises the 'persons' we experience in these hallucinogenic states, since having their own distinct intelligence they exist to teach us, in his assessment, about ourselves and the cosmos. Thus, Hancock blindly assumes these intelligences are beneficent.

Whether we trust these phenomena or deny their existence drives our core interpretation of the universe. Our perspective on the nature of reality is known as *cosmology.*[*] It is "the branch of astrono-

---

* Dictionary.com provides this formal definition of cosmology: It is "the branch of philosophy dealing with the origin and general structure of the uni-

my dealing with the general structure and evolution of the universe."[5] If psychic phenomena do in fact exist, our understanding of humankind and the universe can no longer be a staid 'naturalism'—we must adopt a traditional supernatural view or we migrate toward the 'new reality'. (As we will see in Book Two, there are many in the military who accept this 'fantastic reality' as pure fact, upon which military operations can and apparently should be based.)

Shamanism, the most ancient of religions, connects us to cultures of indigenous tribes worldwide. Shamanism relies upon highly specialized plant compounds containing hallucinogenic drugs.[6] *Shaman* is the politically correct name for 'witch doctor' or 'medicine man', as the Shaman understands the various uses of plants and their ability to heal both physical and psychological conditions. But most notably, Shamans are the priests of 'animism' and facilitate contact with the spiritual realm. In fact, a whole new tourist industry now exists, (popular for the past two decades), in South America and Mexico focused on seekers of spiritual experiences using organic drugs with Shamanic oversight. Psychic experiences 'south of the border' has become a chic method for the religiously disenfranchised to find their way back to some manner of spiritual encounter.

But the trek is hardly a new one. Timothy Leary, the Harvard professor disillusioned with western society, became the most famous drug detective to go south in order to experience the effects of magical mushrooms. And he wasn't the first investigator. Leary was preceded by R. Gordon Wasson, a famous mycologist (*mycology* being the study of fungi). Interestingly, Wasson had been invited to work for the CIA in the early 1950s as part of the infamous and ill-fated MKULTRA project (discussed later in this chapter and in

---

verse, with its parts, elements, and laws, and especially with such of its characteristics as space, time, causality, and freedom."

depth in Book Two). Wasson refused the invitation; nevertheless without his knowing, he was funded by the Geshcikter Foundation for Medical Research, a CIA 'conduit' for its funding, completing his Mexican expedition in 1956. According to Pinchbeck, Wasson retains the title of the 'father' of magical mushrooms to this day. It was indeed Wasson's 1957 article in *Life Magazine* that caught the attention of Leary and compelled him to take his very own magical mystery tour in 1960.[7] Eventually, Leary picked a different drug of choice, LSD, and become an adamant provocateur and strident promoter of hallucinogenic substances, representing them as the needed savior of Western culture. As he famously said, "Turn on, tune in, and drop out."[8] With such glowing words of wisdom, no wonder the 'silent majority' disinherited academia in the 1960s.

The late Terence K. McKenna, still one of the revered leaders of the 2012 'movement' (as the author refers to it—a well-founded label for today's incarnation of *'New Agers'*), would have easily agreed with this assessment. Indeed, he believed that plant-based hallucinogens were the source of humanity's higher consciousness and, ultimately, the impetus for one of its most distinctive features; namely, *language*. Being two of the often-cited traits of the 'image of God' in humankind, the creative power attributed to mushrooms and other plants transform humanity appears to attribute the divine to these chlorophyll-infused life forms. What is ironic, of course, is how far outside of 'standard reality' the hallucinogens take the subject who ingests them. Arguing that *drugs open the door to humanity's distinctiveness*—even divinity—in the author's way of thinking, supposes a leap in illogic that few spiritually-minded in America or elsewhere could easily embrace.

The surprising development of medicine men to complement other forms of holistic treatment is hardly the only stunning development regarding this new way to look at the world. As demonstrated, when we turn to academics, astronomers, mathematicians and cosmologists in today's academia, we discover how reality (nature) is no longer seen as an interaction of mere matter and energy, made known to us through the medium of space-time. As we discussed in the previous chapter, it is far more mysterious. This scientific approach to the 'new reality' decrees more than physics enlivened with a dose of spiritual thinking; it is frequently levered to substantiate the burgeoning occult views discussed above and many other examples enthusiastically celebrated in America's popular culture.

The latest trend toward shamanism, as it turns out, boasts perhaps the most concentrated form of such esoteric and mystical religion. It offers the greatest advocacy for individuals seeking personal power to learn techniques enabling encounter and engagement with supernatural entities—just as Hancock advises. For Hancock and so many others suffused with New Age sentiments, it is through these choice encounters we freely subordinate ourselves to the 'teachers of mankind' who (supposedly) have taught 'spiritual truth' to us for thousands of years as well as proffering humankind's *raison d'être*.[*] Hancock's startling advice boggles the minds of the cautious who travel such darkened and unknown roads prudently suspicious of personal encounters with mysterious strangers.

For those outside the circle of the initiated, it is difficult to grasp the powerful experience these experimenters have had. As Peter Levenda states in his study of 'the doors of perception', "those who have not taken LSD (or other hallucinogens… such as mescaline and psilocybin) cannot appreciate the effects these substances have on one's perception of reality. [Yet] those who have taken the drugs are often considered to be in no position to be objective about them!"[9] In other words, the irony is insurmountable: without trying it, you can't know if you like it. But if you try it and like it—

---

[*] A French phrase meaning reason for existence or "reason for our being."

then you can't be objective. Therefore, once favorably disposed based on personal experience, you ought not to try to convince others why they should follow suit.

However, it is the history of *the personal power quest* in America we wish to address in this chapter. This power quest has a distinctly American character. This amazing history illustrates that American fascination with *spiritualism* (or *spiritism* as it is sometimes called) dominates our religious past far more than many presume. Rather than a follower, America proved out to be a leader and trend-setter in 'pop' religion for almost 300 years, especially as our global influence grew. Today spiritualism continues to be a global ideology surging within intellectual and pseudo-intellectual circles. What we will learn in our brief rundown of spiritualism in America over the past two centuries: although spiritualism commenced in Europe during the Renaissance it was nurtured in America until returned to Europe in the form of Theosophy late in the nineteenth century. The stunning worldwide sway of America's spiritualist movement becomes all the more astounding when one uncovers its humble origins in rural New York from the 1820s through 1870s.[*]

Mormon Magic

Peter Levenda's study on occult aspects of American politics includes a pithy analysis of the founding of Mormonism—that distinctive American take on Christianity—which encapsulates many aspects of the interplay between religion, politics, and the supernatural in America. Levenda writes,

---

[*] Therefore, not only were the English part-time chefs adding to the occult cauldron of Nazi Fascism, but Americans also contributed to the horrendous evil Himmler and Hitler mixed, contributing many influential ideas to the mix.

Joseph Smith was actively involved in the use of ritual magic—ceremonial magic—for the purpose of finding buried treasure. Like a Yankee Doctor Faustus, Joseph Smith conjured spirits to come to his aid. With amulets and talismans, pentacles and swords, sigils and strange alphabets, he stepped from the misty milieu of Continental European magic and into the creation of the quintessential American-born religion, a religion which ties together some loose ends of American archaeology, Christian cabala, Freemasonry, and old-fashioned Bible stories to weave a crazy quilt of millennial paranoia, pseudo-Egyptian magic, and Masonic ritual. In fact, Joseph Smith could be considered one of the godfathers of the American occult scene, the progenitor of such groups as the Church of Satan, the OTO "Caliphate," even the witchcraft revival of the 1970s.[10]

While Joseph Smith initially followed in his father's footsteps using a divining rod and seer stone to find buried treasure, his interests eventually turned to more esoteric matters. He became fascinated with magic stones and gazed endlessly into them. Soon he was seeing visions. Could finding the famous golden plates with the help of the angel Moroni in 1823 have been the byproduct of his honed visionary skill? It is true that several years would go by before he would use seer stones to translate the tablets into the *Book of Mormon*. But Smith's fondness for the mystical continued unabated. Soon it became obvious that the 'realm of the spirit' had bigger things in store for Mr. Smith than simply uncovering colored stones whose use constituted a pair of divine 'dice'. His pietistic persistence led to encounters with personal forces eagerly guiding him to new and many times puzzling enchantments.

Most Mormons have no idea just how 'magical' Smith was. Not only did he grow up in a family of occult practitioners (a channeling mother, a wizard father, as well as an aunt who married an alchemist), he continued practicing ritual magic even after he had founded Mormonism and had written the *Book of Mormon*. Smith led a team of followers into Salem, Massachusetts, a town well-acquainted with magic and witchcraft, seeking hoped-for treasure supposedly hidden in a house there. This incident was in 1836, six years after completing his epic religious revelation on the visitation of Christ to America and the elimination of a white race descended from the lost tribes of Israel. Despite Smith's best efforts in Salem, no treasure was found. After this failure, his focus would be centered mostly on church building until he was killed in 1844. Perhaps he found the pay better from collecting regular offerings than the occasional unearthed treasure using divination.

D. Michael Quinn in his seminal study *Early Mormonism and the Magic World View* provided this important insight:

> Joseph Smith's family owned magical charms, divining rods, amulets, a ceremonial dagger inscribed with astrological symbols of Scorpio and seals of Mars, and parchments marked with occult signs and cryptograms popular in eighteenth- and nineteenth-century English and American folklore. In her 1845 Oral memoir, the family matriarch, Lucy Mack Smith, recalled the Smith's interest in "the faculty of *Abrac*"—a term that might have been lost on some. In fact, *Abrac*, or *Abraxas*, is a Gnostic Term for God that also served as a magical incantation. It forms the root of a magic word known to every child: *abracadabra*.

Quinn also indicates that in the period after the war of 1812, the number of occult books in America multiplied. A listing of various occult books in print or available second-hand from that era was over 100 pages![11] The availability of this material to Smith was no doubt useful as he 'envisioned' his religion into being.

Smith's religious point of view can best be summarized as an amalgamation of select borrowings from Christian doctrine, inspiration attributable to American ingenuity, and the fanciful practice of magical ceremonies. Additionally, when in 1842 Smith was initiated into Freemasonry he obtained substantial additional grist for grinding out his religious views. At the end of the day, Smith was nothing if not a solid American pragmatist, being quite practical about religious matters. Even the polygamist path was a practical revelation. After all, keeping as many wives pregnant as possible couldn't help but grow the movement until the 'latter days' were concluded.

We must ask, "Weren't all these forms of supernaturalism related by the simple fact they were all spiritual pursuits?" And the follow-up question: "Why would there need be any distinction drawn between one form of spiritual practice from another?" In America, the guiding principle seems to be, "*If it works, it must be right.*" As Levenda notes, the Smiths "seemed to be firm believers and... were religious people as well, for whom their occult practices were perceived as complementary—rather than in opposition—to their Christian faith." [12] Levenda's analysis continues with these words:

> Magic was believed to be an extension of religion, and not in opposition to it. Thus, we have many clergymen, scientists, and political leaders involved in those days in practices that can only seem unsavory today. To be sure, many strict fundamentalists opposed to the practice of magic, fearing that it would lead to the excesses of witchcraft and demon-worship. But to the farmer, the villager, the blacksmith, these practices were based on a system of knowledge that was gleaned from the stars and the phases of the moon, things of nature, things that regulated their lives anyway and told them when to plant and when to harvest. [13]

In short, American religion was not particularly discriminating when it came to doctrinal distinctions. Just as certain Renaissance theologians* came to believe that Hermeticism and Christian doctrine should be blended into a composite ideology that it might become more amenable to parties outside the circle of Christian faith, American religion was eager to unite rather than divide spiritual

---

* That is, the Neo-Platonists: Bruno, Marandola, and Agrippa discussed in the previous chapter.

views which shared a regard for supernatural or mystical realities.[14] Such a pluralist approach to religion can't help but be politically correct—even if it winds up being doctrinal dribble.

This tendency to *synthesize*, rather than *distinguish* religious views which may oppose one another, is apparent with the next spiritualist fact, appearing as it does as another intriguing blip on our radar.

American Occultism and Social Good

Although a Christian who proudly traffics in evangelical circles, the author is cautious when it comes to labeling opposing views with extreme remarks.[15] For instance, to make everyone who participates in personal occultism, mysticism, or spiritualism out to be a Satanist would be philosophically naïve and historically inaccurate. Human sociology and psychology are much more complex than this label connotes and any sincere investigation disavows overly simplistic analysis. Plus, name calling doesn't advance the discussion nor factually present the historical record for those characters whose story we seek to accurately portray. This is not to say that the ultimate origins of occultist inclinations cannot be assigned to 'evil' personages, particularly when horrific self-serving aspects of spiritualism are center stage and moral judgments are mandated from concerned and sympathetic people. The Nazis illustrated 'the worst' in spiritualism by leveraging these unusual resources for evil purposes. Examples provided by those close to the action clearly illustrated just how wicked spiritualism without a moral compass can become.[16] In stark contrast, American spiritualism is much more subtle. *Historically, it possesses a strong moral compass.*

Throughout his scholarly analysis of the occult in America, Mitch Horowitz makes this point plain:

> In the public mind, the occultist craved immortality, deific power, and limitless knowledge. It was an image that popular occultists

often fed. The nineteenth-century French magician Eliphas Levi [1810-1875] fancied the occult arts "a science which confers on man *powers apparently superhuman.*" [Emphasis added]   England's "Great Beast" Aleister Crowley extolled self-gratification in his best-known maxim: "Do what thou wilt shall be the whole of the law."

The Standard-bearers of the American occult took a different path. They sought to remake mystical ideas as tools of public good and self-help. The most influential trance medium of the nineteenth century, Andrew Jackson Davis—called the "Pough-keepsie Seer" after his Hudson Valley, New York, home—enthralled thousands with visions of heaven as a place that included all the world's people: black, white, Indian, and followers of every religion. In early America, the occult and liberalism were closely joined, especially in the movement of Spiritualism—or contacting the dead—whose newspapers and practitioners were ardently abolitionist and suffragist. For women, Spiritualist practices, from séances to spirit channeling, became vehicles for the earliest forms of religious and political leadership.[17]

Horowitz documents a particularly colorful example of how women rode the spiritualist religion to public prominence in his account of the 1872 presidential campaign of trance-medium Victoria Woodhull, from the Equal Rights Party, "a consortium of Suffragists and abolitionists:"

Woodhull had gained national prominence the previous year in a historic voting-rights speech before the congressional Judiciary Committee. She was the first woman to appear before a joint committee of Congress. She later told supporters that the Woodhull Memorial, as her testimony was known, had been dictated to her in a dream by a ghostly, tunic-wearing Greek elder—a spiritual guardian who had guided all of her public utterances ever since she was a little girl. Woodhull's presidential campaign was quixotic and short-lived, quickly eclipsed by her twin passions for publicity-mongering and political chicanery. The medium-activist selected Frederick Douglass as her running mate—but without asking him. "I never heard of this," the abolitionist hero later said.[18]

It is also clear that most American practitioners of mysticism, occultism, channeling, et al, saw their spiritualism as a Christian vocation. They recognized no conflict. "In the Church's zeal to erase the old practices—practices that had endured throughout the late ancient world (even Rome's first Christian emperor, Constantine, personally combined Christianity with sun worship)—bishops branded pantheists and nature worshippers, astrologers and cosmologists, cultists and soothsayers in ways that such believers had never conceived of themselves: as practitioners of Satanism and black magic."[19] Horowitz's perspective, of course, is distinctly pluralist.[20]

In summing up the matter, we read, "So heavily did the lines between progressive politics and Spiritualism intersect in the nineteenth century that it was rare to find a leader in one field who had not at least a passing involvement in the other."[21] It is seldom true that anyone sufficiently committed to their spiritual beliefs feels political action is improper or disingenuous. Indeed the opposite is true: in America, one's spirituality should result in political action or the veracity of one's spiritual or religious commitment is questioned. The broad wall that has been fixed by the media between politics and religion in this country during the past few decades, presumed necessary because of the separation of 'church and state', is highly contrary to the spiritual and political temperament of our country since its inception. Likewise, we often hear the question today, "What would Jesus do?" The answer from those who read the gospels carefully is certainly not, 'sit on the sidelines'. *Jesus was an activist as well as a pietist.* Faith and works working together are the sure signs of salvation.

At the conversion of the tax collector (a 'publican', Zacchaeus from Jericho—see Luke 19:1-10—the most hated public official in town), it was only after he pledged to repay what he had stolen from the citizens of his region that Jesus said, "Truly has salvation come to this house." Likewise, social good, even if performed by those whose doctrine is woefully errant, remains worthy of praise. With that being said, we must be cautious regarding the reverse: worthy actions—no matter how meritorious—don't correct bad theology.

America's Most Influential Medium

Few in American religious circles today have heard of *Andrew Jackson Davis,* the namesake of the seventh American President, who was born in 1826 (died in 1910), to an upstate New York family. Jackson's impact upon history is a genuine enigma. The fact that he was born in rural New York and returned to New York City in later

years reinforces a key aspect of the origin of America's spiritualist movement. Rural New York celebrated in Washington Irving's tale of the headless horseman in "The Legend of Sleepy Hollow" (an upper state New York village) turns out to be the spiritual focal point in America for most cults that combine Christianity and Spiritualism.[22] One might say the coincidence of so many cults arising from this area is well, a bit uncanny.

Figure 14 - Andrew Jackson Davis 1847

Andrew Jackson Davis was influenced by local tales of witchcraft, ghosts, and spiritism that pervaded the region. His mother spoke of dreams and visions. Eventually the family moved to Poughkeepsie (hence, his nickname—the "Poughkeepsie Seer"). It was however, the influence of the esoteric German personality identified earlier—Franz Anton Mesmer—that would set Davis on his mystical course.

Mesmer, mentioned before, was much like classical alchemists; he spoke of the aether (the universal 'medium' we discussed in the previous chapter) with a slightly different twist. To him, the aether involved "animal magnetism" which animated all of life. Mesmer partially personified the aether. He enthralled many in the European monarchy (who always possessed time to dabble in the occult) with his ability to put a person into a trance state—literally *mesmerizing* them. Even Marquis de Lafayette was enthusiastic about Mesmer.

Horowitz quotes his letter to George Washington which he penned from Paris on May 14, 1784: "A German doctor called Mesmer having made the greatest discovery upon *Magnetism Animal*, he has instructed scholars, among whom your humble servant is called one of the most enthusiastic—I know as much as any conjuror ever did... and before I go, I will get leave to let you into the secret of

Figure 15 - Franz Anton Mesmer

Mesmer, which you may depend upon, is a grand philosophical discovery."[23] In fact Lafayette carried a letter from Mesmer himself to personally place in Washington's hands. In typical political fashion, Washington politely replied to Mesmer, after receiving a thorough explanation from Lafayette, "[If] the powers of magnetism... should prove as extensively beneficial as it is said it will, [it] must be fortunate indeed for mankind, and redound very highly to the honor of that genius to whom it owes its birth."[24]

In 1843, Horowitz relates how a traveling Mesmerist found Davis an eager subject, easily placed into a trance state (obviously a similar state of mind, if not identical, to being hypnotized). Davis described this state with words oozing euphoria and sentimentality (e.g., "a lightness of being"). After an especially mystical experience involving the appearance of the dead Swedish mystic, Emanuel Swedenborg (1688-1772, his appearance in Davis' vision *ghostly* of course), Davis felt compelled to deliver "lectures on religious or metaphysical topics while in a trance, or magnetized, state. His ideas, he claimed, came from higher regions which he could visit in his psychical flights [no doubt similar to the *out of body* and *remote viewing* experiences we examine in Book Two]. Davis determined he would dictate an entire book this way: It would be the vehicle for the 'new light' Swedenborg told him [in his vision] to deliver to humanity."[25]

After moving to Manhattan in 1845, "Davis entered a trance day after day for months. He dictated visions of other planets, heaven, angels, afterlife realms, and the spiritual mechanics of the entire universe, all recorded by his minister friend for the pages of a massively swelling book."[26] Since these sessions were actually open to the public, a particularly intrigued journalist by the name of Edgar Allan Poe observed Davis' experience of channeled writing (perhaps enviously, since it would make writing much less work!) Being fascinated by Mesmerism, Poe soon would compose one of his most famous short stories, "The Facts in the Case of M Valdemar" (as it was completed later that same year, we conclude Davis was Poe's inspiration). In his fictional account, Poe made his protagonist Valdemar the victim of a Mesmerist who kept him locked in a trance for seven months, until, at the pleading of Valdemar, the Mesmerist 'let his subject go.' Once released from the trance, his body literally and quickly turned into a "liquid mass of loathsome—of detestable putrescence." Most intriguingly, *The Sunday Times of London* would publish Poe's story in 1846 and convey (by omitting any word to the contrary) the account was true (the story entitled, *Mesmerism in America: Astounding and Horrifying Narrative*).[27]

In the account of Davis, Horowitz connects another colorful character mentioned in my previous book *Decoding Doomsday*: Professor George Bush of New York University (during the 1840s, Bush was Professor of Hebrew, famously predicting the physical reestablishment of Israel in the land of Palestine, 100 years before it happened). This Bush was first cousin, five times removed from the first President Bush. Dr. Bush told the *New York Tribune* in regards to Davis' abilities: "I can solemnly affirm that I have heard him correctly quote the Hebrew language in his lectures and display a knowledge of geology which would have been astonishing in a person of his age, even if he had devoted years to the study."[28]

Like other promoters of spiritualism in America, Davis was committed not only to mysticism but to the social gospel. "For many, the true magic of Davis' message was in its liberalism: sexual and racial parity, religions on equal footing, and a universal faith based on reason."[29] A Universalist religion we might acknowledge; but there was a reason some portion of his assertions were more difficult to swallow—Davis' *source for truth* was a channeled spirit. This entity was a wordy supernatural being eager to have his thoughts put down on paper. Should we be surprised? Not really. This pattern is standard operating procedure for occultists. Indeed, *channeled material* is by definition essential to spiritualism. It should be no wonder that Andrew Jackson Davis was a medium given all leaders of New Age spiritualism (from Helena Blavatsky to Alice Bailey, from Benjamin Crème to Phyllis Schlemmer the 'channeler of choice' for THE NINE who we will later consider in Book Two), penned immense works by taking dictation from spirit entities.

However, the legacy of Andrew Jackson Davis would have greater impact than Mr. Davis. This protégé would be one *Henry Steel Ol-*

cott, co-founder of *the Theosophical Society*, traveling companion to *Madame Blavatsky,* and originator of the ideology that found its way back across the pond two decades later, infecting the minds of the English and Germans, whose penchant for spiritualism we've already thoroughly documented. As we will see, the chance meeting of these characters led to their influence upon Nazi Germany (and therefore, the rest of the world). As such, it stands as one of the most important examples of happenstance ever witnessed.

The Birth of Theosophy

Colonel Olcott, as he was also popularly known, grew up a Presbyterian and married the wife of an Episcopal minister. However, despite these Christian leanings, he was fascinated by the occult even as a young lad. At twelve years of age, he took a trip to Poughkeepsie to witness Andrew Jackson Davis make a complete diagnosis of a sick man in his presence with no more than holding a lock of his hair. This one experience would impact Olcott's life work with far reaching consequences.

As a youth, he lived the farmer's life toiling with relatives in Ohio. But as the Civil War drew near, he obtained an Army commission where he developed a new set of skills that would serve him well.

> He was placed in charge of a team of auditors and detectives to investigate fraud and forgery among military contractors, and was promoted to staff colonel to lend weight to his investigations. Exposing a racket of fake provisions sales, Olcott saved the Union army enough money for Secretary of War Edwin M. Stanton to write him that his efforts were "as important to the Government as the winning of a battle." His reputation as an investigator grew. When Lincoln was assassinated in 1865, Olcott volunteered his services. Stanton telegraphed him in New York to "come to Washington at once, and bring your force of detectives with you." During the twelve days that John Wilkes Booth

remained a fugitive, Olcott and his investigators made the first arrests and interrogations of suspected coconspirators."[30]

Figure 16 - Blavatsky & Olcott, London, 1888

After growing rich from government contracts, Olcott became an attorney and began a law practice in New York City. However, he was much more interested in writing. Unsatisfied with the standard fare about which he wrote (becoming bored authoring cultural reviews), "His interest in Spiritualism began to reemerge—especially upon reading press reports of strange happenings at a Vermont homestead." A spirit medium William Eddy and his brother Horatio put on a ghost show with Indians in full regalia and personages from far away. "It was here at the Vermont 'ghost farm' that Olcott had a fateful encounter—one that would send tremors not only through his own life but across other continents."[31]   And radically change history. Horowitz continues the colorful story:

On the sunny midday of October 14, Olcott stepped onto the Eddy porch to light the cigarette of a new visitor: a strange, heavyset Russian woman with whom he grew quickly enchanted. She showed him flesh wounds she said she had suffered fighting beside the revolutionary hero [Italian] Giuseppe Garibaldi in his campaign to unify Italy; she told tales of travels in exotic lands; and she hinted at far deeper truths about the nature of the spirit world than were revealed to the nightly gawkers at the Eddy home. Olcott was perplexed—and utterly fascinated. The college dropout in him seemed somewhat awed by "the arrival of a Russian lady of distinguished birth and rare educational and natural endowments." He marveled over her tales of "traveling in most of the lands of the Orient, searching for antiquities at the base of the Pyramids, witnessing mysteries of Hindoo [sic] temples, and pushing with an armed escort far into the interior of Africa."[32]

Olcott rented an apartment for himself and his new best friend, Madame Helena Petrovna Blavatsky, at West 47th Street and Eighth Avenue. The New York World jokingly referred to their habitat as the *Lamasery*—referencing the lamas' monasteries of Tibet. "It was a cramped Neverland of a place where, amid stuffed baboons, Japanese cabinets, jungle murals, mechanical birds, and palm fronds, New York's spiritually adventurous—ranging from inventor Thomas Edison to Major-General Abner Doubleday—huddled to discuss, argue over, and marvel at arcane ideas."[33]

Edison would admit to Olcott and later to a reporter about his experimenting in the occult, specifically looking at the intersection of the technology of the mind with that of mechanical science—an essential element of Theosophy inasmuch as the ideology wasn't just about 'knowing' but also about 'doing'—specifically physic feats defying logic. (Blavatsky was famous for making things 'go bump in the night', bringing ringing bells to chorus and achieving other poltergeist-like goings-on). Edison built one device to test

whether the mind could create kinetic force and another to communicate with the dead (Note: yet another technologist enamored
with spiritualism). Doubleday not only helped develop and promote
the then-new sport of *baseball* after a highly reputable career in the
military (he lies buried at Arlington National Cemetery), but he contributed to the Theosophy Movement by publishing the first English
translation of French magician Eliphas Levi's occult standard *Ritual
and Dogma of High Magic,* more commonly known as *Transcendental Magic.* After Olcott and Blavatsky left America heading for
India, Doubleday would take over the reins of the American Theosophical Society. Who says baseball and Buddha don't go together?

But why was Blavatsky in America? HPB[*] indicated that she had
been "dispatched to America by a secret order of religious masters—"Mahatmas," or the "Great White Brothers," she would later
call them... Her mission was to expose the limits and fallacies of
Spiritualism and point the way to higher truths. While she admired
the cosmic visions of Andrew Jackson Davis, Blavatsky hinted at
secret teachings that the Poughkeepsie Seer and the trance mediums
who trailed after him could only begin to guess."[34] All this became
firm as fact when,

> One of the turbaned masters materialized before him [Olcott] in
> their West Side apartment. Addressing Olcott as "Brother Neo-
> phyte," one of the Mahatma letters [that Olcott had received,
> penned in gold ink] directed him to stay at Blavatsky's side and
> "not let one day pass away without seeing her." He listened—
> and the two worked together days into nights. They collaborated
> on Blavatsky's epic-in-the-making, *Isis Unveiled*—a dense,
> sprawling, and ultimately extraordinary panoply of occult sub-
> jects. Blavatsky told of a hidden doctrine that united all the
> world's ancient religions and cosmic laws but that unknown to

[*] Her common nickname, self-imposed and liberally used by her followers.

materialist science and modern religion...In the typically blunt fashion that made her a favorite of the New York press, Madame Blavatsky publicly declared, "The Theosophical Society means, if it cannot rescue Christians from modern Christianity, at least to aid in saving the 'heathen' from its influence." The *New York Sun*, never wearying of the Russian Madame, dubbed her the "famous heathen of Eighth Avenue."[35]

Indeed, the story of Olcott and Blavatsky could well be summed up as a furtive campaign against Christianity, its strictures, as well as its 'exclusivist' doctrines. On the positive side, while in India, Olcott and Blavatsky worked hard for the cause of literacy. On the other hand, in contradistinction to his American background, once in Ceylon (now Sri Lanka), Olcott "spoke in temples and open squares, where he urged youths and their families not to relinquish their Buddhist-monastic tradition and to argue against colonialist missionaries... Olcott used the missionaries' own methods against them: He wrote *A Buddhist Catechism*—still read in Sri Lankan Classrooms today—to codify the native faith as missionaries had the Christian one."[36] His 'do-gooding' gained him great respect, raising money for schools and educational programs. Horowitz further indicates Olcott ignited a Buddhist revival causing the number of Buddhist schools to jump from four to over two hundred.

However strange the Theosophical doctrine was to most American's (it remained quite 'off-the-hook'), it wrapped itself in a populist cloak by adding value to society. As most religions of the orient can seldom be accused of performing vast social good or undergirding society in general, the admixture proffered by the odd couple from New York contained a social conscience that was deeply American and earned Theosophy a positive hearing around the globe.

Meanwhile, back in the USA, *Isis Unveiled* was becoming a best seller giving spiritualism a Bible of sorts to satisfy many Americans and their eagerness to grow wise in this new reckoning of reality—an ideology combining *Buddhism, the new discoveries of science, and American individualism.* This combination was the secret sauce that resurrected a decidedly declining interest in oriental mysticism worldwide and made 'being a mystic' fashionable.

> And if there were any hidden Mahatmas who had sent Blavatsky to America and then with Olcott to India, they might have had reason to be proud of their neophytes on other counts. Back in the United States and Europe, Blavatsky's book *Isis Unveiled* popularized the word occultism and made the concept a matter of passionate interest among artists, authors, and spiritual seekers of the Western world—more than it had been any time since Renaissance scholars had marveled over the magical writings of Greek-Egyptian sage Hermes Trismegistus.

The American Spin on Spiritualism

America was primed for Theosophy because of its previous infatuation with *Transcendentalism* spurred to life by another man with a similar sounding name: *Alcott* (that is, Amos Bronson Alcott—Louisa May's father of *Little Women*[37] fame) who, along with Ralph Waldo Emerson and Henry David Thoreau plowed the spiritual ground so Theosophical seeds could be sown.[*] Alcott demonstrated great interest in Hermetic matters studying the 'Egyptian magician' Trismegistus' works in small groups with his highly intellectual neighbors. Alcott was especially influenced by the literary genius of Emerson (1803-1882) who lived across the street. Horowitz quotes scholar Alvin Boyd Buhn from his 1930 study, *Theosophy*, who asserted the *importance of the connection between Transcendentalism*

---

[*] On a personal note, I drove by the houses of these famous Americans who lived in Concord, Massachusetts, most every day for five years when commuting from Nashua, New Hampshire into Boston. Additionally, we celebrated my daughters eleventh birthday by having her and her friends dress up in old New England dresses (*Little Women* style) holding a party for them at the Alcott's house, now open to the public. It was a memorable occasion.

and Theosophy: "Yet, seriously, without Emerson, Madame Blavatsky could hardly have launched her gospel when she did with equal hope of success."[38]

That is why Blavatsky believed America to be the 'Mecca of Spiritualism'. "The opening created by Transcendentalism made the young nation into a magnet for every kind of spiritual experiment. And like many cultural openings, this one appeared so quickly and dramatically that it could leave observers unsure of what was even occurring."[39]

America's excitement regarding Spiritualism may not be easily appreciated by Americans today. But at the time, many American's either discarded their Christian faith entirely or amended it dramatically by seeing it through the lens of Theosophy and other spiritualistic cults.

Figure 17 - The emblem of the Theosophical Society

It was particularly appealing because of the despairing nature of the times for many. Being able to tap into 'the other side' was an enticement that grieving parents couldn't avoid—and there were many such parents in despair. In New York City in 1853, almost 50% of all deaths were children under five years of age.[40] This caused the profession of mediumship to be a method of gainful employment, particularly for women. "In 1850, journalist E. W. Capron counted in Auburn, New York, 'fifty to one hundred' mediums 'in different stages of development,' including those who could induce unseen hands to strum guitars and pound drums." [41] Seeing this musical phenomenon no doubt would have been even more charming than watching the player piano pound the keys at the carnival—both types of playing being about equally mysterious to most audiences.

Horowitz underscores how many newspapers and periodicals sprung to life after 1850 to serve this ascending market. At the peak, those journals almost totaled seventy altogether. His estimates, possibly conservative, suggested that between 10 and 30% of the American population in the latter half of the nineteenth century would have checked the box "spiritualist" if asked to declare their religion. "Spiritualism was not a regional sensation but a national movement." [42]

Even President Lincoln and especially his wife Mary Todd were engaged in séances; some of these social events in the Whitehouse included cabinet members where political matters would be posed to the presiding medium. "Once everyone was seated at the table, according to the Gazette's correspondent, Prior Melton, Lincoln gamely pitched political questions to [Charles] Shockle, the "spirit visitors" who spoke through him, and the two cabinet members, while Mark Todd looked on silently."[43]

After the assassination of the President, Mrs. Lincoln, "so distraught by the death of her husband grew increasingly interested in séances. Ten years after her husband's death, 1875, Mary Todd Lincoln was briefing committed to a sanitorium [sic—committed by her one remaining son Richard], claiming—spuriously—that she was squandering her estate of Spiritualist hoo-ha."[44]

Thus, America produced Theosophy which contributed to the spiritualist mindset and many other myths of the "Black Reich." Authors Pauwels and Bergier, Trevor Ravenscroft, and virtually any other we could cite regard Theosophy as the key to understanding the mindset present in Nazi Germany before World War II. To finish this section with a flourish, it seems appropriate to underscore America's influence on Germany with a quotation from author Christopher Hale, who studied the infamous Nazi expeditions to the Himalayas to track down the roots of the Aryan race (which he called, "Himmler's Crusade," authoring a book by the same title). He drew these conclusions concerning the effect of Theosophy upon Germany and Europe:

> *The Secret Doctrine* made an especially powerful impression in Germany and Austria. Olcott had even considered moving the Theosophical Society headquarters from India to Germany after the English Society for Psychical Research had exposed Madame Blavatsky as a fraud (she was caught out writing the letters which she claimed were 'precipitated' by her mahatmas). Some fifty years later, after 1933, Theosophy would become even more popular as Germans were encouraged to turn away from Christianity and embrace faiths that were considered to be more Aryan. For many, *The Secret Doctrine* appeared to reconcile science and belief, nature and myth, and in Germany, it catalyzed a much older intellectual tradition...[45]

> All over Europe, and in India itself, theosophy became a cult. Its disciples were not the hungry masses who poured into spiritualist meetings and séances desperately seeking solace; they were intellectuals, diplomats, philosophers, and even scientists. United under the Tibetan symbol of the swastika, they infested the salons and laboratories of Europe. As in *The Secret Doctrine* itself, science and occultism lay happily side-by-side in a fetid embrace.[46]

Similar to the intellectual participation of several English literary giants, we pointed out that the evil of Nazi Germany was not an exclusively Teutonic invention. Americans too unwittingly provided ideological support for the Third Reich.

However, the impact of Theosophy is far from concluded here as we will see by tracing its influence on the next stage of Spiritualism in America: *The New Age Movement*.[47] With this more modern form of Theosophy, we see less emphasis upon social gospel and more emphasis upon an eccentric agenda through a sought-after encounter with spirit beings. In the latest incarnation of the ancient wisdom, the personal experience of obtaining *individual spiritual power*—this 'selfish' objective of spirituality—remains the primary thrust.

Spiritualism and the New Age Movement

It is one of the most peculiar themes of latter-day occult philosophy: the insistence that there are a series of "masters" who live in remote places guiding what happens in our world. These masters take various names. Blavatsky labeled them the *Great White Brotherhood;* hers was an update to her grandfather's "unknown Superiors."

Figure 18 - Alice A. Bailey

This tradition continued with her most important disciple, Alice Ann Bailey (1880-1949, typically nicknamed *AAB* by her followers) claiming they should be addressed as the *Ancient Masters of Wisdom.* Bailey, while born in England, lived most of her life in the United States. Once again, Americans can take pride in (or in the author's case, *despair of*) the influence our native spiritualism has upon the rest of the world.

Like Blavatsky, Bailey 'channeled' her messages, claiming to take telepathic dictation from a supernatural source she identified as *Djwhal Kuhl,* aka DK, the *Tibetan.* She wrote over 20 books, from 1919 to 1949 acting as his agent, commenting to the effect that she didn't always agree with DK, but what he said was exactly what she put down on paper. She knew her supernatural superiors as the *Masters of Wisdom,* of which Jesus was but one (and according to her, *not* the supreme Master). In the *Externalization of the Hierarchy,* perhaps her most famous book, Bailey indicates that the time is soon coming when the "Hierarchy of Ancient Masters" will appear before all humanity. A prayer given her by DK—known as the *Great Invocation*, calls out to these Masters, imploring them to leave their "hidden ashrams" behind and live in the cities of the World. For Bailey, the *Christ* translates as a collective title for these various spiritual gurus. The "Return of the Christ" culminates *the divine plan* realized through these spirit guides.

All scholars of merit connect the teachings of Bailey and Blavatsky.[48] Strong evidence abounds to support this conclusion. A case in point: When controversy emerged over who would lead Theosophy and the New Age movement, Bailey and her husband, Foster Bailey, a 32nd degree Freemason, led a "Back to Blavatsky" movement to counter her rival Annie Besant. To this day, a debate remains alive among Theosophists regarding whether Bailey was true to Blavatsky's message.

Nevertheless, Bailey's writings constitute the doctrinal opus of the New Age Movement in America. However, her influence goes beyond her writings. There are numerous organizations she founded with her husband Foster Bailey including *The Arcane School, The Group of New World Servers,* and *Lucis Trust,* originally known as *Lucifer Trust.*[49] After Alice Bailey died in 1949, Mr. Bailey took over Lucis Trust and continued as chief until his own death in 1977.

As with the other oriental religions both past and present, Bailey placed a strong emphasis on transformation, reincarnation, and Karma. Like the Freemasons, she emphasized the mystical powers of *Venus* and *Sirius*. As with Blavatsky, frequent mention is made of *Shamballa*—the divine seat of power for *Sanat Kumara* who is, according to AAB, the ruler of this world and a focal point for occult power and *eternal life*.[50] Also similar to Blavatsky, Bailey evinced anti-Semitic sentiments, believing the Jews "have bad Karma," blame the Gentiles for all their problems, and "require the best for their children no matter what the cost to others." She talked frequently about "the Jewish Problem" and claimed after World War II, that the occupants of the concentration camps were 80% other races and only 20% Jews. One Rabbi said this of her teachings opposing Judaism:

> Bailey's plan for a New World Order and her call for "the gradual dissolution—again if in any way possible—of the Orthodox Jewish faith" revealed that "her goal is nothing less than the destruction of Judaism itself... This stereotyped portrayal of Jews is followed by a hackneyed diatribe against the Biblical Hebrews, based upon the 'angry Jehovah' theology of nineteenth-century Protestantism. Jews do not, and never have, worshipped an angry vengeful god..."[51]

Conclusion: The Ongoing Impact of Spiritualism

In the final analysis of spiritualist religion, there appear two different metaphysical schools of thought, metaphorically speaking. First, there are those advancing a slate of affirmations that most wouldn't quibble with. Horowitz identifies such beliefs with these words:

1. Belief that spiritual ideas have therapeutic value.
2. Belief in there is a mind-body connection in our health.
3. Belief that human consciousness is evolving to a higher stage.
4. Belief that thought determines reality.
5. Belief that spiritual comprehension is available to anyone without pledging allegiance to any one dogmatic religion.[*]

Horowitz suggests these ideas sum up how the occult has influenced America. He concludes: "The encounter between America

---

[*] For the record, I would quibble a bit regarding the final three.

and occultism resulted in a vast reworking of arcane practices and beliefs from the Old World and the creation of a new spiritual culture. This new culture extolled religious egalitarianism and responded, perhaps more than any other movement in history, to the inner needs and search of the individual." [52]

From a popular cultural perspective in America, this summary assessment is essentially true. However, from the standpoint of erstwhile Christian creeds so influential in other aspects of American life from its inception forward, Horowitz's analysis of occult influence, especially in American intellectual history, is utterly innocuous.

It is the 'second school' of New Age thinking—followers of Alice Bailey—who propose a much more radical and directed agenda. We best keep tabs on these spokespersons. Included are Benjamin Crème, David Spangler, Barbara Marx Hubbard, and their disciples in what we call the '*2012 Movement*'. Given their radical antagonism toward American Protestantism as well as their forceful threats for those that do not sing out of their New Age hymnbook, such threats and admonitions raise the hair on the back of this author's neck. For example, Hubbard warns, "People will either change or die. That is the choice."[53] Mel Sanger, an evangelical researcher and contemporary author offers this analysis:

> Unlike the East, where these pagan teachings are familiar, in Western society there is a need to break down traditional monotheistic (and/or atheistic) resistance to them. To ease penetration, New Agers encourage "light encounters," psychic experiences which seem to carry the individual beyond normal consciousness into a new realm of spiritual sensation. Also known as, "a doorway to higher consciousness," the suitably impressed person will be encouraged to seek this experience on a regular basis. The only way to achieve it, however, is through passivity and a willingness to submit one's mind to outside control of a "guide."[54]

There is something especially sinister concerning this segment of the New Age Movement. Like every other spiritualist leader with a theosophical bent, these advisors propose channeling or mediumship as an avenue to advance one's personal spiritual quest. At a minimum, they encourage grasping 'the meaning of life' through opening ourselves to these ultra-dimensional spiritual forces. But to which side are these forces loyal?

David Spangler offers the following less-than-prudent advice:

> The angel of man's evolution, will *(progress us on our)* journey to "godhood" at the new level, which includes a personal experience of the "knowledge of good and evil." New Agers confirm that this knowledge is what Lucifer offered to Eve in the Garden, and it's being offered again today. Only it's been misunderstood, due *to fear inherited from the superstitious Judaic/Christian religion.* Since God has both a good and an evil side [a problematic assumption drawn from Manichaeism], and one cannot attain complete godhood with only one side, Lucifer comes to give us the final gift of wholeness. If we accept it, then he is free and we are free. That is the Luciferic initiation. It is one that many people now, and in the days ahead, will be facing, for it is an initiation into the New Age.[55]

This group, following the lead of Albert Pike (1809-1891), the noted doctrinal authority of Freemasonry, emphasizes the importance of Lucifer, a Luciferic initiation, and the explicit reversal of otherworldly beings from the standpoint of who is the 'good guy' and 'the bad guy.' While most commentators dismiss any suggestion that true Freemasonry (let alone New Age team just mentioned) is anti-Christian, *such authorities apparently haven't read or choose to ignore the pertinent remarks regarding Freemasonry's search for Luciferian enlightenment.* So should we, likewise, dismiss what these authorities say about themselves and avoid taking them at their word? Isn't it relevant that many in Germany in the 1930s dismissed the notion their country soon would be headed down the path to Fascism? Isn't such incredulity increased when we include the possibility such an outcome would be energized by spiritual forces?

Yet, this is exactly the same situation in America today. Who could possibly believe that 'power players' concealed with the nation's most elite families press for hegemony in regards to our national government? If it is too fantastic to fathom, it must be false.

Despite all such reasonable doubt, we must proceed with caution concerning many of the New Age recommendations for spiritual achievement. Indeed, we should especially take into account the form of freedom that Spangler espouses. His 'liberty for life' is normally considered bondage by most psychologists, particularly by those who have engaged with such spiritual forces over the long haul. Likewise, picking up the story from whence we began in this chapter—taking drugs to prompt a personal spiritual encounter— promises even stouter cases of addiction and self-destruction. Yes, there is a difference between ritual drug taking and reducing your stress, just as there is a difference between a hunting rifle and an AK-47.   However, no matter the intent, just as the experienced know to be careful with fire arms and exercise caution in their use, taking hallucinogenic drugs demands equal prudence. Surely, this guidance for spiritual experience can't be dismissed by third-parties as harmless counsel merely because it originates from well-meaning New-Age-cum-2012 authors attempting to propagate their 'universalist' philosophy. The stakes for the psychological health of the individual are much too high to imbibe hallucinogens with only an ounce of blind faith as a chaser.

Besides these 'pop-religions' of the American masses, another vital force in America influenced the ideology of our nation, commencing even before the creeds of our Founding Fathers. In the pages ahead we will learn that the blueprint for America was completed well before the first permanent English colony, Jamestown was established precariously on the Virginia coast.   To this subject and other highly astonishing facts we now turn.

NOTES

[1] The movement was so-named by Alice Bailey and her followers in American in the 1930s but became widespread in the 1960s and 70s. Today, it could be relabeled the '2012 movement' since it is typically accompanied by predictions for massive change in the consciousness of humankind in the year 2012, when supposedly *the New Age dawns.*

[2] "Shamanism is a range of traditional beliefs and practices that involve the ability to diagnose, cure, and sometimes cause human suffering by traversing the axis mundi and forming a special relationship with, or gaining control over, spirits. Shamans have been credited with the ability to control the weather, divination, the interpretation of dreams, astral projection, and traveling to upper and lower worlds. Shamanistic traditions have existed throughout the world since prehistoric times. Shamanism is based on the premise that the visible world is pervaded by invisible forces or spirits that affect the lives of the living. In contrast to animism and animatism, which any and usually all members of a society practice, shamanism requires specialized knowledge or abilities." See www.crystalinks.com/shamanism.html.

[3] Pinchbeck, *Breaking Open the Head*, 62.

[4] Hancock, Graham, *Supernatural: Meetings with the Ancient Teachers of Mankind* (New York, NY: The Disinformation Company, 2007), 244.

[5] "Cosmology," *Dictionary.com Unabridged*, Random House, Inc., accessed June 30, 2011, http://dictionary.reference.com/browse/cosmology.

[6] Alkaloids such as *dimethyltryptamine*, aka DMT, or *mescaline,* a phenethylamine, both of which are considered *entheogens*, aka psychoactive agents to stir up the "god within us."

[7] Wasson and his wife studied the possibility and concluded that hallucinogens underlie all of humankind's ancient religions. This view is shared by Daniel Pinchbeck and Graham Hancock in the respective books cited here. In other words, to them, God is a magical mushroom, or at least lives within one! "All of our evidence taken together led us many years ago to hazard a bold surmise: was it not probably that, long ago, long before the beginnings of written history, our ancestors had worshipped a divine mushroom?" There is a fungus among us. But this author certainly doesn't believe it is God (Pinchbeck, *Breaking Open the Head*, 48).

[8] "Turn on, tune in, drop out," *Wikipedia*, last modified March 24, 2011, http://en.wikipedia.org/wiki/Turn_on,_tune_in,_drop_out. It was likely the hysterical nature of Leary and his mad ranting about western culture and

the necessity to use hallucinogens to save our souls that 'turned off' (rather than 'on') the American "psyche" to LSD. Today's advocates for the spiritual value of drug-taking blame Leary from doing far more harm than good in educating the masses about the personal usefulness of such compounds.

[9] Levenda, Peter, *Sinister Forces: A Grimoire of American Political Witchcraft*, TrineDay, Waterville, Oregon, 2005, p. 215.

[10] Ibid., p. 28.

[11] Ibid., p. 33.

[12] Ibid., p. 31.

[13] Ibid., p. 36.

[14] Levenda comments on page 40, "As Americans, we have been moving too fast and forgetting too much to realize that we have a unique cultural contribution to make, one that unites religion with mysticism at the very bedrock of human experience... and then transforms this alchemical tincture into a political and scientific Philosopher's Stone capable of causing tremendous change in the human psyche." Levenda's celebration of this indiscriminate combination of spiritualism with Christian supernaturalism is, unfortunately, inconsistent with his acknowledgement that many 'forces' are sinister, just as his book title asserts. If so, the need to distinguish good from evil is mandated and a requirement for any form of Christian faith that takes the Bible's warnings about spiritualism seriously. Discernment and differentiation go hand in hand as do their opposites: deception and consolidation.

[15] Yes, I do realize that my remarks just penned on Mormonism are quite disparaging. My defense: these facts are historically verified by multiple sources and tell the story of Mormonism's beginnings. Its status today is highly sophisticated and bears little resemblance to its origins. However, even this acknowledgement should concern those who are members of the LDS. Christianity's origins are highly regarded and offer positive behavioral models. Not so with Mormonism. Indeed, the most compelling aspects of Mormonism lie in its emulation of the early 'church model' and evangelistic methods of the Christian church, not the Mormon version which arose from a spiritualistic, even magical genesis.

[16] Of course, this can be said of most any religion. When any ideology harms the individual and the society, that religion becomes untrustworthy. In fact, members of society are responsible to question the viability of any religion whose affects consistently demonstrate breaking what our Founders called 'natural law' which protects basic rights of individuals and communities. We see the recent story of Warren Jeffs and his polygamist cult as a prime example.

17 Horowitz, Mitch, *Occult America: The Secret History of How Mysticism Shaped Our Nation,* Bantam Books, New York, 2009, p. 3.

18 Ibid., p. 63.

19 Ibid., p. 7.

20 His is an attempt to be non-judgmental or 'politically correct', inasmuch as pluralism attempts to embrace all points of view as equally valid. I would expect very few who endorse such forms of 'religion' to explain their conduct as consorting with the devil even if they were unwittingly practicing pagan methods. I doubt many Shamans see themselves doing anything other than 'serving the public good'—often self-descriptively viewing themselves as caretakers of their community. Those engaged in these practices (channeling, drug taking, holding séances), from their vantage point, aren't seeking to harm—they certainly seek to help and strive to find personal meaning as a byproduct. Value judgments on what they are doing, from a Judeo-Christian perspective is ultimately based upon a comparison to what biblical directives present as proper or improper—indeed, judging occult practices as forbidden and reprehensible. (See Isaiah 47:11-13) In the New Testament, sorcery, also translated witchcraft, is itself a "sin of the flesh" (See Galatians 5:20) — human beings perform it quite naturally. The New Testament word for witchcraft and sorcery is *pharmakeia* from which our word pharmacy is derived. It takes little imagination to see the link between drug usage for spiritual purposes and sorcery as asserted in the Christian Bible. In the hands of the user, such tools seek to empower the individual to manipulate, not just explore, the entities that inhabit this 'supersensible' realm. This comprises the most personal and mystical power quest of all.

21 Ibid., p. 64

22 Ibid., p. 23. Joseph Smith found his golden plates in western New York, apparently another hotbed for occultism.

23 Ibid., pp. 32-33. His letter is taken from *Abnormal Hypnotic Phenomena, Vol. 4: The United States of America* by Allan Angoff, edited by Eric Dingwall (J.& A. Churchill, 1968).

24 Ibid., p. 33. The Washington letter was drawn by Horowitz from *Franklin in France, Volume II*, by Edward Everett Hale (Roberts Brothers, 1888).

25 Ibid., p. 36.

26 Ibid., p. 37.

27 We might infer tabloid journalism in London had already hit stride 165 years before Rupert Murdoch and the Fox News Corp in 2011 began eaves dropping on voice mail in the name of sensationalism!

[28] Ibid., p. 39. Professor Bush in 1848 published a short book predicting that the nation of Israel would physically become a nation once more. Ironically, 100 years later, Bush was proven a prophet. It is also interesting that Bush eventually left his mainline denominational affiliation and became a follower of Swedenborgism (aka, The New Church), a mystical amalgam of spiritualism and Christianity. It was "founded by the followers of Emmanuel Swedenborg in the late eighteenth century, especially its assertion that Christ is God Himself and not the Son of God, and its reliance upon accounts of mystical appearances of Christ to Swedenborg." (See *www.thefreedictionary.com /Swedenborgism*). Horowitz also points out that the legendary Johnny Appleseed was the most famous member of this group.

[29] Ibid., pg. 41.

[30] Ibid., p. 44.

[31] Ibid., p. 44.

[32] Ibid., pp. 44-45.

[33] Ibid., p. 45.

[34] Ibid., p. 46.

[35] Ibid., p. 47.

[36] Ibid., p. 48.

[37] Louisa May Alcott enjoyed some very special teachers to be sure: "Alcott's early education included lessons from the naturalist Henry David Thoreau. She received the majority of her schooling from her father. She received some instruction also from writers and educators such as Ralph Waldo Emerson, Nathaniel Hawthorne, and Margaret Fuller, who were all family friends. She later described these early years in a newspaper sketch entitled 'Transcendental Wild Oats.'" See *en.wikipedia.org/wiki/ Louisa_May_Alcott.*

[38] Ibid., p. 50.

[39] Ibid., p. 53.

[40] Ibid., p. 55.

[41] Ibid., p.55.

[42] Ibid., p. 57.

[43] Ibid., p. 59. And another story illustrating Lincoln's wit and charm: "When Shockle's spirits did get around to giving their inevitable military advice—through the channeled words of no less than Henry Know, secretary of war to George Washington—Lincoln was unimpressed: 'Well, opinions differ among the saints as well as among the sinners. They don't seem to understand running the machine among the celestials much better than we do. Their talk and advice sounds very much like the talk of my Cabinet.' Lincoln then asked his discomforted cabinet secretaries whether they agreed that the spirits knew little better how to proceed than the mortals—

which elicited stammering assurances from Navy Secretary Gideon Welles that, uh, well, sir, he would certainly consider the matter." (Ibid., pp. 60-61).

44 Ibid., p. 59.

45 Hale, Christopher, *Himmler's Crusade,* Hoboken, New Jersey: Wiley and Sons, 2003, p. 26.

46 Hale, op cit., pp. 29-30.

47 Mitch Horowitz's analysis of a number of twentieth century American churches, such as Christian Science, The Unity School, the Church of Religious Science, and several others may or may not be classified as spiritualist depending upon your definition. I interpret these offshoots of Christianity to be focused on 'mind over matter' and the spirit as an inspirational aspect of reality. Some are more or less orthodox in terms of core Christian doctrines. For instance, Norman Vincent Peale (and the contemporary Robert Schuller) might be accused of believing in a less-than-personal God that enhances our lives when we 'take charge' and become positive influencers on people and situations around us. However, in my reading of these authors I find no reason to include them amongst spiritualists as there is neither evidence nor promotion of channeling, mediumship, etc., and in the case of Peale and Schuler, there is a strong commitment to core Christian doctrines such as the Deity of Christ, sacrificial atonement, and the like. This is not true in the case of Christian Science, Unity, Church of Religious Science, and a very up-to-date flavor of this manner of belief totally without reference to Christian doctrine in the book (and later movie) *The Secret* (Rhonda Byrnes, 2006). These latter belief systems strongly reflect *Gnosticism* (or Manichaeism) and not orthodox Christian affirmations.

48 See Lewis, James R. and Melton, J. Gordon. *Perspectives on the New Age.* SUNY Press. 1992.

49 Lucis Trust continues operating today closely associated with the United Nations. Members include such interesting individuals as George Schultz, Henry Kissinger, David Rockefeller, and Paul Volker. This fires the flames of conspiracy to be sure.

50 Shamballa was also the city Marco Polo tried to find that contained the fountain of youth, or the "tree of life."

51 *http://en.wikipedia.org/wiki/Alice_Bailey#cite_note-Gershom-149* .

52 Ibid., p. 258.

53 Hubbard, Barbara Marx, *Happy Birthday Planet Earth*, Ocean Tree Books, 1986, p.32, quoted by Sanger, Mel, Mel, *2012 – The Year of Project Enoch?* Rema Marketing, 2009, Part II, p. 13.

54 Sanger, Mel, *op. cit.,* Part II, p. 17.

55 Spangler, David, *Reflections on the Christ,* p.37, quoted by Sanger, op. cit., p. 12, 13.

CHAPTER FOUR:
FREEMASONRY, OUR FOUNDING FATHERS, AND THE PLAN FOR AMERICA

It is in America that the transformation will take place, and has already silently commenced.

Madame H.P. Blavatsky, *The Secret Doctrine*, 1888

Those mystical extrasensory perceptions viewed with suspicion by the materialist would then be developed according to the disciplines of the sciences, and all learning would be consecrated to the supreme end that men become as the gods, knowing good and evil.

Manly P. Hall, *The Secret Destiny of America*, 1944

As Weishaupt [founder of the radical society, the Illuminati] lived under the tyranny of a despot and priests, he knew that caution was necessary in spreading information, and the principles of pure morality. This has given an air of mystery to his views... If Weishaupt had written here [i.e., in America], where no secrecy is necessary in our endeavours to render men wise and virtuous, he would not have thought of any secret machinery for that purpose.

Thomas Jefferson, from his *Letter to Rev. James Madison*, 1800

The Founding Fathers and Religious Freedom

The history of America is in one sense, the record of secret societies who sought to establish a new nation, free of monarchy, church dogma, and in particular all prejudices against mysticism and spiritualism. It is traditionally construed due to the Enlightenment that reason rather than religion was exalted to a preeminent place in the revolutions of the eighteenth century. While true that in France this principle was put into effect, in America, the story is much more nuanced. No doubt our revolutionary leaders believed themselves reasonable men who would govern society based upon a measured point of view. But that didn't mean that our leaders were pure rationalists. Indeed, the real story is surprisingly different. Those most influential persons in the American Revolution extolled esoteric mysticism more than mere mental acuity. America wasn't committed to a political philosophy based on pure reason—despite the fact that they often said so (note the quote from Jefferson in the epigraph). That would be left to the French and Robespierre, perhaps the greatest icon of secular humanism, whose radical commitment to *anti-theism* left no room for compromise.[1] The French would craft an idol of both liberty and reason (literally so, parading this 'goddess' around Paris). No doubt their motives were heavily weighted with vindictiveness toward the Church. But in America, there was no such open worship of the goddess. The trappings of Christianity, at the very least, were regarded as a necessary aspect of social life and virtuous behavior.

What was most hated by ambitious 'liberal' leaders was *authority solely vested in the hands of Monarchs and Priests,* an authority claimed because of 'the divine right of kings' or the sanction the Church maintained it held to rule a 'Christian' society. Certainly, like any other political power—whether kings or priests—the first order of business was to eliminate any manner of thinking that could uproot the then-current order. In France, resistance always met with far more than stiff rebuke. The price of seeking 'free speech' charged the highest fare imaginable—the dungeon, or even more likely, losing one's head.

Consequently, we shouldn't be surprised that 'free thinkers' would see in the New World an opportunity to break from the customs and conventions of the Old. In general, whatever we may think of the appropriateness of what they professed, we can understand why members of spiritualist sects in Europe, who had been so horribly persecuted by the Catholic Church (and later, to a lesser extent, the Protestant Churches in Switzerland and Germany), sought in the

New World respite from the ubiquitous intolerance of European Christianity in the sixteenth and seventeenth centuries.* While the Monarchy and the Church played a constant game of political chess with the loser financially the worse off; when threatened, they rushed to one another's aid in any number of ways to maintain the duopoly of power they enjoyed. Power sharing with the burgeoning middle class was unthinkable. *Democracy* was the dirtiest non-four letter word in Europe.

Another misconception common to most patriotic Americans: the assumption our Founders sought religious freedom to allow worship of God according to personal preference. This too, is only partially true. Catholicism would be treated with suspicion until America elected its first Catholic president, John F. Kennedy in 1960. Community leaders may have casually acknowledged religious freedom but they were mostly prejudiced toward the Protestant path to God.

However, when we carefully study early influences upon America—that is, what happened before America declared its independence—it is much more accurate to argue that the most prominent revolutionary leaders seeking to liberate the colonies from English rule, sought freedom *to worship a non-Christian God.* At the very least, they sought relief from any and all theology which denigrated the place of individual devotion and personal experience. In essence, America was established by its better known founders to give *esoteric spiritualism, paranormal rituals, and many forms of eccentric or emotional piety* a place to be practiced without threat of persecution. These were the underlying and heart-felt convictions of the elite intellectuals who championed an independent America.

---

* Along these lines, we likely overlook the fact that the Spanish Inquisition had been an ongoing reality for many centuries—not just a few decades as most suppose (established in 1480 it wasn't disbanded until 1834).

Not that the masses who braved the frightening waters of the cold Atlantic were eager to practice witchcraft once they arrived in Massachusetts (although, as we know, later some did). For the most part, these were genuine and sincere Christians, eager to break free from Catholicism and even the Church of England they saw as a compromise to Roman paganism. These were the Puritans who sought *total purification* in the Church (hence their well-known nickname). What better way to accomplish this than to leave the tainted church of the Mother Country behind and flee to a New World?

A wonderful little book written by fellow Okie, Sarah Vowell (*The Wordy Shipmates*, 2008) provides a colorful and comedic history of the Plymouth colony where it is readily established that Puritan virtues were most strictly observed beginning in 1620. Indeed, the beginning of 'evangelical' Christianity in America can trace its roots to the arrival of these early pilgrims which founded Plymouth, as well as those following in the 'Great Migration' when 20,000 English settled in New England. This period was "between 1629, when King Charles I dissolve[d] the Puritan-friendly English Parliament, and 1640, when the English Civil War [began] and the Puritans under Oliver Cromwell eventually behead Charles and [ran] the country."[2]

The pressure exerted by Charles in his return to Catholicism, caused members of The Massachusetts Bay Colony to believe that God was calling them to America, to first 'help the savages' (however, ironic that may seem today), but also to depart a country they deemed to be falling apart. John White and Francis Higginson wrote that "The departing of good people from a country does not cause a judgment, but warns of it."[3] Thomas Hooker, a fiery puritan preacher states, "So glory is departed from England, for England hath seen her best days, and the reward of sin is coming on apace; for God is packing up of his gospel, because none will buy his wares..."[4] In effect, America was to be the fulfillment politically of Jesus' parable of the 'Wheat and Tares'. The Master taught his disciples that in the period following His resurrection, the 'good grass and the bad weeds' would grow together. It will be impossible to rid the Kingdom of the tares without destroying the wheat—the two must grow together. What should be surprising to most Americans, however, is how plentiful the tares were and how early they sprouted in the soil of our great nation.

The Early Sowing of Tares into American Soil

Manly P. Hall summarizes the evidence for the 'making of America' by secret societies with his recital of relevant Masonic red-letter dates in his work, *America's Assignment with Destiny*. We read:

> In 1730, Daniel Coxe of New Jersey was appointed Provincial Grand Master of the provinces of New York, New Jersey, and Pennsylvania by his Grace, Thomas, Duke of Norfolk, Grand Master of the Premiere Grand Lodge of England. Benjamin Franklin became a Mason in 1731, and was Provisional Grand Master of Pennsylvania in 1734. George Washington took his first degree in the Lodge at Fredericksburg, Virginia, in 1752. The early American Lodges met in taverns or inns, and the first Masonic Temple in America was built in Boston in 1832. It cannot be learned that Thomas Paine was a Mason, although he wrote an essay dealing with the origin of Freemasonry. He attempted to trace the Fraternity to the Celtic Druids. Of Masonry, George Washington wrote in 1791: "Being persuaded a just application of the principles on which Free Masonry is founded, must be promotive of virtue and public prosperity, I shall always be glad to advance the interests of this Society and be considered by them a deserving brother."[5]

> It is believed that the Boston 'Tea party was arranged around a chowder super at the home of the Bradlee brothers, who were Masons, and that mother Bradlee kept the water hot so that they could wash off the disguises. "Who were these 'Mohawks,' Sons of Liberty, in paint and gear?" asks Madison C. Peters. "Free Masons,

members of St. Andrews Lodge, led by the Junior Warden, Paul Revere."[6]

Surely, the recital of Freemasonry's role is indeed a long and compelling one. Hall recounts many additional facts:

> The first Continental Congress, on the motion of George Washington, selected Peyton Randolph, past Grand Master of Masons of Virginia, to preside over its deliberations. Later, John Hancock, another Mason, succeeded him. It was Hancock who signed the Declaration of Independence with a signature so bold that "the King of England could read it without spectacles." It is believed that Thomas Jefferson became a Mason in France. Of the fifty-six signers of the Declaration of Independence, nearly fifty were Masons [most authorities admit to only nine although their names are among the most famous]. Only one is known with certainty not to have been a member of the Order.

> At Bunker Hill, on June 17, 1775, fell General Joseph Warren, Grand Master of the Massachusetts Grand Lodge. There is a report unverified that George Washington personally made Lafayette a Mason in military Lodge No. 19. at Morristown, New Jersey... Baron von Steuben, who received the first offer of surrender from Lord Cornwallis at Yorktown, was made a Mason in New York State... Other Masonic leaders included General Nathaniel Green and Major General Henry Knox. All but two of Washington's Brigadier Generals were Masons, as was Ethan Allen of Green Mountain Boy fame. Of the fifty-five members of the Constitutional Convention, all but five were Masons. [7] [Comment added]

Why was there such a commitment by Masons to the causes of the American Revolution? Hall suggests such action was motivated by a philosophical assumption that was part and parcel of Freemasonry: "The esoteric side of the rites [of Freemasonry] and symbols [is] impressive to scholarly minds, and the Masons regarded themselves as the responsible custodians of a vast project dedicated by earlier adepts to the emancipation of humanity from ignorance and tyranny."[8] Furthermore, Masonry allowed persons with spiritual inclinations to give regard to mystical matters without making commitments to particular theological creeds. "Masonry also successfully bridged many religious differences and discords. The Brethren could practice Christian principles without emphasizing theological differences, thus supplying a spiritual horizon necessary to offset the conflict of sects."[9] In other words, charitable aspirations were encouraged, but any attempts to articulate essentials of Christian orthodoxy would be anathema to those with the Masonic mindset.

The impetus toward revolution and overthrowing the powers of King and Church was the particular agenda set forth by Adam Weishaupt when in 1776 he founded the *Illuminati* in Bavaria. Quoting from my earlier work, *Decoding Doomsday*, I summarized there the relationship between the Illuminati, Freemasonry, and their revolutionary ambitions with these words:

> The Illuminati were radical revolutionaries out to destroy the Church and the Monarchy. It's usually asserted they had only a mild affect upon America's revolution, while they had an enormous impact upon the French version. At issue is [whether] the reality of an infiltration of the Illuminati into the Masonic organization [is true at] the highest levels of its leadership. Some academics judge this notion a by-product of an overactive imagination. While it's a favorite of conspiracy theorists, the facts nonetheless seem to point to its genuineness.

> One particularly telling piece of literary history provides a summary judgment. John Robison, a Mason invited to join the Illuminati in late 18th century (100 years after the founding and supposed dissolution of the secret society of Illuminism), wrote a book with a not-so-succinct title, *Proofs of a Conspiracy Against All the Religions and Governments of Europe Carried on in the Secret Meetings of the Free Masons, Illuminati, and Reading Societies.* Robison, a professor at Edinburgh University, quoted from one of Weishaupt's letters to his fellow Illuminati: "The great strength of our Order lies in its concealment. Let it never appear in any place in its own name, but always covered by another name, and another occupation. None is fitter than the three

lower degrees of Freemasonry; the public is accustomed to it, expect little from it, and therefore takes little notice of it."

Of particular import was a 1782 Masonic convention at Wilhelmsbad in Hesse. According to historian Nesta Webster, it was at this order that both Illuminism and the Order of Strict Observance... apparently were covertly merged into the Freemasons. For neither was publicly noticed from that time forward.

Jim Marrs comments: "With divisive issues settled and the Illuminati safely hidden away within the Freemasons, the Convent [sic] of Wilhelmsbad proved a turning point for the order. Although attendees were sworn to secrecy, the Count de Virieu later wrote in a biography, "The conspiracy which is being woven is so well thought out that it will be... impossible for the Monarchy and Church to escape it." "From the Frankfurt Lodge, the gigantic plan of world revolution was carried forward," [William] Still wrote. "The facts show that the Illuminati, and its lower house, Masonry, was a secret society within a secret society." "Even though the Illuminati faded from public view, the monolithic apparatus set in motion by Weishaupt may still exist today," Still commented. "Certainly, the goals and methods of operation still exist. Whether the name Illuminati still exists is really irrelevant."[10]

Trustworthy witnesses to the same are cited by Peter Levenda:

Winston Churchill, in a statement published in the *Illustrated Sunday Harold* of Feb. 8, 1920, famously announced, "From the days of Sparticus-Weishaupt [Adam Weishaupt, Sparticus-sic-being his code name] to those of Karl Marx, to those Trotsky, Bela Kuhn, Rosa Luxembourg and Emma Goldman, this worldwide conspiracy has been steadily growing. This conspiracy played a definitely recognizable role in the tragedy of the French Revolution. It has been the main-spring of every subversive movement in the 19th Century..." [11] [Comment added]

Even George Washington at the outset of the American age wrote in one of his letters: "It was not my intention to doubt that the doctrine of the Illuminati and the principles of Jacobinism[*] had not spread to the United States. On the contrary, no one is more satisfied of this fact than I am."[12]

Figure 19 - Manly P. Hall

Of all Freemasons, Benjamin Franklin was perhaps the most famous and influential. Not only was he the Master of Freemasons in Philadelphia, but his reach extended to England and France. He was responsible for recruiting and initiating an elderly and declining Voltaire into the Lodge of the Nine Sisters in Paris. Hall comments that "the sentiments of the French people were appropriately touched when Dr. Benjamin Franklin and Voltaire embraced each other with fraternal tenderness of the floor of the Lodge of the Nine Sisters. It was only natural that under Franklin's guidance this Lodge should have enlarged its scope to become a veritable university of world political philosophy."[13] Hall continues:

> The Lodge of the Nine Sisters, guided by the impressive scholarship of Court de Gébelin,[14] was the most philosophical, mystical, and esoteric of the French Lodges. Its membership included such extremes as Prince Charles de Rohan and Monsieur Danton. Lafayette was, of course, involved, and in 1785 the Marquis also joined the Egyptian Masonry of Cagliostro and proclaimed his absolute confidence in the Grand Cophte. When Anton Mesmer

---

[*] Jacobinism was the political movement to overthrow the reigning dynasty in England with the progeny of King James—the English equivalent of Jacob.

arrived from Vienna with his theories of animal magnetism, Lafayette was one of his first customers.[15]

Lafayette, as mentioned in the previous chapter, said of himself, "I know as much as any conjuror ever did." Hall provides the following bit of his history and influence: "The Marquis revisited America in 1784, called upon General Washington at Mount Vernon, and on this occasion presented Washington with a beautiful white satin apron, elaborately embroidered with Masonic emblems in red, white, and blue, the handiworks of Madame, the Marquise de Lafayette. Washington wore this apron when he was present at the Masonic ceremony on the occasion of the laying of the cornerstone of the District of Columbia."[16] Hall asserts that "Lafayette is a direct link between the political societies of France and the young American government" and more specifically the revolutions of the two countries." Hall quotes the editor from *The Theosophist Journal* (Madras, October 1883), who he speculates is Madame Blavatsky:

> Yet it is as certain though this conviction is merely a *personal* one, that several Brothers of the Rosy Cross—or 'Rosicrucians,' so-called—did take a prominent part in the American struggle for independence, as much as in the French Revolution during the whole of the past century. We have documents to that effect, and the proofs of it are in our possession... it is our firm conviction based on historical evidence and direct inferences from many of the memoirs of those days at that French Revolution is due to *one* Adept. It is that mysterious personage, now conveniently classed with other 'historical charlatans' (i.e., great men whose occult knowledge and powers shoot over the heads of the imbecile majority), namely, the Count de St. Germane[17]—who brought about the just outbreak among the paupers, and put an end to the selfish tyranny of the French kinds—the 'elect, and the Lord's anointed.' And we know also that among the *Carbonari*—the precursors and pioneers of Garibaldi [the Italian revolutionary that ultimately brought Italy together as a single country[18]]—there was more than one *Freemason* deeply versed in occult sciences and Rosicrucianism. [Emphasis in original, comment added][19]

We can safely conclude a major sect within Freemasonry was intent on ridding the world of monarchical tyranny and religious dogma. Few would argue that Freemasonry retains revolutionary ambition today (it seems preposterous to most scholars and of course meets with vehement if not condescending denials by Masonic leadership), but such radical objectives surely played a part in revolutions past.

When Did Freemasonry Enter America?

Amongst Freemason historians there exists much debate about what groups and at what time the esoteric 'wisdom' of the Secret Societies was exported from Europe into the American colonies. Hall provides the following analysis:

> It is certain, however, that between 1610 and 1660 a mass of material concerned with the development of *the Great Plan for America* was transferred from Europe to the Western Continent for preservation and future use. It is shallow thinking to assume that the Secret Societies operating in Europe—the Freemasons, the Rosicrucians, and the Fellows of the Royal Society—had no representation among the colonies until the beginning of the eighteenth century [when Freemasonry can be documented]. The confusion is due not to the lack of such activity, but to the inadequacy of available records.[20] [Emphasis added]

Hall quotes Rev. Edward Patterson, in his *History of Rhode Island,* "In the spring of 1658, Mordecai Campaunall, Moses Packeckoe, Levi, and others, in all fifteen families, arrived at New Port (American), from Holland. They brought with them the first three degrees of Masonry, and worked them in the house of Campaunall, and continued to do so, they and their successors, to the year 1742."[21]

Hall asserts "the best-publicized candidate for the honor of having brought the Esoteric Schools to the New World was the German theological student and mystical Pietist, Magister Johannes Kelpius (1671-1708), author of *Kabbala Denudata.*[22] Kelpius was twenty-three years old when he arrived at Germantown in April, 1694 and a 10-week voyage on the *Sarah Maria*. Hall discloses, "[Once] here they formed themselves into the Society of the *Woman of the Wilderness*, where they consecrated their efforts toward spiritual preparations for the millennium. The brethren became known as the *Hermits of the Ridge,* and combined their spiritual ministrations with horoscopy, magic, divination, and healing."[23]

> Kelpius, writing in 1699, explained the origin and doctrines of his Order. The Pietists were conscientious objectors to the corruptions existing in organized theologies. Their reforms were accompanied by ecstasies, revelations, inspirations, illuminations, inspeakings, prophecies, apparitions, changing of minds, transfigurations, translations of bodies, fastings, [and] paradisiacal representations of voices, melodies, and sensations.[24]

Pietism, a seventeenth century movement, drew upon the mystical teachings of Jacob Böhme (1575-1624)[25] and was based upon a reaction against an orthodox German Protestantism that had little interest in a personal connection between the believer and God. "The Principal emphasis was upon religious experience as the direct means of attaining Christian insight. The Moravians are considered a direct offshoot of Pietism, as to a degree was the Methodist revival under John Wesley."[26] "Some of the Pietists gave thought to alchemy, attempted the calculation of the millennium, located water with the divining rod, and wore magical amulets and talismans. They were Second Adventists, and a few believed that they would be translated bodily into the spiritual world without suffering physical death."[27]

Hall argues effectively, however, that the Pietist movement was *not* what brought a Rosicrucian or Masonic doctrine regarding American destiny to the New World.

> The Pietists were channels through which books on cabalism, alchemy, astrology, and the Hermetic arts reached the New World. Thus they contributed to the westward motion of the Philosophic

Empire. Their own practices, however, detracted seriously from their usefulness as reformers or educators, and their influence was limited to the neighborhood wherein they dwelt. Kelpius was a devout man, possibly well-learned, but most of his followers were more earnest than informed, and there seems to have been no vision among them of a broad or enduring ministry.[28]

While Hall demonstrates that Kelpius wasn't the locus of esoteric wisdom's founding, the account reinforces the usefulness of America to serve as home to those Europe considered heretics and non-conformists. America was a dumping ground for Europe to rid itself of the spiritually 'undesirable'. We think of the poem, *The New Colossus*, associated with the Statue of Liberty:

> *Give me your tired, your poor,*
> *Your huddled masses yearning to breathe free,*
> *The wretched refuse of your teeming shore.*
> *Send these, the homeless, tempest-tost to me*
> *I lift my lamp beside the golden door!*[29]

And might we add, "I'll also take your spiritual mystics and free thinkers who wish to be free from dogmatic religion of any kind." Here in America, they certainly found a home.

The Great Plan and Francis Bacon

"The history books tell us that the colonists made the long and dangerous journey in small ships in order to find a place where they could worship God, each according to the dictates of his own conscience. There is however much more to the story than our historians have dared to suggest."[30] In short, at work was *The Great Plan* devised by Secret Societies through the ages, but assembled into a strategy to be executed in the New World by none other than Francis Bacon. "Bacon's secret society was set up in America before the middle of the seventeenth century. Bacon himself had given up all hope of bringing his dream to fruition in his own country, and he concentrated his attention upon rooting it in the new world."[31]

According to Hall, when Bacon served a diplomatic apprenticeship at the Court of Navarre with the Spanish King, Phillip II, he was initiated into…

> [T]he new liberalism represented throughout Europe by Secret Societies of intellectuals dedicated to civil and religious freedom. He returned to England fully aware of the intentions of Philip II, the Spanish king [resolved to control England with helpful espionage by the ambassador of Spain to England residing in the Court of Queen Elizabeth]. Later, when the moment was propitious, he threw the weight of his literary group with the English colonization plan for America in order to prevent Spanish dominations of the New World. The same political considerations apparently also induced him to develop Freemasonry as a further bulwark against the encroachments of the Spanish plot. Cherishing as he did the dream of a great commonwealth in the *New Atlantis*, Bacon was resolved to prevent his plan from being frustrated by a dominant clergy, supporting and supported by an entrenched aristocracy. [32]

According to Hall, we learn Bacon identified representatives to bring 'The New Atlantis' into reality (*The New Atlantis* being Bacon's title for his allegory dedicated to the 'Great Plan'). His "mystic empire of the wise had no national boundaries and its citizenry was made up of men of good purpose in every land. The Alchemists, Cabalist, Mystics, and Rosicrucians were the incisive instruments of Bacon's plan. Representatives of these groups migrated to the colonies at an early date and set up their organization in suitable places."[33]

Elite Europeans had their eyes on America five centuries ago—but specifically those there who sought to change the political power structure for centuries to come:

The brotherhoods met in their rooms over inns and similar public buildings, practicing their ancient rituals exactly according to the fashion in Europe and England. These American organizations were branches under European sovereignty, with the members in the two hemispheres bound together with the strongest bonds of sympathy and understanding. The program that Bacon had outlined was working out according to schedule. Quietly and industriously, America was being conditioned for its destiny—leadership in a free world.[34]

As we indicated earlier, Benjamin Franklin, the most influential and powerful Mason in America served as 'project director'.

Franklin spoke for the Order of the Quest, and most of the men who worked with him in the early days of the American Revolution were also members. The plan was working out; the New Atlantis was coming into being, in accordance with the program laid down by Francis Bacon a hundred and fifty years earlier. The rise of American democracy was necessary to a world program. At the appointed hour, the freedom of man was publicly declared.[35]

The Origin of Secret Societies in America— Jamestown and the Virginia Company

Since so many elements of American colonization hinged on Francis Bacon's plan, it is easy to question whether Hall's endorsement is at best a case of hero worship (fudging the facts to make his hero larger than life), or at worst rewriting history to overstate the importance of secret societies. Indeed, alternative historians Michael Baigent and Richard Leigh argue a more modest view—that the American Revolution was not *purely* the culmination of a Masonic conspiracy in America, although Freemasons provided key leadership and the drive behind it.

We know that the first documented Freemason in America was Jonathan Belcher, "who on a visit to England in 1704, was initiated into an English lodge" and would later be governor of Massachusetts and

New Hampshire in 1730.[36] But they insist the influence of Freemasonry was nevertheless substantial:

> Most historians of the American War for Independence have tended, so far as Freemasonry is concerned, to fall into one of two camps. Certain fringe writers, for example, have sought to portray the fray exclusively as a 'Freemasonic event'—a movement engineered, orchestrated and conducted by cabals of Freemasons in accordance with some carefully calculated grand design. Such writers will often cite lengthy lists of Freemasons— which proves little more than that they have lengthy lists of Freemasons to cite, and there is certainly no shortage of such lists. On the other hand, most conventional historians circumvent the Freemasonic aspect of the conflict entirely. Philosophers such as Hume, Locke, Adam Smith and the French *philosophes* are regularly enough invoked; but the Freemasonic milieu which paved the way for such thinkers, which acted as a kind of amniotic fluid for their ideas and which imparted to those ideas their popular currency, is neglected.[37]

Their moderate view modulates the Masonic enthusiasts (like Manly Hall) and reconciles the 'propaganda' with traditional academics. Consequently, they are suited to supply a reasoned summation:

> Ultimately, the currents of thought disseminated by Freemasonry were to prove more crucial and more pervasive than Freemasonry itself. The republic which emerged from the war was not, in any literal sense, a 'Freemasonic republic'—was not, that is, a republic created Freemasons for Freemasons in accordance with Freemasonic ideals. But it did embody those ideals, it was profoundly influenced by those ideals; and it owed much more to those ideals than is generally recognized or acknowledged. As one Masonic historian has written:
>
> > Freemasonry has exercised a greater influence upon the establishment and development of this [the American] Government than any other single institution. Neither general historians nor the members of the Fraternity since the days of the first Constitutional Conventions have realized how much the United States of America owes to Freemasonry, and how great a part it played in the birth of the nation and

the *establishment of the landmarks of that civilisation...*[38] [Emphasis added]

Even if Freemasonry came late to the party (and it likely didn't), the real issue remains, "How formative was the influence of those men like Francis Bacon, Christopher Wren, Elias Ashmole (members all of the *Invisible College* and later, the *Royal Society*) on promoting colonization in America and for what particular reason?"

Hall cites many sources which testify to the influence of Bacon, one of history's most influential men. Dr. Alexander Brown is cited by Hall from his *Genesis of the United States:* "May not Bacon have aided Shakespeare in compiling some of his plays? Bacon always had a fancy for such things."[39] This connection between Bacon and Shakespeare (and the fact that many speculate Bacon may have used *Shakespeare* as his pseudonym for the many plays attributed to him) was due to the connection of Bacon's usage of the word *tempest* in a particular way in his musings on his own political decline. Dr. Brown writes of Bacon's participation in the settling of Newfoundland that it was "due to the Great Chancellor's influence that the king granted the advances and issued the Charters to Bacon and his associates in Guy's Newfoundland Company."[40] Several specific letters with exact details are then mentioned to substantiate this fact. Hall provides an extensive quote from *The Personal History of Lord Bacon*, written by William Hepworth Dixon, in 1861:

In no History of America, in no Life of Bacon, have I found one word to connect him with the plantation of that great Republic. Yet, like Raleigh and Delaware, he takes an active share in the labours, a conspicuous part in the sacrifices through which the foundations of Virginia and the Carolinas are first laid. Like men of far less note, who have received far higher honours in America, Bacon pays his money into the great Company [Virginia Company], and takes office in its management as one of the Council [equivalent to a Board of Directors]. This other glories therefore must be added that of a Founder of New States...

All generous spirits rush to the defense of Virginia. Bacon joins the Company with purse and voice. Montgomery, Pembroke, and Southampton, the noble friends of Shakespeare, join it... A fleet, commanded by Gates and Somers, sails from the Thames, to meet on its voyage at sea those singular and poetic storms and trials which add the Bermudas to our empire and *The Tempest* to our literature.

One hundred and seventy-five years after Walter Raleigh laid down his life in Palace Yard for America, his illustrious blood paid for by Gondomar in Spanish Gold, the citizens of Carolina, framing for themselves a free constitution, remembered the man to whose genius they owed their existence as a state. They called the capital of their country Raleigh. The United States can also claim among their muster roll of Founders the no less noble name of Francis Bacon. Will the day come, when, dropping such feeble names as Troy and Syracuse, the people of the Great Republic will give the august and immortal name of Bacon to one of their splendid cities?[41] [Comments added, with apologies to citizens of Troy and Syracuse]

Hall notes a personal testimony, dated 1618, from a dedication placed upon manuscript copy of *His Historie of Travaile into Virginia Britania* by William Strachey: "Your Lordship ever approaving yourself a most noble fautor (favorer) of the Virginia plantation, being from the beginning (with other lords and earles) of the principal counsel applied to propagate and guide yt."[42]

More records of Bacon's involvement would be available had a fire not burned at Whitehall in 1618 destroying many records stored there. However, Hall provides a half-dozen other references, remarks from speeches, and quotations from other sources to solidify the role that Bacon played in the startup of American colonies. Furthermore, many who formed the Bacon Society left England and settled in Virginia:

It was through them that the Great Plan began to operate in America. There were most fortuitous marriages between the families of the original custodians of the philosophical legacy. From the minglings [sic] of the bloods of the Bacons, the Wottons, the Donnes, the Herberts, and the Mores, the Virginia colony derived many of its prominent citizens. Lord Bacon guided the project and probably outlined the program to be followed after his death.[43]

Hall points out the many descendants of Bacon in Virginia. Even the *Bacon Rebellion* as it is known, was led by a direct descendant Nathanial Bacon, happening perhaps ironically 100 years to the month before the Declaration of Independence (July, 1676). The presence of family members in Virginia yields substantial support to the claim that Bacon's legacy in America continued well after his death in England.

Lastly, Baigent and Leigh argue that a substantial reason that the British relinquished the colonies was due to the sentiment of brotherhood often expressed between Freemasons *on both sides of the conflict.* Since they found themselves frequently fighting with fellow Masons, the British military's heart 'wasn't in it.'

> Throughout the American War for Independence, there are accounts of the warrants and regalia of field lodges being captured by one side or the other and duly returned. In one instance, the regalia of the 46th Foot—later the 2nd Battalion of the Duke of Cornwall's Light Infantry—was capture by colonial troops. On the instructions of George Washington, it was sent back, under a flag of truce, with the message that he and his men 'did not make war upon institutions of benevolence'. On another occasion, the warrant of the 17th Foot—later the Leicestershire Regiment— was similarly captured. It, too, was returned, with a letter from General Samuel Parsons. This letter is eloquently typical of the spirit fostered by Freemasonry in both armies and all ranks:
>
> Brethren,
>
> When the ambition of monarchs, or the jarring interests of contending States, call forth their subjects to war, as Masons we are disarmed of that resentment which stimulates to undistinguished desolation, and, however our political sentiments may impel us in the public dispute, we are still Breth-

ren, and (our professional duty apart) ought to promote the happiness and advance the weal [good fortune] of each other. Accept, therefore, at the hands of a Brother, the Constitution of the Lodge 'Unity, No. 18' held in the 17th British Regiment, which your late misfortunes have put it in my power to restore to you.

I am, your Brother and obedient servant,
Samuel H. Parsons.[44]

Freemason Ideology and its Influence on America

So if Freemasonry was so vital to the establishment of America, are its ideals worthy of the nation to which it was dedicated?

While its principles may be worthy, its theology is in fact a genuine retreat into *paganism*. In my book, *Decoding Doomsday,* I offer an extensive exploration into Egyptian paganism (see pages 215-219) and its incorporation into Masonic beliefs and dogma. Here provided for the reader's convenience are only a few concerted comments. For the interested party, I encourage reference to the 'prequel' of this book. For now:

> From…"The Great Work in Speculative Freemasonry," *The Dormer Masonic Study Circle* (1930) offered this commentary:
>
>> It is now generally acknowledged by those competent to judge, that of all *the ancient peoples the Egyptians were the most learned in the wisdom of the Secret Doctrine*; indeed, there are some who would have it that Egypt was the Mother of the Mysteries, and that it was on the banks of the Nile that the Royal Art was born. We can affirm, without entering into any controversy on the matter, that the wisest of philosophers from other nations visited Egypt to be initiated in the sacred Mysteries; Thales, Solon, Pythagoras and Plato are all related to have journeyed from Greece to the delta of the Nile in quest of knowledge; and upon returning to their own country these illumined men each declared the Egyptians to be the wisest of mortals, and the Egyptian temples to be the

repositories of sublime doctrines concerning *the history of the Gods and the regeneration of men.*[45] (*Emphasis mine*)

What's truly at the heart of *the Secret Doctrine*?

In the early dynasties of ancient Egypt, the obelisk was known as the *ben ben* stone. It was a monument to the sun god, *Ra*. Later Pharaohs dedicated their obelisks to *Osiris*, the brother of *Isis*. Osiris was the god of this world, the underworld, and supposedly the afterlife. The Egyptian myth revolves around the conflict between Osiris and Seth, Osiris' evil brother. Seth kills Osiris, but Osiris is resurrected by his son Horus. This resurrection is facilitated by "the lion's grip." In the symbolism of Freemasonry, this same grip is used to "raise to life" the initiate in the Third Degree ceremony. The scholars of Freemasonry agree *the story of Osiris' resurrection is essential to the lessons of their Order.* We [commonly] use the phrase, "giving someone the third degree," inferring we are giving someone a difficult time. Little do we realize the phrase relates to Masonic initiation, to the more intense process to achieve the rank of Third Degree Freemason. Even less do we recognize that upon receiving the Third Degree, the initiate has taken part in a ceremonial resurrection from the dead that's at the heart of Freemasonry. Masonry isn't just a social club.[46]

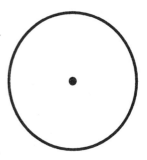

Figure 20 –Symbol of the Phallus of Freemasons

Several pages later, this author specifies the essence of the spiritual truth underlying Freemason theology, specifically, the issue of "What God do they worship?" (The critique applies only to those Freemasons that truly understand the secrets to which they've pledged themselves).

Albert Mackey, in his book *A Manual of the Lodge*, admits that Freemasons join with most pagans through the ages *as worshipers of the sun.* Furthermore, as the emphasis on the obelisk bears witness (a not-so-subtle symbol of the phallus), Freemasons (almost all, *unsuspectingly* and *unwittingly*) participate in a fertility cult. Even the simple circle "with a dot in the middle" is a symbol signifying "the phallus" to Freemasons. Mackey states, "The point within the circle is an interesting and important symbol in Freemasonry... The symbol is really a beautiful but somewhat abstruse [puzzling] allusion to the old Sun-Worship, and introduces us for the first time to that modification of it, known among the ancients as the worship of the phallus."[47] It's unexpected to say the least.

Albert Pike would correct Mackey inasmuch as he believed that Masons worship not the sun-god, but the god behind the sun, the bringer of light, or *Lucifer*. According to [Jim] Marrs, "Pike wrote that *Adonai*, one of the biblical names for God, was the rival of Osiris, the Egyptian sun-god, a prominent figure in Masonic Traditions... "Thousands of years ago, men worshipped the sun... Originally they looked beyond the orb [our solar system's sun] to the invisible God... The worship of the Sun [the invisible God] became the basis of all the religions of antiquity." [48] But their invisible god didn't use the same name as the Hebrew God (Adonai). To sharpen Pike's point: *Lucifer good, Adonai bad.* Certainly, Pike would decry any charge of Satan worship. He considers the Masonic teaching "Luciferian" and not Satanic. However, should we take comfort in Pike's qualification?[49] The Bible warns its adherents "And no marvel; for Satan himself is transformed into an angel of light" (II Corinthians 11:14). *"Luciferic truth" is the very disguise that Satan hand picks.* Pike's denial is in reality an admission that [his] opponents' allegations are right on target.

As we dig further, we find even more unsettling ties to Alchemy and Hermetic science[50] embedded within Freemasonry. Mackey wrote, "There can be no doubt that in some of what are called the [Masonic] High Degrees there is a very palpable infusion of a Hermetic element. This cannot be denied." Marrs says, "The mythical and magical practice of alchemy was passed down from the Egyptians." Then he quotes Picknett and Prince who explain: "The [Hermetic science] practice embraced a fine web of interlinking activities and modes of thinking, from magic to chemistry, from philosophy and Hermeticism to sacred geometry and cosmology. *It also concerned itself with what people today call ge-*

netic engineering and methods of delaying the aging process, and of trying to attain physical immortality"[51] [Emphasis added].

Additionally, as documented by many scholars and in my previous book, our nation's capital is dominated by Egyptian pagan symbols. From the world's largest obelisk we call *The Washington Monument* to our very own version of *The Pantheon* (aka, our Capitol building) the architecture of Washington DC is a panorama of paganism (albeit beautiful and emotionally stirring).

As I point out in *Decoding Doomsday*, "Even David Ovason who became a Mason after he wrote *The Secret Architecture of our Nation's Capital: The Masons and the building of Washington, D.C.,* "argues effectively that the city's layout intentionally incorporated the esoteric belief system of Freemasonry, especially as it involved astrologically aligning the capital with the constellation Virgo (Isis)."[52] These important Egyptian gods would be known as Venus and Apollo in Roman mythology. Their story, as Tom Horn discloses in *Apollyon Rising: 2012,* provides a glimpse into some of the more mysterious aspects of the Book of Revelation and its identification of the notorious personage we know as Antichrist.[*]

In essence, before declaring its independence and then afterward and ever since, America *remains a symbol of freedom*—from tyrants and despots—be they monarchs or ecclesiastics. However, at its inception not only was it a safe haven for puritan Protestants (exemplified by the pilgrims of Plymouth), it became a sanctuary for spiritualists wishing to practice esoteric rituals based on mystical belief systems. *We are not just the home of the free and the brave—we are home to*

---

[*] Revelation 9:11 discloses his name and its link to the ancient god Apollo: "And they had a king over them, [which is] the angel of the bottomless pit, whose name in the Hebrew tongue [is] *Abaddon*, but in the Greek tongue hath [his] name *Apollyon*."

mystics and to paranormal practitioners. Such is our melting pot—not quite a witches cauldron—but a concoction of spiritual recipes that are as much a part of our national composition as... well, apple pie. And judging by the sentiments expressed directly by our Founders, their ideology aligns closely with Freemasonry and much less with Christianity—despite what our rosy tradition has taught.

David Wilcock in his very recent book, *The Source Field Investigations,* has this to say tying the mythology of Egypt to the 'Great Plan' in America (as he discusses the inclusion of the 'Precession of the Equinox' in Egyptian 'symbology', i.e., the pyramid):

> One of the first major clues was apparently built into the Great Pyramid of Giza—which may forecast nothing less than a messianic event for humanity as we head into the Age of Aquarius [which he speculates may be in 2012-1214 timeframe). Once I understood the symbolism, the symbol on the back of the U.S. dollar bill became much more interesting. The founding fathers of America appear to have been very well aware of these archaic prophecies—and gave us a new and improved version of the same prophecies we see in Sumer, Babylon, India, Egypt, Greece and Rome. The American eagle is the new version of the Egyptian Bennu bird [the Phoenix]. The pyramid the baetyl—a symbol of the awakened pineal gland.[*] The founding fathers may have even started the United States to help usher these prophecies in. And once you understand the seemingly impossible miracles of the Great Pyramid's construction, it becomes much easier to see how this may have been considered as *the ultimate living proof that gods had once openly assisted humanity* here on earth.[53] [Emphasis added]

---

[*] Wilcock proposes it is the physical crossover point for 'nature and supernature' in human consciousness—see Chapter Seven for a discussion on this topic.

The Founding Father's Speak Their Minds Plainly

Chris Pinto in his Preface for Tom Horn's book, *Apollyon Rising: 2012*, recounts comments made by our Founding Fathers regarding their true (and surprising) religious sentiments. When we assemble these quotations into one message, we will be shocked by the anti-Christian bias they represent. For instance, Thomas Paine wrote:

> When I see throughout the greater part of this book [the Bible] scarcely anything but a history of the grossest vices and a collection of the most paltry and contemptible tales, I cannot dishonor my Creator by calling it by His name.

> What is it the Bible teaches us?—rapine, cruelty, and murder. What is it the Testament teaches us?—to believe that the Almighty committed debauchery with a woman engaged to be married, and the belief of this debauchery is called faith.

> It is the fable of Jesus Christ, as told in the New Testament, and the wild and visionary doctrine raised thereon, against which I contend. The story, taking it as it is told, is blasphemously obscene.[54]

Thomas Jefferson said the following in his letter to Alexander Smyth of January 17, 1825:

> The greatest of all the Reformers of *the depraved religion* of his own country was Jesus of Nazareth. Abstracting what is really His from *the rubbish in which it is buried,* easily distinguished by its luster from the dross of his biographers, and as separable from that as the diamond from the dunghill. [Emphasis added]

Likewise, Jefferson conveyed the same testimony in another letter to William Short, dated April 13, 1820:

> Among the sayings and discourses imputed to Him by His biographers, I find many passages of fine imagination, correct morality, and of the most lovely benevolence; and others, again, of so much ignorance, so much absurdity, so much untruth, charlatanism and imposture... I separate, therefore, the gold from the

dross… and leave the latter to the stupidity of some, and roguery of others of His disciples. Of this band of dupes and impostors, Paul was the… first corruptor of the doctrines of Jesus.[55]

Jefferson's bias against orthodox Christianity could hardly be more eloquently stated.

Benjamin Franklin's record of personal morality has been the subject of a number of documentaries on the *History Channel* and the *Discovery Channel*. It is well-documented there of his participation in the *Hell Fire Club* of England. Consequently, his reputation is well-known and in no need of further establishment. Suffice it to say, the goings-on with this group of English nobleman made all of them, including Franklin, much less noble. Regarding his stated beliefs concerning Jesus Christ:

As to Jesus of Nazareth, my Opinion of whom you particularly desire, I think the System of Morals and his Religion, as he left them to us, the best the world ever saw or is likely to see; but I apprehend it has received various corrupt changes, and I have, with most of the present Dissenters in England, some Doubts as to his divinity.[56]

I have some doubts as to Franklin's sincerity. His words smack of 'political correctness' since they were reduced to print for posterity.

Next, Pinto relates John Adams' comments *opposing the notion of the crucifixion of Christ* as providing any religious benefit given he was a Unitarian in good standing in Massachusetts.

Regarding George Washington, it is well-known the Father of our Country attended Church regularly but would dodge the question regarding the divinity of Christ and the validity of God's revelation of Himself in the Bible. None dare challenge his greatness. But Washington was a man who necessarily neither admired nor endorsed the Christian faith. As such, Pinto closes his Preface with these words:

Yes, there were most certainly Christians who came to this country through the Puritan/Pilgrim movement, but they were not alone. With them came the secret societies that saw America as "the New Atlantis" envisioned by Sir Francis Bacon. There is even a 1910 Newfoundland six-cent stamp (with three sixes on it no less) with the image of Bacon that reads: "Lord Bacon, the Guiding Spirit in Colonization Scheme..."

If one reads *The New Atlantis*, where Bacon describes a society with tall buildings, flying machines, weapons of mass destruction, health spas, the magnification of sound, and experiments with poisons on animals for the purpose of curing human beings, it becomes readily discernible that our country has followed his blueprint from the start.

Masonry's Mission Going Forward

Manly P. Hall, like Albert Pike, cannot be considered a friend to Christian orthodoxy.[57] We see this plainly below in his passionate rebuke of Christianity which brings into focus the core of what Freemasonry and other esoteric secret societies believe. He asserts,

> Once Christianity had rejected paganism, it refused to recognize the Esoteric Orders of the pre-Christian world. It regarded them as detrimental to its own prestige, and sought relentlessly to exterminate them. This was impossible, but the Church refused to accept and to teach a universal religion or a universal philosophy. The spiritual mysteries of life belong to no one faith, race, or school. In order to advance itself as the supreme custodian of salvation, ecclesiasticism had to reject the Mystery system. In doing so, it did not destroy that system, but *forfeited its own place as an instrument for the fulfillment of the Great Plan.*[58] In its effort to usurp this high destiny for itself, *the Church obscured the very essentials of human progress* and discouraged its followers from those noble and unselfish convictions which might long ago have supplied the incentives for a Universal Reformation of mankind.[59] [Emphasis added]

Hall continues his assault on the Christian religion and its core tenet of salvation achieved by personal acceptance of the death of Christ (as orthodox Christians maintain, to purge us from true moral guilt and sin ascribed by a just—yet loving—God, eager to forgive):

> When legitimate authority passed from the Church to the Orders of the Quest, this secret ecclesia drew to itself those who truly loved mankind. Even with the passing of centuries, the right has not been mended. Theological groups still emphasize a personal salvation achieved by miraculous means. In this case, the very word miraculous stands for the rejected esoteric tradition. It is the undefined and, for the theological, undefinable [sic] science of human regeneration. It is not sufficient to say that beyond the Church is only the unknown sphere of God. Actually, beyond the Church are the Mysteries, guarded by the shepherds of men...[60]

When reading the pronouncements of Manly P. Hall, one might suppose that the mission of Freemasonry could still threaten the status quo in many regions of the world where tyranny or dogmatic religion of any kind may still reside; for he exalts the esoteric wisdom of secret societies and its clandestine mission with these words:

> The Secret Societies are now engaged upon a broad reformation of the world-educational concept. The great universities and schools must fulfill the destiny which conceived them and sustained them through long and troublous times. Humanity cannot be preserved by the three "R's," unless *the universal truths locked within the forms of the arts and sciences are released.* Just as *mysticism once opened and revealed the secrets of religion,* so it must now open and reveal the secrets of the sciences.[61] [Emphasis added]

Furthermore, this vision must be spread far and wide—and embraced by many:

> This vision must be communicated. It must be extended throughout human society *until humanity **redeems itself** by the experience of enlightenment.* The security that the world seeks cannot be bestowed; it must be earned. When a sufficient number has attained

this degree of true leadership, the imperishable democracy of the sages will become a fact in the mortal sphere. [Emphasis added]

Therefore, we see how Hall preached a *gospel of intellectual growth over one's entire lifetime*. This is for him the nature of Masonic salvation: *it is earned through study*. No wonder Hall chided the New Age movement, with its populist campaigns and slogans as no more than pitiful fluff. Mitch Horowitz summarizes Hall's reaction to Eden Gray's simplistic revelation of Tarot Cards in 1960 (*The Tarot Revealed*) and other 'easy methods' to the esoteric with these words: "Gray's writing was friendly, informal, and practical. It would not please everyone. Manly P. Hall, born the same year as Gray, believed the New Age generation cheapened esoteric ideas, proffering quick fixes rather than demanding a lifetime of study. Regardless, the new era belonged to Gray."[62]

Hall, as a member of the generation before the greatest generation, looking at the average American embracing *The Secret* or ritual use of drugs in the twenty-first century, would no doubt lament how Americans haven't progressed in their spiritual pursuits quite the way he envisioned. We have gotten lazy, reckless, and utterly self-indulgent. This was certainly not what Hall or Francis Bacon had in mind for a country dedicated to enshrine 'The Great Plan'. Mysticism is apparently hard work with few willing to sign up to its exacting standards.

Conclusion: Is America the New Atlantis?

In conclusion, any moralist and proponent of liberty would enthusiastically endorse most aspects of what Freemasons promote. The emphasis upon freedom of religion, in and of itself, is a compelling and proper cornerstone of a free society. Likewise, representative democracy envisioned by Masonry is rightly embraced by all who call themselves American patriots.

However, if and when Freemasonry connects these principles with pagan mysticism, intentional diminution of nationalism, and support for a global democracy led by the intellectual elite, anyone who continues to believe in the wisdom of independent states and the survival of national autonomy will dramatically lower the volume of his or her accolades for the esoteric brotherhood. Quoting Hall once more:

> It is reasonably conceivable that in secrecy and anonymity well-ordered aid has been given to the struggle for human equity and justice that has been America's destiny through the past to our present time. It is our duty and our privilege to contribute what we can to this Universal plan. It will go on, served by the unknowns, until the Platonic empire is established on the earth, and the towers of the new Atlantis rise from the ruins of a materialistic and selfish world.[63]

But if the motive behind global democracy is to assure humanity the freedom to pursue the Masonic ideal of 'becoming as the gods', Christians of all persuasions (both conservative and liberal) should find common ground and sound the alarm.

When we stop to reflect, we realize those who believe they have become gods are not likely to play well in their sandboxes with those who doubt their 'inherent divinity'. This is especially so for those who conscientiously oppose the quest for divinity sought by Freemasons and New Agers.

History's gravest lessons power this opposing viewpoint; for when human leaders believe themselves to be gods, governments cease to serve the people—they serve those who would be god, for only *they* are worthy. In the case of the French revolution where the secret societies reigned openly,[64] liberty was commandeered by these 'gods' resulting in tens of thousands beheaded when they appeared a threat to the revolution. Likewise, in Nazi Germany where esotericism became the dogma of those heading the government, the leadership subordinated the good of the 'volk' (folk) to evoke the Übermensch—man transformed into 'Gôt'. These men, once unfettered from traditional spirituality, soon committed unspeakable acts.

The Bible calls for all leadership to be servant-like and accountable to authority. These leaders should be guided by biblical principles. However, seldom has the world yielded leaders with this motive. It is most unfortunate that many, who claimed Christianity as their inspiration, damaged its message of love with accountability by their own despicable actions. On the other hand, the record of atheistic humanist leaders provides little to be of proud either, doing no worse than tying for first place in the race to garner the 'most evil' of evil deeds.

However, the mawkish view of most New Age proponents asserts we are destined to become 'as the gods'. Supposedly, all who embrace this hope stand the cusp of this new divine life. David Wilcock puts this quixotic belief into words which connect American destiny with *the coming of gods and realization of our godhood*:

> From this passage [Virgil's Ecologue IV where he quotes the Sybil of Cumae whose phrase inspired *Novus Ordo Seclorum* on our Great Seal], we see that the gods are indeed predicted to return—and that humans on earth will "receive the life of gods" themselves. This is the Great Seal of the United States—printed right on the dollar bill. Clearly we are expected in these prophecies *to be seen as gods ourselves* once this process is complete. These Sibylline prophecies therefore represent a bold prophecy of a coming Golden Age, in which "the Golden One shall arise again in the whole earth"—meaning everyone who is here.[65] [Comment and emphasis added]

In closing: nothing is more alluring than power. Gaining that power and keeping it, remains the primary objective of any political leader. But could this maxim be a dominant factor influencing America's behavior today? Has America become an evil presence in the world? Is 'American *exceptionalism*' actually anything more than our self-applied rationalization of an arrogant demeanor? Is it an excuse to pursue our self-interests at the expense of other nations? *Or could it be that in gaining insurmountable military advantage over all nations, the power players of our world intend America to be the 'enforcer' of the 'Great Plan', insuring that all the world come under the guidance of 'the golden one' when he arrives on the world scene?*

In the next chapter, we will examine the nature of political power in the latter half of the twentieth century and its connection with the paranormal powers we've highlighted. We will examine what arises as the single most important factor motivating American involvement in world politics—and why, as a result, we became an empire.

NOTES

[1] Maximilien Robespierre (b. 1758) was the mouthpiece and icon of the French Revolution, who would eventually to fall victim to Madame Guillotine in 1794. Robespierre's downfall, ironically, was when he donned a toga and appeared in the heart of Paris on a float extoling the Great Architect of the Universe (a familiar Freemason label for God) on Pentecost, June 6, 1793. This led the masses to conclude he had fallen off his rocker. He took this ill-advised walk on the float because he came to believe (when he saw the Revolution failing due to its insatiable appetite for violence and death), that the construct of God was good for a civil society. While he burned an effigy of 'atheism' he led, along with many others, a defrocking of 20,000 Catholic priests and nuns. Consequently, while claiming that atheism was evil; his actions of anti-theism were the order of the day. Bauval and Hancock assert in *The Master Game*, that the Revolution was dedicated to the cult of Isis, which many French scholars claim is the goddess for whom the city of Paris was built and dedicated (See their chapter, The New City of Isis).

[2] Vowell, Sarah, *The Wordy Shipmates*, Riverhead Books, Penguin, New York, 2008, p. 23.

[3] Ibid. p. 28. Quoting John White and Francis Higginson from their pamphlet, *Reasons to be Considered for Justifying the Undertakers of the Intended Plantation in New England, and for Encouraging Such Whose Hearts God Shall Move to Join with Them in It.* Ca. 1630.

[4] Ibid., p. 29.

[5] Given in writing to the offers of St. Andrew's Lodge at Newport, Rhode Island, quoted by Manly P. Hall, p. 228.

[6] *The Masons, Makers of America,* quoted by Manly P. Hall, p. 228.

[7] Ibid., pp. 228-229.

[8] Hall, Manly P., *The Secret Destiny of America*, originally published in 1944. Penguin Group edition, New York, 2008, p. 221.

[9] Ibid. p. 222.

[10] Woodward, S. Douglas, *Decoding Doomsday*, Defender Books, Crane, Mo. 2010, pp. 213-214)

[11] Levenda, op. cit., p. 42.

[12] Ibid., p. 42.

[13] Ibid., p. 222.

[14] "Antoine Court who named himself Antoine Court de Gébelin (ca.1719 – May 10, 1784) was a former Protestant pastor, born at Nimes, who initiated the interpretation of the Tarot as an arcane repository of timeless esoteric wisdom in 1781." See en.wikipedia.org /wiki /Antoine_Court_ de_G%C3%A9belin.

[15] Ibid., p. 222.

[16] Ibid., pp. 226-227.

[17] Compte de St. Germain (Germane) was another fascinating character in the history of the occult in Europe.

> When the man who first became known as Saint-Germain was born is unknown, although most accounts say he was born in the 1690s. A genealogy compiled by Annie Besant [a rival of Alice A. Bailey] for her co-authored book, *The Comte De St. Germain: The Secret of Kings*, asserts that he was born the son of Francis Racoczi II, Prince of Transylvania in 1690. Other accounts, taken less seriously by most, say he was alive in the time of Jesus and attended the wedding at Cana, where the young Jesus turned water into wine. He was also said to be present at the council of Nicaea in 325 A.D.
>
> What is almost unanimously agreed on, however, is that Saint-Germain became accomplished in the art of alchemy, the mystical "science" that strives to control the elements. The foremost goal of this practice was the creation of "projection powder" or the elusive "philosopher's stone," which, it was claimed, when added to the molten form of such base metals as lead could turn them into pure silver or gold. Furthermore, this magical power could be used in an elixir that would impart immortality on those who drank it. Count de Saint-Germain, it is believed, discovered this secret of alchemy.

See http://paranormal.about.com/od/humanenigmas/a/saint-germain.htm.

[18] Little do most American's know that Garibaldi was so famous in his day he offered to lead the Union Army, an offer considered by Abraham Lincoln. Ultimately, he was granted a lesser post, but still a significant commission. We read, "At the outbreak of the American Civil War (in 1861), Garibaldi volunteered his services to President Abraham Lincoln. Garibaldi was

offered a Major General's commission in the U.S. Army through the letter
from Secretary of State William H. Seward to H. S. Sanford, the U.S. Minister
at Brussels, July 17, 1861. On September 18, 1861, Sanford sent the following reply to Seward:

> He [Garibaldi] said that the only way in which he could render service, as
> he ardently desired to do, to the cause of the United States, was as Commander-
> in-chief of its forces, that he would only go as such, and with the additional con-
> tingent power—to be governed by events—of declaring the abolition of slav-
> ery; that he would be of little use without the first, and without the second it
> would appear like a civil war in which the world at large could have little inter-
> est or sympathy.

According to Italian historian Petacco, "Garibaldi was ready to accept
Lincoln's 1862 offer but on one condition: that the war's objective be declared as the abolition of slavery. But at that stage Lincoln was unwilling to
make such a statement lest he worsen an agricultural crisis." On August 6,
1863, after the Emancipation Proclamation had been issued, Garibaldi
wrote to Lincoln: "Posterity will call you the great emancipator, a more en-
viable title than any crown could be, and greater than any merely mundane
treasure." See http://en.wikipedia.org/wiki/Giuseppe_Garibaldi.

[19] Hall, op. cit., pp. 227-228.

[20] Ibid., p. 211

[21] Ibid., p. 211.

[22] Ibid., p. 212.

[23] Ibid., pp. 212-213

[24] Ibid.

[25] Böhme had mystical experiences as a youth. His theology was something of an attempt to combine alchemy (Paracelsus was a favorite of his)
with his Lutheran Theology. The emphasis was on direct revelation. "While
Böhme was famous in Holland, England, France, Russia and America during
the seventeenth century, he became less influential during the eighteenth
century. A revival, however, occurred late in that century with interest from
German Romantics, who considered Böhme a forerunner to the movement.
Poets such as John Milton, Ludwig Tieck, Novalis and William Blake found
inspiration in Böhme's writings. Böhme was highly thought of by the German philosophers Baader, Schelling and Schopenhauer. Hegel went as far as
to say that Böhme was "the first German philosopher." See en.wikipedia.org
/wiki /Jacob_Boehme#cite_ref-23.

[26] Hall, p. 215.

[27] Ibid., p. 215. Note: Here is a very early appearance, ca. 1700, of the
Rapture of the Church in American religious thinking.

[28] Ibid., p. 217.

[29] "'*The New Colossus*' is a sonnet by Emma Lazarus (1849–1887), written in 1883 and, in 1903, engraved on a bronze plaque and mounted inside the Statue of Liberty." See en.wikipedia.org/wiki/The_New_Colossus.

[30] Hall, p. 92.

[31] Ibid, p. 92.

[32] Ibid., p. 195.

[33] Ibid., p. 93.

[34] Ibid., p. 94.

[35] Ibid., p. 95.

[36] Baigent, Michael and Leigh, Richard, *The Temple and the Lodge*, Arcade Books, New York, p. 202.

[37] Ibid., pp. 218-219.

[38] Ibid., pp. 219-220. Quoting Heaton from *The Masonic Membership of the Founding Fathers*, p. iv.

[39] Hall, op. cit., p. 200.

[40] Ibid., p. 201. We are directed by Hall to the *History of Newfoundland*.

[41] Ibid., p. 202.

[42] Ibid., p. 205.

[43] Ibid., p. 208.

[44] Baigent and Leigh, op. cit., pp. 254-255, quoting Milborne, 'British Military Lodges in the American War of Independence', pp. 37-38.

[45] See *http://www.mt.net/~watcher/greatwork.html*, pg. 1.

[46] Ibid., pp. 215-216.

[47] Mackey, Albert, *A Manual of the Lodge* p. 329.

[48] Jim Marrs, *Rule By Secrecy*, Harper, New York, p. 263.

[49] Indeed Pike and other Masons believe that God has both a good and bad side. Lucifer is the good side. Even if Christians don't react to the Lucifer assertion, they would strongly disagree that the God they worship *has a bad side*. Christians may be accused of having a *Manichean* theology (*Mani*, a 3rd Century Persian believed that there is a good god and a bad god – this same view was embraced in *Gnosticism*); however, Christian orthodoxy does have a reasonable explanation for evil in the world. Eastern thought conceives of the Ying and the Yang, the black and white symbol, of which the Masonic symbol of the black and white checkerboard is actually a parody. The meaning: God is both good and evil. Christians must repudiate a theology that maintains this perspective. At the very core, Masonic theology is closely associated with the primary notions of *Gnosticism*.

[50] Hermeticism is defined as a combination of the Greek God *Hermes* and the Egyptian God, *Thoth*. There are pseudo-graphical writings of a Hermes Trismegistus. The combined god is considered a god of knowledge, writing, and magic. Trismegistus means "thrice great" and may be dated

from Egypt as early as the third century BC. *Hermes* in Greece, *Thoth* in Egypt and *Teuton* in Germany (whence comes Teutonic), *Mercury* (the Roman version of Hermes), all likely refer to the biblical person Enoch that the Book of Enoch indicates was considered the author of writing. He was known as 'the scribe'. The concept of *messenger* is derived from this fact.

51 Marrs, *Rule By Secrecy*, citations of Picknett and Prince, *Templar Revelation*, p. 113.

52 Horn, Thomas, *Apollyon Rising*, Defender Books, Crane, Mo., 2009, p. 111.

53 Wilcock, David, *The Source Field Investigations: The Hidden Science and Lost Civilizations behind the 2012 Prophecies*, New York: Dutton/ Penguin Group, 2011, p. 117.

54 Ibid., pp. 4-5, quoting Thomas Paine, *The Age of Reason,* Part 1, Section 5 and Part 2, Section 20, (See www.ushistory.org).

55 Ibid., p. 6.

56 Ibid., p. 11, quoting from "Benjamin Franklin, " *The Encyclopedia Americana, Vol. XII* (*Encyclopedia Americana*, 1919), 11.

57 Freemasonry and Catholicism remain enemies to this day. Historically, the reason for the enmity (originating with a Papal Bull on April 24, 1738 forbidding Catholics to be Masons), was well stated by Michael Baigent and Richard Leigh in the book we've referred to previously: "The point is that Rome feared, not entirely without justification, that Freemasonry, as an international institution, stood a reasonable chance of offering a philosophical, theological and moral alternative to the Church... Freemasonry threatened to become, in effect, something like the League of Nations or United Nations of its day" (*The Temple and the Lodge*, Arcade Books, New York, p. 191).

58 *The Great Plan*, if not already made clear to the reader, is to establish a world democracy to protect the freedom of humankind from the tyranny of priests or kings; an empire built in America with American power ensuring its longevity. We may be in the very last stages of this 'great plan'.

59 Ibid., pp. 243-244.

60 Ibid., p. 244.

61 Ibid. P. 244.

62 Horowitz, op. cit., p. 250. Horowitz continues: "And, in her own shorthand style, she offered many of the same ideas as Hall and the more "serous" esotericists. New York publishers began to reprint her work and look for more. By the early 1970s, Tarot and occult how-to guides numbered in the hundreds."

63 Hall, op. cit., p. 123.

64 Baigent and Leigh, op. cit. p. 263, provide a good summary of how the American Revolution led Freemasonry to take on more radical aspects which became important to the advancement of the revolution in France.

[65] Wilcock, op. cit., pp. 134-135. However, Wilcock throughout his discussion repeatedly asserts this hope without support from Virgil's passage, or "Lieutenant Totten's letter" from which he draws the interpretation (again unsupported) that 'the golden one' refers to all humanity. The more likely reference by the Cumae is to *Apollo*, the god of the Cumae (as she was the 'oracle of Apollo') who she indicates in the poetic prophecy was the offspring of Jove (Jupiter or Zeus, of whom Apollo was his most notable offspring). As Tom Horn points out in *Apollyon Rising: 2012*, the 'golden boy' is certainly a hoped for Messiah –a demi-god by the kings of the earth— however, his true identity is Apollyon, Abaddon, or Antichrist. There is no reason to arrive at the conclusion of Mr. Wilcock however winsome and well-intentioned his supposition may seem, and apply the 'hoped for one' to all of humanity.

CHAPTER FIVE

IS THE FOURTH REICH ALIVE IN AMERICA TODAY?

The maxim that society exists only for the well-being and freedom of the individuals composing it does not seem to be in conformity with nature's plans... If classical liberalism spells individualism, Fascism spells government.

Benito Mussolini

For Nazism or Fascism is by no means an Italian or German specialty. It is as international as murder, as greed for power, as injustice, as madness...If we don't stamp out the Nazi underground, it will make itself felt all over the world; in this country too. We may not have to wait ten years, perhaps not even five. For many years in the past we closed our eyes to the Nazi threat. We must never allow ourselves to close them again.

Curt Reiss, from *The Nazis Go Underground*, 1944

*[Imperiled Civilization's] united efforts have ground the German war machine to fragments. But the struggle has left Europe a liberated yet prostrate land where a demoralized society struggles to survive. These are **the fruits of the sinister forces** that sit with these defendants in the prisoner's dock... What makes this inquest significant is that these prisoners **represent sinister influences** that will lurk in the world long after their bodies have returned to dust.*

Robert Jackson's "Opening Statement" at the Nuremburg Trial

Who Really Won World War II?

Contrary to the outrageous claims of some conspiracy theories, Adolf Hitler did not escape Germany at the end of World War II. He committed suicide with his new bride, Eva Braun, and their bodies were burned together outside his bunker in Berlin on April 30, 1945 as Russian troops crept ever closer. [1]

However, contrary to the best-known annals of American history, unlike Hitler, Fascism and Nazism clandestinely escaped Germany to be revived in institutions, both governmental and private, throughout the Western Hemisphere (as well as Russia) from 1945 forward. Ironically, while the 'Allies'—the United States, England, France, and the Soviet Union—celebrated their victory over the Third Reich, tens of thousands of German scientists, engineers, and spies (who proved too valuable to imprison or execute despite their horrendous war crimes) were slipping through Nuremburg's loosely fashioned grip. This, the true 'great escape' of World War II, was thanks to meticulous plans developed over a year earlier by Martin Bormann, Hitler's second-in-command. In fact, even while the victors were sorting through the pieces of war-torn Europe negotiating over the spoils, the Nazis were already engaged in the next war—a war that today, however posthumously, they appear to have won. Upon closer inspection, the Cold War wasn't just the story of how Capitalism conquered Communism; it was the story of how Nazi Germany, despite its near total defeat and the stunning devastation of its greatest cities, became a deciding factor in the ongoing battle between these two alternative competing ideologies, and how the real winners would be the elite bankers, European aristocracy, multi-national corporations (many of which were infected with Nazis), and even the royalty of the world who played one political ideology against the other to achieve their agenda—gaining a foothold to restore for themselves the power to rule the world once more.

Jim Marrs, the author we reference frequently in this chapter, (mostly from his book, *The Rise of the Fourth Reich*, 2008), explains how many Nazi's escaped justice at the end of World War II holding the world's most advanced technology as their trump card while being financed with the largest treasure even known stolen and stashed away in Swiss Banks. It is the greatest story *never* told. "The Germans were defeated in World War II... but not the Nazis.

They were simply forced to move. They scattered to the four corners of the world. Many of them came to the United States and penetrated what President Dwight D. Eisenhower termed 'the military-industrial complex'."[2]

Marrs continues in his introduction to make a statement the author believes is slightly exaggerated yet holds forth prophetic warning for the immediate future: "At the beginning of the third millennium after Christ, by most criteria, the once-free constitutional republic of the United States had become a National Socialist nation, an empire of the creators of the Third Reich—a Fourth Reich."[3] His argument hinges not upon the extent of German accents in high places but upon impregnable collusion between big business and government in 'this here United States', coupled with the infusion of Nazi technology, personnel, and their well-known Illuminati maxim, 'the end justifies the means'—a guiding principle for 'doing business' whether in the public sector or private.

By definition, Fascism[*] (to remind the reader) consists of a governmental order when business and government so closely combine that 'the People' become servants of the State and exist for the good of the collective. *Individual liberties are sacrificed in the name of shared economic prosperity.* To underscore this point: we must acknowledge that while remaining heavily tilted in favor of the wealthy, Fascism is nevertheless a compelling substitute for Communism, since most workers benefit as 'rising tides raise all boats'. We should recall that Hitler turned around the German economy in five years, put millions back to work, and even developed the 'Volkswagen'—the car of the people—to make transportation af-

---

* Italian Dictator Benito Mussolini coined the terms Fascism, from his 'black shirts' labeled the *Fascisti*. As we will see, the fascist connection to some famous American symbolism is striking and frighteningly straightforward.

fordable. At the beginning of World War II, Hitler was loved. Someone once said that if the War had not broken out, Hitler might have been deemed a saint for the economic miracles he worked.

Consequently, we are compelled to ask, "Are we already a fascist country?" The answer lies in whether or not one believes that big

business controls government through relentless lobbying of lawmakers and various ways of patronizing powerful politicians. While the media appears to argue either for the liberal or conservative perspective, typically in the name of Socialism versus Capitalism (the supported ideology seems to depend upon which cable television channel you watch!), the plain truth as stated at the

Figure 21 - The Fasces on the American 'Dime'

outset of this book, is the country moves down the path toward a third political ideology seldom mentioned because it seems too dreadful to contemplate: namely, National Socialism aka Fascism.

In our case, we are wont to ask, "If the People elect a government that cannot support the vast majority of its population because of commitments made to corporate interests and Wall Street, are the People really in control their government?" In other words, in America today, the People's voice appears not to make much difference in what happens on the national scene—in regards to the biggest issues, much more powerful interests prevail.

So is this a fair description of our politics? Marrs comments:

Party politics, slogans, and social issues are employed to distract the masses. The world's elite deal in only one commodity—*power*. They seek to gain and maintain the controlling power that comes from great wealth, usually gained through the monopoly of ownership over basic resources. *Politics and social issues matter little to the globalist ruling elite, who move smoothly between corporate business and government service.* The desire for wealth with its attendant power and control drives their activities. It is this unswerving attention to commerce and banking that lies behind nearly all modern world events. It is the basis for a "New World Order" mentioned by both Hitler and former president George H.W. Bush. [Emphasis added][4]

Figure 22 - The Fasces in the Statue of Washington, Federal Building, Manhattan, New York

The emblem of fascism, the *fasces*, is actually a common image located on many of our governments' seals. It is featured in the Seal of the Senate, the Mace of the House of Representatives, and the Seal of the United States Courts, as well as protruding from the front of Lincoln's chair at the Lincoln Memorial, and lying beneath the cloak of George Washington in his statue at Federal Hall, Manhattan. The fasces are a bundle with an axe sporting a metal blade bound amidst a band of other wooden rods which lack the same. It symbolizes authority. It was carried before ancient Roman magistrates emblemizing their power.[5] The fact that it appears amidst so many of our federal government symbols is a yet another surprising example of our fondness for mystical allusions to Rome so common in America.

It's Not Personal—It's Just Business

A subtle joke is often voiced amongst business people that the only parties who make money in a lawsuit are the lawyers. Likewise, twentieth century history suggests that the only parties who make money in a war are the *bankers*. This proverb would be completely true if we threw in businesses that make munitions, chemicals, and war machines. This is most certainly so in the case of Germany with its remarkable ascent to power between World Wars I and II. The astounding circumstances of how American industrialists befriended Hitler, perhaps seeing in him a means to keep communist Russia at bay, are blatant, plentiful and incriminating.

> By the mid-1930s, with the government, military, and the German cartels now firmly in hand, Hitler knew it was time to strengthen his influence over international bankers and businessmen. Despite his declared intentions to nationalize German businesses and curtail the power of international business and finance, Hitler initially had little trouble getting funds from corporate sponsors who saw his National Socialism as a necessary alternative to worldwide Communism. [6]

When we study the economic goings-on between American and German industry, well-known names such as Warburg, Bush, Morgan, Rockefeller, emerge again and again in various banking entities, law firms, inter-locking directorates, and conglomerates. What follows is a cursory chronicle of the various ways that America's business and banks helped Hitler build his formidable regime.

For starters, American business provided substantial propaganda and intelligence for Hitler:

Another solid conduit for Nazi propaganda and intelligence activities was the Hamburg-Amerika shipping line. Max Warburg, a leader of Deutsche Bank, sat on the board of Hamburg-Amerika Steamship Line along with Prescott Bush, father and grandfather of two future U.S. presidents. Max Warburg was the brother of Paul Warburg, America's first chairman of the Federal Reserve System and the man in charge of U.S. finances in World War I.[7]

And Yankee ingenuity was also forthcoming:

Automobile-maker Henry Ford became a guiding light to Hitler, especially in the realm of anti-Semitism. In 1920, Ford published a book titled *The International Jew*. As Hitler worked on his book, *Mein Kampf*, in 1924, he copied liberally from Ford's writing and even referred to Ford as 'one great man.' Ford became an admirer of Hitler, provided funds for the Nazis, and, in 1938, became the first American to receive the highest honor possible for a non-German: the Grand Cross of the Supreme Order of the German Eagle... In July 1940, at a meeting in Dearborn, Michigan, between ITT's Westrick and the Fords, it was decided that rather than build aircraft engines for beleaguered Britain, the Ford company would build five-ton military trucks for Germany, the "backbone of German Army transportation..." Albert Speer once told him [Bradford Snell, who reported this in the *Washington Post* in 1998] that Hitler would never have considered invading Poland without the synthetic fuel technology provided by General Motors.[8]

Even the early seedlings of high technology growing in the form of tabulating machines from IBM (International Business Machines) significantly aided the Third Reich. Its president, Thomas J. Watson, was virtually Hitler's personal account manager.

Watson kept in close contact with his German subordinates, traveling to Berlin at least twice a year from 1933 to 1939. Watson never sold IBM machines to the Nazis. They all were merely leased. This meant that all machines were dependent on IBM punch cards, parts, and servicing. Interestingly, IBM punch cards of that time were not standardized [into 80 column punches]. Each batch sent to Nazi Germany was custom-designed by IBM Engineers... Watson, a well-connected Freemason, proclaimed "World Peace through World Trade" in 1937, while in Berlin to be named president of the International Chamber of Commerce. In that same year, President Franklin D. Roosevelt named Watson U.S. commissioner general to the International Exposition in Paris, and Hitler created a special medal for Watson, called the Merit Cross of the German Eagle with Star, to "honor foreign nationals who made themselves deserving of the German Reich."[9]

Marrs indicates that Joseph P. Kennedy, at the time America's Ambassador to England, was recalled in 1940 because he, along with Ben Smith a Wall Street player, had met with the Nazi head of the Luftwaffe, Chief Hermann Goering in Vichy, France sometime earlier. After this meeting, Kennedy (father of President John, and U.S. Senators Robert and Edward) donated large sums to the Nazi cause. Apparently, many elite Americans who were disgusted with the left leanings of President Franklin Roosevelt viewed the German fascist cause with great hope (Roosevelt's lasting legacy is his social policies—not the various 'works' programs, but his most famous creation, *Social Security*). The disdain was so intense important industrialists Irénée du Pont (Director on the Boards of Du Pont and GM) and General Motors president William S. Knudsen "in early 1934 planned to finance a coup d'état that would overthrow the president [Roosevelt] with the aid of a $3 million-funded army of terrorists, modeled on the fascist movement in Paris known as the *Croix de Feu*."[*]

> The undoing of this scheme was retired Marine Corps major general Smedley Butler, the most decorated marine in U.S. history, who was approached by the plotters and urged to head the new military government. Butler, who had openly attacked Roosevelt's New Deal programs, however, proved to be a loyal citizen and immediately informed Roosevelt of the treasonous conspiracy. "Roose-

---

[*] The *Croix de Feu* was a French far right league during the Interwar period, led by Colonel *Francois de la Rocque*, which failed in a coup attempt there.

velt... knew that if he were to arrest the leaders of the houses of Morgan and Du Pont, it would create an unthinkable national crisis in the midst of a depression and perhaps another Wall Street crash. Not for the first or last time in his career, he was aware that there were powers greater than he in the United States.[10]

Marrs informs us that a congressional investigation verified the facts and stated that the players and their intentions were exactly as Major Butler had indicated, although Roosevelt had much earlier leaked the story to the press along with a dismissive statement downplaying its validity.

As if there is insufficient proof adduced so far to make the point that many American elite were sympathetic to Hitler, we can add the witness of the U.S. Ambassador to Germany, William E. Dodd "who told reporters upon his arrival back home in 1937, 'A clique of U.S. industrialists is hell-bent to bring a fascist state to supplant our democratic government and is working closely with the fascist regime in Germany and Italy. I have had plenty of opportunity in my post in Berlin to witness how close *some of our American ruling families are to the Nazi regime.*'"[11] [Emphasis added] Dodd published "The Bible of a Political Church," in *The Nazi Primer: Official Handbook for the Schooling of Hitler Youth*, in which he made a number of unequivocal statements regarding Hitler's ideology, his plan for world conquest, and his intention to eliminate Jewish influence, during the course of evaluating what the Germans were teaching their children:

> Several policies were adopted during the first two years of the Nazi regime; the first was to suppress the Jews... They were to hold no positions in University or government operations, own no land, write nothing for newspapers, gradually give up their personal business relations, be imprisoned and many of them killed.... [The Primer] betrays no indication of the propaganda activities of the Nazi government. And of course there is not a word in it to warn the unwary reader that all the people who

might oppose the regime have been absolutely silenced. The central idea behind it is to make the rising generation worship their chief and get ready to "save civilization" from the Jews,[12] from Communism and from democracy—thus preparing the way for a Nazified world where all freedom of the individual, of education, and of the churches is to be totally suppressed.

Perhaps American politicians should have listened more closely to their German Ambassador. Then again, perhaps they weren't surprised by what he had to say.[13] They just simply chose to ignore it.

Rudolf Hess and the Plot to Overthrow Churchill

If Roosevelt feared being overthrown by American industrialists, Winston Churchill recognized he was threatened by his own King. This intrigue likely led to one of the most amazing stories of World War II—the personal peace mission of Rudolf Hess, Hitler's top aid, originator of the infamous hand gesture, "*Heil Hitler*" ("Hail Hitler") and most likely the real author of Hitler's *Mein Kampf.* King George VI,[*] father to Queen Elizabeth II, along with other English royals were "sensitive about their German extraction. Peace with their relatives would have been very desirable during the war years. In 2000, senior British government sources confirmed that private letters between the Queen Mother and Lord Halifax showed hostility toward Churchill and even a willingness to submit to Nazi occupation if the monarchy was preserved."[14]

There is little dispute amongst historians that King Edward VIII, the duke of Windsor who abdicated the throne supposedly for the love of the American, Wallis Simpson (Duchess of Windsor), was 'tight'

---

[*] This is the King who was the subject of the 2010 film, *The King's Speech* written by David Seidler and directed by Tom Hooper.

with the Nazis. Scott Thompson in his article, "The Nazi Roots of the House of Windsor" pulls no punches when he asserts:

> One of the biggest public relations hoaxes ever perpetrated by the British Crown is that King Edward VIII, who abdicated the throne in 1938, due to his support for the Nazis, was a 'black sheep', an aberration in an otherwise unblemished Windsor line. Nothing could be further from the truth. The British monarchy, and the City of London's leading Crown bankers, enthusiastically backed Hitler and the Nazis, bankrolled the Führer's election, and did everything possible to build the Nazi war machine, for Britain's planned geopolitical war between Germany and Russia.[15]

Agreeing with Thompson, Marrs recounts that Germany saw Russia as its biggest threat and preferred the English to be their ally against Communism. Hitler was well aware of the insanity of a war on two fronts, even blaming Germany's defeat in World War I on this ill-advised strategy by the Kaiser. In *Mein Kampf*, he had written, "With England alone [as an ally], one's back being covered, could one begin the new Germanic invasion [of Russia]."[16]

Traditional history teaches that Hitler was the aggressor with Stalin stunned by Hitler's attack. However, a source close to the situation Vladimir Rezun (writing under the pen name of Viktor Suvorov), provided a very different view. His testimony: Hitler felt forced into a preemptive strike. "While Suvorov's conclusions grate against the conventional view of Hitler's attack on Russia, he has provided a compelling argument. Suvorov pointed out that by June, 1941 Stalin had massed vast numbers of troops and equipment along Russia's European frontier, not to defend the Motherland but in preparation for an attack westward. Stalin's motive was to bring Communism to Europe by force, a plan he expressed in a 1939 speech."[17] Marrs quotes U.S. Department of Defense official Daniel W. Michaels who wrote, "Stalin elected to strike at a time and place of his choosing. To this end, Soviet development of the most advanced offensive weapons systems, primarily tanks, aircraft, and airborne forces, had already begun in the early 1930s... The German 'Barbarossa' attack shattered Stalin's well-laid plan to 'liberate' all of Europe."[18] This documented truth stands as one of the most important overlooked facts of history.

Marrs suspects the globalists were behind Roosevelt's decision to arm the Soviets in violation of the Neutrality Acts of 1935, 1936, and 1937. Only by the end of 1940, with all Europe under German control and Britain threatened, did they likely determine to stop Hitler. Other sources Marrs quotes, along with a few historians, believe "Hitler's strange order to halt the German advance at Dunkirk allowed the British Army to escape the continent. Hitler wanted his future ally intact."[19] If true, this policy was soon to change.

These factors set the stage for the strange flight of Hess on May 10, 1941. Hess climbed into his specially modified ME-110 Messerschmitt heading to an airstrip near Hamilton, Scotland. He flew there to "negotiate peace terms with an anti-Churchill faction and then be flown to Sweden as the first leg of a return trip home. This faction was prepared to oust Churchill and agree to a ceasefire with Germany."[20]

> This proposition may not be as absurd as it first sounds. [Authors] Picknett, Prince, and Prior noted, "The extravagant postwar mythologizing of Churchill has obscured the fact that he remained in a very insecure position politically for at least the first two years of his premiership, largely because it was well known that he did not—to put it mildly—enjoy the support and confidence of the King."[21]
>
> The notion of an internal coup against Churchill was even broached to President Roosevelt by FBI director J. Edgar Hoover. In a memorandum written only a week before the Hess flight, Hoover informed Roosevelt, "[I]t was reported that the Duke of Windsor entered into an agreement which its substance was to [the] effect that if Germany was victorious in the war, Hermann Goering through his control of the army would overthrow Hitler and would thereafter install the Duke of Windsor as the King of England."[22]

As fate would have it, Hess missed his landing spot and low fuel forced him to bail out. Upon touching down, he broke his ankle. His troubles were worsened since he had landed on the property of a patriotic farmer (armed only with his sharpened pitchfork) who quickly captured Hess, spoiling the plot. Although in the hands of MI6, the situation wasn't over. Intelligence leaders there knew of the attempt to secretly reach peace between Hitler and the British Government—a policy that many in the institution favored. However, despite the conundrum and their hesitancy of what to do, the steps of Hess eventually led him to the Tower of London.

Was this incredible action just the crazy whim of a deranged Nazi acting alone? That is what historians assert—another 'lone gunman' theory providing a more comforting explanation.[23] Despite the public disavowal of Hess by Hitler—probably to avoid tipping his hand to Stalin that he was planning to attack eastern Russia—the logic of the plot to overthrow the British government seems to fit the facts.[*] When we consider the process leading to the ill-fated flight and several other details surrounding the story, the puzzle appears solved: *The English Monarchy was plotting against Churchill.*

Quoting extensively from Marrs:

> A detailed study of Hess's flight clearly indicates that it was not just a sudden whim of an unstable individual. There is evidence of foreknowledge in Germany. Hess prepared for the flight meticulously over a period of months, even having famed aircraft designer Willy Messerschmitt modify a twin-engine Messerschmitt-110. Hess also received special flight training from Messerschmitt's chief test pilot, as well as Hitler's personal pilot, Hans Baur—evidence that Hitler had knowledge of Hess's plans. On his flight, Hess carried the visiting cards of both

---

[*] Stalin could easily deduce Hitler's plan to attack once he realized Hitler sought England to 'cover his back' as he had written in *Mein Kampf.*

Haushofer and his son, Albrecht Haushofer, yet another indication of his intent as a peace mission, since the elder Haushofer had long been an advocate of maintaining friendly relations with Britain as a cornerstone of German politics.

According to the French scholars Michel Bertrand Jean Angelini (writing under the name of Jean-Michel Angebert), Haushofer passed along to Hess the names of members of the *Order of the Golden Dawn,* an occult society in England, as well as names of supporters of a peace initiative, such as the duke of Hamilton, the duke of Bedford, and Sir Ivone Kirkpatrick. The Golden Dawn, most popularly connected to England's foremost occultist, *Aleister "the Beast" Crowley*, was an outgrowth of the Theosophical Society, from which much Nazi mysticism was derived, and had close ties with the *Thule Society.*

According to some theories, British Intelligence manipulated Hess's belief in the occult to provoke his flight to England. Oddly enough, this scheme involved Crowley as well as British Intelligence agent Ian Fleming, who would later write the popular James Bond novels. "Via a Swiss astrologer known to Fleming, astrological advice was passed along to Hess (again, via the Haushofer's and by Dr. Ernst Schulte-Strathaus, an astrological adviser and occultist on Hess's staff since 1935) advocating a peace mission to England," wrote [Peter] Levenda. "May 10, 1941, was selected as the appropriate date, since an unusual conjunction of six planets in Taurus (that had the soothsayers humming for months previous) would take place at that time." Once in England, Hess was to be debriefed by fellow occultist Crowley.[24] [Emphasis added]

Later, Albert Speer, Hitler's armaments minister wrote that Hess assured him in all seriousness the idea had been inspired by a dream supplied *by supernatural forces*. This followed the now explainable meeting between Hess and the Duke of Hamilton at the 1936 Olympic Games in Berlin, where Hess apparently hoped to open the lines of communication and move the ill-fated strategy forward.

Several other facts add depth to the conspiracy theory: First, some suggest that there were two Hess's. One was the real one, captured in England and put to death by Churchill in secret, another held in

Germany who pled ignorance of the whole affair at the Nuremburg trials indicating he had lost his memory and couldn't speak to the questions raised (certainly a convenient excuse if you never were Rudolf Hess). Allen Dulles, serving as High Commissioner of Germany after the war, had one Dr. Donald Ewen Cameron examine Hess at Nuremburg (Cameron becomes notorious in later years for his experiments on mind control). Dulles believed that this Hess was not the real deal.

> Dr. Cameron was a Scot who pioneered brain washing techniques before the end of the war, at the Allen Memorial Institute at McGill University, funded by *the Rockefeller Foundation.* He went on to become president of the American Psychiatric Association as well as the first president of the World Psychiatric Association. He also became *part of the CIA's notorious MKULTRA mind-control program.* Various researchers have wondered if Dulles's choice of Dr. Cameron to study Hess might have grown from the knowledge or suspicion that the man posing as Hess had been brainwashed into actually believing he was the Nazi deputy fuehrer. Mind-control experimentation was much further along—particularly in Europe… than most people realize. [Emphasis added]

Hess had previous well-known and documented scars from the World War I that would have been easy for any doctor to detect. Why send Cameron? Clearly, it must have been due to Cameron's 'specialty'. If the Hess held in captivity was the subject of some manner of 'mind control', Cameron would spot it.

Another colorful anecdote: the last person to dine with the Duke of Kent before his death was Prince Bernhard of the Netherlands (the Duke of Kent was the younger brother of King George VI who may have served as 'point man' for the royals in the affair until his plane fatefully crashed in Scotland, August 25, 1941). "The dinner represented an unusual gathering of the British royals at Balmoral Castle in Scotland, which, in addition to the duke and Prince Bern-

hard, included King George VI and Queen Elizabeth."[25]   Marrs
continues underscoring the future significance of Prince Bernhard:

> But it is Bernhard's presence that has caught the interest of re-
> searchers. Prince Bernhard originated meetings of the Bilder-
> berg Group, a collection of world movers and shakers so secre-
> tive they have no proper name. Bernhard was a former member
> of the Nazi SS and an employee of German's I.G. Farben [the
> conglomerate and massively powerful chemical company] in
> Paris. In 1937, he married Princess Juliana of the Netherlands
> and became a major shareholder and officer in Dutch Shell Oil,
> along with Britain's Lord Victor Rothschild.

Bernhard moved to London when Germany invaded Holland. On
the surface, his true loyalties are difficult to assess. However, the
link between Bernhard and the globalist conspiracy is a direct one:
Bernhard chaired the Bilderberg's until 1976, when he resigned in
disgrace after being charged with receiving kickbacks from Lock-
heed to promote their sale of airplanes to Holland, his native land.[26]

With all these machinations, it is little wonder that conspiracy theorists contend the evidence for the global takeover of the world system proves to be a longstanding and still highly active affair—with
the 'royals' at its very heart. The story of Rudolf Hess opens the
door ever so slightly for others to view what transpires behind those
heavy and generally closed doors amongst the royals, the bankers,
and the world's most powerful politicians.

It is also easy to see why we should bemoan and belittle what we
were taught in school. Our American history education was candy
coated in red, white and blue. Surely, when one is a child truth is a
hard commodity to come by. However, even as an adult in America
today, the truth evades us still since we aren't often inclined to question the agenda of the rich and powerful; we doubt our ability to alter it if we did. We have learned not to tug on Superman's cape.

The Secret Escape of Nazism

Even before D-Day in June, 1944, warnings about the Nazi strategy to escape defeat was in published form. Quoted as one of two items in this chapter's epigraph, Curt Reiss, an English correspondent who had traveled throughout Europe during the war, published his prescient book, *The Nazis Go Underground.* Marrs cites Reiss's words that sound as if they were written in 2004 rather than in 1944:

> "They [the Nazis] had better means for preparing to go underground than any other potential underground movement in the entire previous history of the world. They had all the machinery of the well-organized Nazi state. And they had a great deal of time to prepare everything. They worked very hard, but they did nothing hastily, left nothing to chance. Everything was thought through logically and organized to the last detail. Himmler [along with Bormann] planned with the utmost coolness. He chose for the work only the best-qualified experts—the best qualified, that is in matters of underground work."[27]

According to Reiss, Himmler had said, "It is possible that Germany will be defeated on the military front. It is even possible that she may have to capitulate. But never must the National Socialist German Workers' Party capitulate. That is what we have to work for from now on." Plus, the reader should recall that American capitalists had hundreds of millions invested in German corporations ($471 million by 1941 to be exact)—they had no intention of losing those assets. Secreting the business know-how, financing, and management out of Germany was in everyone's best interests—except those who fought and died to stop the fascist war machine.

It was Bormann who masterminded the project known as *Operation Eagle Flight.* While Hitler was bouncing back and forth from depression to hysteria, Bormann coolly assembled his team and put in place plans that would ultimately create 750 foreign front corporations broken out as follows: 58 in Portugal, 112 in Spain, 233 in Sweden, 214 in Switzerland, 35 in Turkey, and 98 in Argentina.[28]

> According to Paul Manning, a CBS Radio journalist during World War II and the author of *Martin Bormann: Nazi in Exile*, Bormann "dwelled" on control of the 750 corporations. He wrote: "[Bormann] utilized every known device to disguise their ownership and their patterns of operations: use of nominees, option agreements, pool agreements, endorsements in blank, escrow deposits, pledges, collateral loans, rights of first refusal, management contracts, service contracts, patent agreements, cartels, and withholding procedures." Copies of all transactions and even field reports were maintained and later shipped to Bormann's archives in South America.[29]

In other words, amenable local citizens of each country agreed to be titular head of these companies, but Nazis acting behind the scenes or under assumed names would wield control of the businesses they established to carry on the Reich's work.

Enter the Elite

According to John Loftus, Nazi War Crimes prosecutor for the U.S. Department of Justice, "much of the wealth was passed out of Germany by German banker Fritz Thyssen through his bank in Holland, which, in turn, owned the Union Banking Corporation (UBC) in New York City."[30] Two prominent U.S. business leaders who supported Hitler and served on the board of directors of the Union Banking Corporation were George Herbert Walker and his son-in-law Prescott Bush, father of George H.W. Bush and grandfather of President George W. Bush. The attorneys for these dealings were John Foster Dulles and his brother Allen. John later became secretary of state under President Dwight D. Eisenhower while Allen became one of the longest-serving CIA directors before being fired by President John F. Kennedy in 1961. Both were original members of the Council on Foreign Relations. Their commitment to German companies and indirectly, to Nazism is well documented by no less than the U.S. government itself.

> On October 20, 1942, the office of U.S. Alien Property Custodian, operating under the "Trading with the Enemy Act" (U.S Government Vesting Order No. 248), seized the shares of UBC on the grounds that the bank was financing Hitler. Also seized were Bush's holdings in the Hamburg-America ship line that had been used to ferry Nazi propagandists and arms. Another company essential to the passing of Nazi money was the Holland American Trading Company, a subsidiary of UBC. It was through Fritz Thyssen's Dutch Bank, originally founded by Thyssen's father in 1916, that Nazi money was passed. The Dutch connection tied the Bush and Nazi money *directly to former SS officer and founder of the Bilderberg Group, Prince Bernhard of the Netherlands*, who was once secretary to the board of directors of I.G. Farben, with close connections to the Dutch Bank. Loftus noted, "Thyssen did not need any foreign bank accounts because his family secretly owned an entire chain of banks. He did not have to transfer his Nazi assets at the end of World War II, all he had to do was transfer the ownership documents… from his bank in Berlin though his bank in Holland to his American friends in New York City: Prescott Bush and Herbert Walker. Thyssen's partners in crime were *the father and father-in-law of a future president of the United States.*[31] [Emphasis added]

We should also mention the leading shareholder of UBC was E. Roland Harriman, brother of Averell Harriman, also an owner and later U.S. ambassador to Russia (so named by Roosevelt in 1943); who along with the Bushes, were members of the Yale secret society *Skull and Bones*. It has also been documented as recently as 2003 by the *New Hampshire Gazette* that the Prescott Bush failed to divest himself of holdings in the Silesian-American Corporation, a Nazi front company providing much needed coal to Germany during the War.[32] Publisher and historian Edward Boswell recounts the story:

The story of Prescott Bush and Brown Brothers Harriman is an introduction to the real history of our country. It exposes the money-making motives behind our foreign policies, dating back a full century. The ability of Prescott Bush and the Harrimans to bury their checkered pasts also reveals... collusion between Wall Street and the media that exists to this day.[33]

As we will discuss in Book Two, nestled amongst these facts, is an easily deduced and highly probable rationale as to what caused John F. Kennedy to be killed. Specifically, the explanation surfaces that Kennedy's assassination resulted from his ostensible threat to expose the German 'invasion' of America. We can also connect the Bush family, the Harrimans, and the Dulles Brothers who worked together to achieve shared goals with European royalty, headed by Prince Bernhard, the former SS officer of the Nazis, Prince of the Netherlands, and future head of the Bilderberger group. We will explore the depth of the evidence in Book Two of Power Quest.

The Treasure of Solomon

Another intriguing story recounted by Marrs regards how the Nazi's apparently obtained the fabled Treasure of Solomon, supposedly stolen by the Knights Templar from under the Temple Mount in Jerusalem during the first Crusade in the twelfth century. The importance of the story, as far as the 'great escape' of Fascism is concerned, regards the enormous financing it provided the Nazis. This 'found' money fueled their incursion into the Western hemisphere.

In Marr's retelling of the story, we see all the same characters that supplied the backdrop for Dan Brown's *The Da Vinci Code*. Most notably, it is the story surrounding the French Priest François Saunière that commences the legend (his name is borrowed by Brown for the father of Sophie Neveu Saint-Clair in the novel). Specifically, François Bérenger Saunière (1852-1917) was a priest in the French village of Rennes-le-Château in the South of France. While some researchers have proposed that Saunière's unexpected wealth was attributed to learning of the true nature of the Holy Grail and using this information as blackmail against the church in Rome (according to Brown's fictional account, the 'grail' constitutes the blood line of Christ through Mary Magdalene). The research of German occult author Otto Rahn proposes instead that the true source of wealth was the discovery of the Treasure of Solomon, spirited out of Jerusalem by the original nine French noblemen who comprised the original Knights Templar. After excavation and removal of the treasure, they hid its vast cache of jewels, gold, and other precious artifacts for safe keeping within the great caves in the *Languedoc* region (at the foothills of the Pyrenees separating France from Spain).

Rahn published his book, *Crusade Against the Grail* in 1933. The book came to the attention of Heinrich Himmler who sought after anything and everything involving historical or legendary relics as long as they could bring wealth or other occult powers to benefit the Reich.[*] In 1936, Himmler made Rahn a lieutenant in the SS.

> Himmler and his cronies must have been entranced with Rahn, who had drawn connections between the Cathar fortress of Montségur and a fabulous cave housing the Holy Grail called Montsavat, mentioned in *Parzival* by Wolfram von Eschenbach in the thirteenth century. Rahn believed he had discovered the final resting place of a great treasure of antiquity, which included the Tables of Testimony[34], the Grail Cup known as Emerald Cup, and perhaps even the long-lost Ark of the Covenant.

Marrs relies upon the research and personal experience of a highly credible source, Colonel Howard Buechner, former medical officer

---

[*] So the American public learned, from my favorite movie, *Raiders of the Lost Ark*—the great joint effort of George Lucas and Stephen Spielberg in 1981.

with the 45th Infantry Division, professor emeritus of medicine at LSU and professor of medicine at Tulane University for the details of the story.

To begin with, we learn Rahn lost heart with the SS and resigned his commission in 1939. It was the work of Otto Skorzeny, a man of great physical stature (who we will meet again), who was the Nazi version of 'Indiana Jones'... eventually discovering Solomon's amazing stockpile in a cave in the Languedoc region. With a one-word telegram from Skorzeny to Himmler, "Eureka" (I found it!), we had word of the discovery. While pilgrims* surrounded this sacred area on March 16, 1944, Himmler sent a sky writer to place a Celtic cross above the throng to celebrate the discovery. The Colonel relates that "the pilgrims on the mountaintop were awestruck and reacted as if a miracle had occurred. They had no idea that the fabulous treasure of the Cathars had been discovered only a short time before and that the plane was saluting the victorious expedition."

Marrs continues the astounding account:

> According to Colonel Buechner's sources, the treasure was carried out of the Pyrenees by pack-mule train to the village of Lavelanet, where it was loaded onto trucks for the journey to a rail head. Guarded rail cars carried the treasure to the small town of Merkers, located about forty miles from Berlin, where it was catalogued by hand-picked members of the Ahnenerbe SS and then moved to other locations, including Hitler's redoubt [stronghold] at Berchtesgaden, where some of the treasure was

---

* The pilgrims were descendants of the Cathars massacred during the The Albigensian Crusade or Cathar Crusade (1209–1229) which was a 20-year military campaign initiated by the Catholic Church to eliminate Catharism in Languedoc. The Cathars, likely influenced by the Templars and their discovery, had heretical views which are connected to the plotline of Dan Brown's book *The Da Vinci Code*. Hancock and Bauval explore them in depth in their book, *The Master Game*.

carried into the extensive tunnel system, large parts of which remain inaccessible today.[35] [Comment added]

For what it's worth (which is a staggering amount), the estimated value of the treasure by Colonel Buechner and other researchers is over $60 billion depending upon the price of gold (which in 2011, compared to the time of Buechner's estimate, would make it now worth almost $100 billion). As Marrs concludes: "Such wealth made it possible for Bormann and other Nazis to misdirect West German investigations and silence foreign governments and news organizations. And it provided the means to infiltrate and buy out numerous companies and corporations, both outside the United States and within."[36] If true, this provides yet another painful insult to the world's Jews, inasmuch as the treasure of King Solomon financed the ongoing influence of Nazism after World War II.

Conclusion—Do We Now Live in Amerika?

The amazing story of National Socialism's survival is one of the least recognized dynamics influencing today's geo-political situation. The amount of documentation to substantiate the connections between America's ruling elite, international bankers, and European royalty is remarkable. What is equally stunning: the common man in America (or woman!) knows little to nothing about these chronicled details.

America's native historians in the latter half of the twentieth century have done little to investigate these truths and rewrite the reality of American involvement in Nazi Germany's ascendancy. Perhaps this reluctance to document the truth stems from Academia's reliance upon research grants originating with these moneyed and powerful dynastic families. For whatever reason, the truth still has never been explained in popular forums or even exposed to the public.

Furthermore, even the mere suggestion there resides a ruling elite in America (which can be easily traced through the last 100 or more years), is surely branded worse than audacious! If proven to be true, an unsavory conspiracy is now plainly documented. Therefore, it is easy to see why the story, despite its veracity, remains off-limits.

Nevertheless, this author considers the testimony to be without taint; *it is not a matter of opinion or conjecture.* The Nazis survived World War II and their fascist influence continued long afterwards—even to this day as will become obvious when we present Book Two.

While this chapter has focused little on the 'supernatural' element per se, we nonetheless have documented how much the occult influenced the principles of National Socialism (and the elite who espouse it) in the matters of political ideology and key historical events. The Americans who helped Fascism grow in Germany were very likely heavily influenced by Secret Societies as well, given the membership of most of these players in Yale's *Skull and Bones*. In the final analysis, it is this combination of both political commitment and ideologies that constitutes the unspoken but sinister power behind many of the most vital personalities in the recent past, no doubt playing an important role in shaping many of the most memorable events of our lifetime. In the next chapter, we will summarize our study so far and provide an update of the contemporary state of spiritualism in America. The paranormal continues to be, as they say, very much 'in play'.

NOTES

[1] Conspiriologist William Lyne, a fascinating and *occasionally reliable* writer believed that Adolf and Eva, "were flown out of Germany in a flying saucer piloted by the famous German pilot Hanna Retisch and German Luftwaffe ace Hans Ulrich Rudel! As if that were not enough, he adds that they lived happily ever after in Kassel, Germany, protected by a secret NATO agreement, and that on the invitation of President Lyndon Johnson, visited

the San Antonio World's Fair in Texas..." (See Joseph P. Farrell, *The SS Brotherhood of the Bell*, Kempton, Illinois, Adventures Unlimited Press, 2006).

[2] Marrs, Jim, *The Rise of the Fourth Reich*, HarperCollins Publishers, New York, 2008, p. 4.

[3] Ibid., p. 5.

[4] Ibid., p. 7. The question of course is, "How different are these two versions?" In other words, "Is Bush's vision just a kinder, gentler Fascism?"

[5] Answers.com indicates the word means "A bundle of rods bound together around an ax with the blade projecting, carried before ancient Roman magistrates as an emblem of authority."

[6] Ibid., p. 26.

[7] Ibid., pp. 26-27.

[8] Ibid., pp. 30-31.

[9] Ibid., pp. 31-32.

[10] Ibid., p. 33.

[11] Ibid., p. 34.

[12] Communism was seen as a Jewish creation, as Marx was a Jew.

[13] Dodd, William E., "The Bible of a Political Church," in *The Nazi Primer: Official Handbook for the Schooling of Hitler Youth* (Harper & Brothers, 1938), 256ff.

[14] Ibid., p. 40.

[15] Thompson, Scott, "The Nazi Roots of the House of Windsor," *The American Almanac*, August 25, 1997, p. 1. Readers should remember that the family name is not Windsor, but Battenberg, after first being made Mountbatten—the monarchs took the name of Windsor Castle to, shall we say, appear to be more English. "Most members of the family, residing in the United Kingdom, had renounced their German titles in 1917, due to rising anti-German sentiment among the British public during World War I, and changed their name to 'Mountbatten', an Anglicized version of Battenberg." See http://en.wikipedia.org/wiki/Battenberg_family.

[16] Marrs, op. cit., p. 41. Quoting Hitler's *Mein Kampf.*

[17] Ibid., pp. 41-42.

[18] Ibid., p. 42.

[19] Ibid., p. 44.

[20] Ibid., p. 44.

[21] Ibid., p. 44 . Quoting Lynn Picknett, Clive Prince, and Stephen Prior, *Double Standards: the Rudolf Hess Cover-up*, London, Little, Brown and Company, 2001, p. 112.

[22] Ibid., p. 44.

[23] The lone gunman theory, that Oswald killed Kennedy, is often justified; despite the likelihood it isn't true, because Americans 'can't handle the

truth'. Likewise, if Hess didn't act alone, the British public might not be able to handle the truth either! The King, with German roots, wanted Churchill gone and the Monarchy in England reinstated with full power. This appears to be what the German leaders were willing to guarantee.

[24] Ibid., p. 39.

[25] Ibid., p. 48.

[26] Scott Thompson comments: "Prince Bernhard first became interested in the Nazis in 1934, during his last year of study at the University of Berlin. He was recruited by a member of the Nazi intelligence services, but first worked openly in the motorized SS. Bernhard went to Paris to work for the firm IG Farben, which pioneered Nazi Economics Minister Hjalmar Schacht's slave labor camp system by building concentration camps to convert coal into synthetic gasoline and rubber. Bernhard's role was to conduct espionage on behalf of the SS. According to the April 5, 1976 issue of *Newsweek*, this role, as part of a special SS intelligence unit in *IG Farbenindustrie*, had been revealed in testimony at the Nuremberg trials." Thompson, op. cit. p. 1.

[27] Ibid., p. 107. Quoting Curt Reiss, *The Nazis go Underground.*, p. 2.

[28] Ibid., p. 111.

[29] Ibid., p. 111.

[30] Ibid., p. 116.

[31] Ibid., pp. 116-117.

[32] Ibid., p. 117.

[33] Ibid., p. 188. See http://www.georgewalkerbush.net/ bushnazidealingscontinueduntil1951.htm.

[34] Marrs speculates that "the Sumerian Table of Destiny is thought to be the same as the Tables of Testimony mentioned in Exodus 31:18. Other Bible verses—Exodus 24:12 and 25:16—make it clear that these tables are not the Ten Commandments... British author Laurence Gardner believed this ancient archive was directly associated with the Emerald Table of Thoth-Hermes, and that its author was the biblical Ham. "He was the essential founder of the esoteric and arcane 'underground stream' which flowed through the ages," stated Gardner. This table of knowledge was passed from Egypt and Mesopotamia to Greek and Roman masters, such as Homer, Virgil, Pythagoras, Plato, and Ovid. In more recent times, it was passed through such secret societies as the Rosicrucians and Knights Templar and on to the Stuart Royal Society in England. (Marrs, *The Rise of the Fourth Reich*, p. 95)

[35] Ibid., p. 103. Quoting: Colonel Howard Buechner, *Emerald Cup—Ark of God: The Quest of SS Lieutenant Otto Rahn of the Third Reich*, Metairie, LA, Thunderbird Press, 1991, pp. 39-42.

[36] Ibid., p. 105.

CHAPTER SIX

THE SPIRITUALISM OF CONTEMPORARY AMERICA

2012 is most often described as a choice point, a time of intensified possibility and opportunity, rather than an apocalyptic time bomb destined to explode at midnight on December 21, 2012... Opening to the possibilities of 2012 required us to open to mystery, to open to the powers of the cosmos that are transhuman.

Tami Simon, *The Mystery of 2012* (2009)

The encounter between America and occultism resulted in a vast reworking of arcane practices and beliefs from the Old World and the creation of a new spiritual culture. This new culture extolled religious egalitarianism and responded, perhaps more than any other movement in history, to the inner needs and search of the individual.

Mitch Horowitz, *Occult America* (2009)

The Guiding Principles Governing America

Spiritualism in America reflects the American spirit. While not intended to be a mere 'well-turned phrase' or pun, this sentence represents an accurate yet crisp statement defining our interest in matters *beyond the senses.*

America's culture and national philosophy emphasizes the individual and the pragmatic. We celebrate independent thinking, shun excessive religiosity, and value doing 'whatever it takes to get it done'. Merely being told to follow the rules is never enough. We need to know why we should follow the rules. This 'libertarian spirit' encapsulates what makes America and its people great.

But as we've documented so far, a vast majority of Americans also believe in an underlying faith in spiritual realities. While our national leadership from its inception embodied the drive for independence from both royalty and the priesthood—believing that government should be driven by reason and not religion—it nevertheless was unashamed in its passion for 'the wisdom of the ages'. As we've seen, from Washington to Franklin, from Adams to Jefferson, the sentiment of the Founders was dominated by Freemasonry and the pagan symbolism of the Egyptians. Although a controversial claim to the closed-minded, even the architecture of our nations' capital city bespeaks the high regard our Founders had for ancient Rome, Greece, and especially Egypt.[1] This commitment wasn't just ceremonial—purely for form and decorum—it was sincere and serious in its ritual; calling upon powers beyond nature to aid our republic's rise to stability and ultimately to become the greatest power in the world.

One ritual in particular stands out: "To modern Freemasons the *cornerstone ceremony* remains one of paramount importance. It serves not only as a link to their 'operative' ancestors who built temples and cathedrals, but also as a potent symbol of renewal and 'rebirth'. It expresses itself with particular force in the Masonic aspiration (whether taken literally or metaphorically) to 'rebuild Solomon's Temple' in Jerusalem and to lay its cornerstone."[2] (Emphasis added) Masonic author David Ovason comments:

> Symbolically speaking, the crypt is the burial place. It is the earth into which the seed of wheat must be dropped, to grow and resurrect emerging as a sprouting plant from the coffin. In Masonry, the crypt is the burial place of the Master Mason, under the Holy of Holies... This idea of rebirth is continued even in modern times in the formal ritual of the Freemasonic cornerstone ceremonials, in which participants in the ritual scatter wheat upon the floor, and sometimes even link this seeding with the stars.[3]

It is a perplexing point: How could the revolutionary ideology of the American Founding Fathers, as well as the more radical French revolutionaries, espouse humankind's *'reason alone'* as the guiding light of liberty, when the gods *they revered and worshiped (the gods of Egypt), led to performing mystical rituals invoking their support?* This paradox seems lost on Americans throughout the centuries.[4]

As we stated earlier in Chapter Four, the Founding Fathers were assuredly not atheists—however, they certainly weren't orthodox Christians either. Even evangelicals, who are passionate about their faith and their country, mix the two passions together and credit the Founding Fathers with a Protestant faith to which most of the most notable founders did not accept. Indeed, some like Thomas Paine strenuously repudiated such beliefs. Nonetheless, for the most part our population remains unwilling to accept this surprising fact. We prefer to instead deify the Founders, recounting their actions as 'larger-than-life'. One need only recall the recent televised programs of Glenn Beck, lauding our Founders without regard to their own written record of their true religion. We have created our own legends, remembering the Founders in the way we want. Never let the facts get in the way of a good story.

The Meaning of Being Spiritual to Most Americans

When it comes to individual piety, most Americans readily admit their interest in 'spiritual things', if not openly identifying themselves as spiritual beings. No doubt the meaning of this profession of faith varies widely from one person to the next. For some it may mean reverence and recognition for past sacrifices others have made. For many, it includes what today we call being 'centered'. Most would readily agree we shouldn't overlook the societal standard to participate in rites and ceremonies commemorating important events—from family member's graduations to anniversaries and patriotic ceremonies. As such, Americans demonstrate an abundant sense of 'transcendence'. We eagerly celebrate those things 'greater than ourselves' that add meaning to our lives. This is a 'baseline' spirituality to which 99.9% in our culture are committed.

If we dig deeper, we discover the most essential element of the highly regarded Twelve Step Program (developed to help the addicted), is *the recognition of a 'higher power'*—whose adherents believe superintends our health and well-being. This higher power serves those 'cooperative' in spirit, always reliant to manage their lives favorably. Although vague, this 'higher power' is undoubtedly a populist idea also favored by a vast majority across our nation. The mainstream would likely agree it serves as a 'minimum shared belief in God'. It is my supposition our culture recognizes this affirmation so universally we consider it essential to enable our population to be 'well-socialized' and 'solid citizens'—indeed, it seems a core element of an *unwritten social contract between the citizenry.*[5] From this standpoint, there are very few atheists in our society. This much appears central to the American 'spirit'.

In stark contrast, most other cultures in our world do not share even this minimalist 'theistic' conviction about what lies at the foundation of the cosmos. Countries dominating by communism are suffused in a dismal milieu brought about by decades of atheistic materialism. Most cultures in Europe reflect an environment affected by three centuries of disbelief in transcendence, depressed by massive wars fought on their soil, characteristically parochial, some serving as the well-spring of tyrants brandishing blatant fascism, and mistrusting any form of spirituality no doubt due to nearly a millennium of widespread religious persecution. There resides little optimism individuals can 'make a success of themselves' unless they come from the right family, have an impeccable education, and 'keep in line' as it regards political processes. The vocal minority—when demonstrating publicly—isn't credited with exercising a right to protest and exhibit free speech; the majority regards the minority's actions as a step toward anarchy; it is the first sign of revolution. (In the summer and fall of 2011, the riots in Athens motivated by a failed economy, stand out in this respect). This negative consensus permeates Europe and Latin American simply because, all too often, such suspicions have proven true. There the social contract is much more tenuous.

Most Christian scholars would regard the 'Christian legacy' (what intellectual Francis Schaeffer called, our cultural "Christian memory") more lively in America than in these other cultures; thus, it remains dominant despite its diminished 'power' to influence behavior during public protests. As I write these words, a disorganized movement of several hundred, self-named 'Occupy Wall Street', have gathered in lower Manhattan, protesting the disparity of wealth and excesses of bankers who plunged our country into recession. Their ire is partially traced to the astonishing fact not a single instance exists so far of anyone 'going to jail' because of their greed or misconduct. Will this group remain non-violent? Is it too small to matter? It has already spread to other cities with consistent violence seen in Oakland. Could we be on the cusp of anarchy in America? Very few would argue this to be so.

However, we should recall it was another disorganized crowd of no more than 800 who stormed the *Bastille* in Paris on July 14, 1789, launching the French Revolution. Their first act: cut off the heads of the guards, put them on a pike, and parade them through the streets.

It would seem such actions lie outside any possible scenario in America, because it is so out of character for Americans to mistrust the 'powers that be'. Indeed, for those who call themselves American, observing the way the rest of the world behaves, we remain grateful we live in this land where freedom and stability are reckoned as certain as the sun rising tomorrow. We trust that riots will be quelled and the majority will never stand for such rascally behavior. Nevertheless as we will exhibit in Book Two of our study, this confidence could be misplaced—perhaps the 'powers that be' no longer merit our trust. Yet for now, staying the course has little opposition.

A Recap of America's Modern Spiritual Principles

As described above, the characteristics of our 'social contract' and commitment to spirituality make us a great people; however, they often make many of us prone to spiritual excesses that are, by definition, *esoteric*—even bordering on the eccentric. In Chapter Three, we charted the history of spiritualism in America. From the seventeenth century onward, we noted how vast numbers of the population dabbled in the occult. Consulting with mediums was commonplace. Many more sought spiritual demonstrations with viewings of ghosts, divinations to predict the future by some mystical means, and spiritual doctrines falling outside the bounds of orthodox Christianity. Additionally, numerous American cults came into being, most notably Mormonism, which was an strange mixture of the arcane traditions of magic, rituals of Freemasonry, a big dollop of Christian theology, divination through the use of religious instruments to hunt treasure (in the beginning), and the traits of a sex cult with polygamist practices promising to win one's ticket to the after-life.

We also pointed out that America gave birth to Transcendentalism in the eighteenth century and the more objectionable Theosophical Society in the nineteenth; ultimately influencing twentieth-century European esotericism and Nazism. As noted earlier, Madame Blavatsky was especially exuberant about the American spirit and believed it was in America that the rebirth of the esoteric would begin and flourish. It appears she was mostly accurate in her assessment.

In the first half of the twentieth century, while many of the 'enlightened' and well-educated turned away from traditional spiritual sources (such as Christian evangelicalism—a substantial movement in England and America from about 1840 onward), the American philosophy of positive thinking and religious science arose and grew popular. It sought to reconcile an empirical methodology for discerning truth with an *esoteric philosophy of power from the subconscious, super-conscious, or 'higher conscious'*. In this approach to spirituality, at best God became a power to be engaged by meditative prayer; at worst, God could be coerced to meet the physical and financial needs of the individual. Seventy-five years before, Theosophy had basically claimed to accomplish the same thing—by synthesizing scientific findings with a 'Buddhist-like' understanding of the cosmos—but Theosophy's tone was much more arcane as well as adamant in its pronouncements.[6] Both American spiritualistic approaches promoted the view that *the divine* was ultimately an aspect of humanity which could be 'manipulated' to help the individual achieve their personal goals (that is to say, everything from obtaining a sense of *unity-with-what-is* or 'oneness'; to realize self-seeking fiscal objectives in the quest for wealth). The theosophical view was the much more extreme—an 'erudite' person's philosophy—while religious science and 'positive thinking' (essentially identical to what was presented in the best-selling 2006 book, *'The Secret'*) were accessible to the less sophisticated.[7] Oftentimes, these notions were referred to as 'the self-help movement' so characteristic of the American spirit. 'Self-help', whether invoking the spiritual or not, remains a popular category at the top of the charts even today. Americans still find it sage advice to 'pull oneself up by the bootstraps' rather than relying upon handouts and entitlements.

As the twentieth century progressed toward its close (during its last three decades), the works of Alice A. Bailey were rekindled by Marilyn Ferguson, David Spangler, Barbara Marx Hubbard, and a score of others (including actress Shirley MacLaine), who espoused the teachings of the 'New Age', which were often linked to a political socialism and a notion of the 'New World Order'. Their teachings are properly labeled *Luciferian* and acceptably so even by these authors.

In summary, this ideology advocates that Lucifer, as a being of light, provides enlightenment and wisdom to humankind.

For Christian evangelicals among whom the author counts himself, this form of spirituality is even worse than it sounds. Luciferians regard the teachings of the Bible as dogmatic, restrictive, pernicious, stultifying, and solely for the simple-minded. For the Luciferian, *Jehovah constrains—Lucifer liberates*! Consequently, for many Americans (to the disbelief of most others), *Lucifer and liberty appear to go hand-in-hand*. Centuries of teaching 'the secret doctrine' by those advocates of Rosicrucianism and Freemasonry, have led to this twisted understanding.

The all-too-common argument nowadays—to identify the concept of God with 'higher consciousness'—finds a surfeit of scientific support in the revised depictions of reality as provided by the 'new physics'. The idea of an aether or universal medium with its peculiar behaviors (be it *time, space-time,* or *consciousness*) permeating all-that-is, implies to the thinkers of the New Age the essence of true spirituality lies with adopting and applying this conception to humanity; specifically, its message of human identity with what we have traditionally understood to be 'God'. The 'connection' between the consciousness of humankind and its effect upon material objects, giving occasion to the sometimes weird behavior of 'nature', causes many authors as well as scientists to conclude that the 'stuff' of *consciousness and material reality* may be far more closely related than we've ever been willing to recognize before.

It is for this reason that in Chapter Two we investigated the new physics, and its 'source field' as author David Wilcock calls it (we will delve into his work in the next chapter). Wilcock discusses *remote viewing*—a form of clairvoyance—exploited by our military (a key subject to be discussed in Book Two). He refers to authors that shine a light on this hidden activity, who "suggest that everything in the Universe is ultimately One Mind—as the consciousness of the viewer can project into any remote location and experience it as a part of his own awareness."[8] Given this assumption (that mind and matter are connected), Wilcock wonders aloud, "If we all share a collective consciousness, are there practical things we can do to improve the world, by nothing more than the power of our own thoughts?"[9] In other words, if our minds come together in one method of thinking, will the goal of Nimrod at the Tower of Babel be accomplished? As the Lord God said (paraphrasing colloquially), "Once they come together, they will be able to accomplish anything they put their minds to." Mind over matter really matters.

C.S. Lewis remarked in numerous original works, such ideas as these are continuously hailed by proponents to be 'new' and revelatory[*]; but in reality we should recognize them to be 'old as the hills' (or perhaps the 'mounds' of ancient paganism, the center of their spiritism). This conception of the divine is aptly categorized as *pantheism*. Lewis, in a characteristically sassy moment states (closely paraphrased), "Just because the shoe fits, doesn't mean it's a new shoe." He went on to indicate that pantheism is, pure and simple, *the natural bent of the human mind.*

Even if there is a 'mind-matter' connection that can be worked to advantage, the Bible warns against exploiting it. Apparently, for reasons not fully explained, the God of the Bible desires his followers to avoid seeking such spiritual enticements because they pull the individual away from Him and into their 'self' (and sometimes the demonic)—inevitably (and mistakenly) supposing our psychic power supplies evidence we are 'gods' or on the verge of becoming

---

[*] To be specific: 'new age', 'new thought', 'new science', 'new physics', 'new order of the ages', and 'New World Order' just to name a few 'news'.

god-like.[10] The promise of the snake in the Garden now seems well-within our reach.

Not to over-play my hand, but the author's assessment corroborates Madame Blavatsky's enthusiasm for our nation and its people with her quotation as cited earlier in the epigraph to Chapter Four (from *The Secret Doctrine*): "It is in America that the transformation will take place, and has already silently commenced." Simply put, however unsavory, *Americans may be far more likely to believe in folk religions and ancient paganism than any other people on earth, with the possible exception of those ensconced in voodoo cults and Wicca.* Americans are spiritual people—but their spiritual aspirations are not always directed to a noble source (namely, the biblical God).

In Book Two of this study, we will dive into the political implications of the New Age ideologies, its 'technologies', and its many top-secret incarnations in America's military and intelligence services. However, in the remaining portion of this chapter, my intent is to paint with broad brush strokes the current (twenty-first century) landscape of paranormal thinking in America by looking at some of the most prominent entrants into spiritualism today: (1) the '2012 Movement', (2) 'Awakening as One', and the (3) stunning widespread presence of Satanic cults and the thousands (if not millions) of victims affected by this malignant element inherit in the not-so-new spirituality. The presence of this very 'dark side' is one of America's best kept (and gravely astonishing) secrets.

Therefore, upon completing this recap of American spirituality, we ask, "Where are we now, one decade into the twenty-first century?"

Doomsday Today!

Since the 1987 announcement and subsequent lackluster event known as the 'Harmonic Convergence'—sponsored and promoted by New Age and Mayan authority, José Argüelles—a growing movement of spiritualists and doomsday purveyors have predicted the beginning of a new golden age in 2012. The few who warn of doom focus on the fact that the Mayan calendar ends its 26,000 year 'long count' [aka *precession* or 'movement' which signifies the earth's wobble upon its axis] on December 21, 2012. Supported by other legends and obscure prophecies from ancient cultures around the world besides the Maya, this watershed moment portends everything from hallucinogenic visions to crop circles fashioned near *Stonehenge*. These claims, that *the end is near,* arise from a few (but not most) of the '2012 authors'. David Wilcock comments: "Many authors want to sound the alarm about what they feel is imminent doom associated with this cycle [of precession]—and its apparent due date of 2012. Some of the people I've spoken to who worked in various classified projects would agree with them. There is compelling evidence that significant Earth Changes do occur at the end of each of these cycles, but remember—we are already seeing those changes now."[11] [Capitalization in original]

Wilcock references Giorgio de Santillana from his important book *Hamlet's Mill* (1969, co-written by Hertha von Dechend)[12] which indicates legends exist from all parts of the world asserting conditions will grow worse and worse until the 'new age' arrives.

Likewise, from the fore-telling of Edgar Cayce (the *Sleeping Prophet*) and the prophecies of the *Mahabharata*, a sacred Hindu text, we learn of the *Kali Yuga*, an experience of 'hell on earth' which adherents contend we must pass through before we can experience a rebirth. Additionally, one author in particular, John Van Auken is quoted by Wilcock from the March-April 2009 issue of the Association for Research and Enlightenment's magazine *Venture Inward*. In this article Van Auken speculates that accompanying the New Age will be a fresh body for humans through a 'fifth root race' to be "more accommodating to soulful consciousness." Gushing, he proposes that this will be a "souped up model that allows for more cosmic consciousness while incarnate."[13]

But will there be a Golden Age on the other side of the possible 2012 cataclysms—or just the end of the world, *period*?

Perhaps the best written of the doomsday books, *Apocalypse 2012* by Lawrence Joseph, chronicles a slew of untimely phenomena including: the 'solar maximum' (hyperactive heating from our sun); the movement of our solar system into an area of the Milky Way experiencing a massive magnetic storm (with negative implications for our earth); deadly climate changes (the greenhouse effect 'on steroids'), and even comet collisions destined to destroy or at the very least, radically transform our planet. But compared to another author, Patrick Geryl (whose pronouncements are the most radical of all 2012 doomsday authors), Joseph's warnings sound like the earth is destined to experience nothing more than 'a few bad days'.

Geryl predicts a complete destruction of the surface of the earth from the slippage of the crust across the face of the earth's 'mantle' involving a relocation of the magnetic poles and all the distresses that come along for the ride. Geryl's bases his pronouncements on the peculiar view that a cosmic cycle (citing a particular, irregular event associated with a well-known constellation—the *Seven Sisters* or the Pleiades)[14] is soon to repeat itself once more in 2012. According to Geryl, this coincidental and rare movement of the Planet of Venus (moving backwards against the face of the Pleiades—a 'retrograde motion' as it is known in astronomy), was first detected and recorded by the ancients, connected to the destruction of Atlantis about 9,700 BC. Subsequently, Geryl is now hiding out high up in the Spanish Pyrenees convinced a global flood will occur in 2012 with the rest of us everywhere else awash in high water—over our wet heads so to speak.

Other aficionados of doomsday cite the 'return of Planet X' (aka Nibiru) at this very same time which spells the end of our civilization. This prediction of the rare return of the '12th planet' (discovered by author Zecharia Sitchin from his study of the Sumerian cuneiform-clay tablets) is one of the most controversial of all predictions. The controversy rages despite the fact there is little to no evidence that such a planet or 'brown dwarf star' has been detected by science, as well as the rather obvious timing problem pointed out by Sitchin himself. He claims the event occurs every 3,600 years and the next rendezvous is still 1,000 years away (circa 3012). Although Sitchin remains with us no longer, he believed 2012 posed no special threat. But other experts aren't so sure.

One such author David Wilcock cites is Peter Lemesurier in the *Great Pyramid Decoded,* a French scholar of the *Institut Geographique National* who interprets the symbology of the Great Pyramid to insist the 'Age of Aquarius' begins in 2011. Most authorities suggest the 'dawn of Aquarius' may not break for another 150 years. But like the dreaded 'Kali Yuga' whose arrival also is open to debate, doomsayers cite all such portents as virtual facts.

Still, the majority of authors writing 2012 books testify that the world won't end—at least not for those who are ready for the New Age. As Tami Simon, editor of *The Mystery of 2012* states (cited in the epigraph): "2012 is most often described as a choice point, a time of intensified possibility and opportunity, rather than an apocalyptic time bomb destined to explode at midnight on December 21, 2012... Opening to the possibilities of 2012 requires us to open to mystery, to open to the powers of the cosmos that are transhuman".[15]

Simon's comments about the 'transhuman' may cause the hairs on the back of some reader's necks to stand on end. This is especially so given the possibilities which many 'New Age' authors discuss concerning non-human entities frequently experienced by initiated persons during 'cosmic consciousness', visionary sessions incited by hallucinogens, and the highly controversial alien abduction phenomena, about which even pop-singer Katy Perry is singing in her song, *E.T.* Selecting a few of the more provocative lyrics from Perry's hit:

> *You're so hypnotizing*
> *Could you be the devil?*
> *Could you be an angel?...*
> *You're from a whole other world*
> *A different dimension...*
> *[I] Wanna be a victim*
> *Ready for abduction...*
> *Boy, you're an alien*
> *Your touch so foreign*
> *It's supernatural... Extraterrestrial*

Miss Perry is sometimes known as a Christian vocal artist—or at least a vocalist who is a Christian[16]. If so, she is definitely blazing a new path amongst Christian singer/song writers. Methinks instead she is roaming dangerously through the darkened woods. Many of this author's evangelical friends and acquaintances are guaranteed to come unglued over this one (as they should).[17]

Other authors also chime in about the great expectations of the days ahead. Author Greg Braden (who has written a number of books crossing the line from 'New Age' to '2012') writes, "There is nothing in any of the prophecies that tells us unconditionally that the world itself will end on this date. What they do say is that the world as we have known it will enter a time of change on this date. How we respond to that change will define how we experience it and our lives in the next age of our existence." [18] His opinion is shared by almost all of the experts in this mysterious genre. Indeed, another author, Peter Russell offers a similar assessment:

> The global crisis we are now facing is, at its root, *a crisis of consciousness* – a crisis born of the fact that we have prodigious technological powers but still remain half awake. We need to awaken to who we are and what we really want. Throughout human history, there have been individuals who appear to have become fully awake.

These are the enlightened ones – the mystics, seers, saints, rishis, roshis, and lamas who in one way or another have discovered for themselves the true nature of consciousness... Aldous Huxley called this the "perennial philosophy" – the timeless wisdom that has been rediscovered again and again through the ages. [19]

In essence, *2012 is the moment when the 'New Age' begins*—at least according to those who are immersed in the ancient wisdom that is not only labeled the 'perennial philosophy' of Huxley, but is always perennially declared 'new' no matter how many centuries it continues to hang around (as noted before by C.S. Lewis with his 'new shoe' quip). This ideology seems, like hope itself, to spring eternal.

Awakening as One

The ideology of this watershed moment—the crisis of consciousness—is adamantly stated in the numerous videos available for viewing at *www.awakeningasone.com*. Various Mayan authorities are featured there such as John Major Jenkins and Carl Calleman. Key resources and subject matter are also identified: The Dark Rift (of the Milky Way galaxy) and the Mayan Cosmology; the 2012 conjunction with this 'Dark Rift'; *Mayan Cosmogenesis* by author Jenkins; the *Cygnus Mystery* by author Andrew Collins. Virtually anyone who is connected with the 2012 'gospel' participates in the 'hope' of this new golden age in which we shall be transformed—changed in an instant of time. In fact, this aspect of its imminence and instantaneous character amounts to a 'pagan rapture' for those who believe in the coming of *higher consciousness*. Barbara Marciniak, another New Age author and channeler, writes in her book *Bringers of the Dawn* about the need to eliminate those who are holding back the Earth from her next Golden Age: "The people who leave the planet during the time of Earth changes do not fit in here any longer, and they are stopping the harmony of Earth. When the time comes that perhaps 20 million people leave the planet at one time there will be a tremendous shift in consciousness for those who are remaining." [20] Marciniak is receiving this information directly from her cosmic, extraterrestrial sources.

Why do many millions need to be physically removed from the earth? The E.T.'s tell us why, if we trust Marciniak's channeled message:

> If human beings do not change—if they do not make the shift in values and realize that without Earth they could not be here—then Earth, in its love for its own initiation and its reaching for a higher frequency, will bring about a cleansing that will balance it once again. There is the potential for many people to leave the planet in an afternoon. Maybe then everyone else will begin to wake up to what is going on.

What isn't so new about this New Age promotion? At best, religious persecution is to be expected—at worst, we should anticipate those not 'singing out of the same hymnbook' will be exterminated. And then, once again, we see the talk of 'frequencies' and a soft allusion to science 'proving' the validity of the spiritualist sentiment.

There is almost nothing about the vision that isn't apocalyptic—including identifying those who will be damned because they are not 'resonating' with everyone else who is prepared to enter into this new cosmos. From the web site, we learn how this *new awakening* is the latest incarnation of the perennial philosophy. See if you can identify the many connections to Blavatsky, Bailey, and their esoteric ilk from this quotation found there:

> This is a typical occurrence at the close of each world cycle, and one that necessarily precedes the return of the anointing light to the Earth. The purpose of such 'timely intensity' is to provide humanity the necessary challenges and trials that will afford us the opportunity for our spiritual evolution. For it is widely accepted in both *ancient spiritual practices* and in *modern day physics* that "All things come from *One*, and that to *One* we will return." …Yet, this Peace, this Paradise, this heaven or this Kingdom will never be found by trying to affect change outside of oneself. For

the masters tell us that "Faith is the Key that will unlock *the king-dom within*"... And in so doing we will learn to see that Heaven is not a place, or a prize... but rather, *it is a state of mind.*" [21] [Emphasis added, capitalization in original]

My summary of their message, having masticated all the very well-produced videos at the site [absorbed but not so easily digested], comes from my presentation entitled, 'The Dark Side of 2012':

- It is *the Plan* fulfilled (as taught by Blavatsky and Bailey)
- It is timed to occur on 12-21-2012 (the dawn of the new age),
- It is a *syncretistic* approach to religions (combining the theosophist hope to merge empirical science with mystical Buddhism);
- The 'duality' of theism must be relinquished (we must realize that *all is one*—that matter and mind are the same—'duality' is an illusion' holding us back from salvation);
- We must resonate with nature and the earth (as all of reality at its lowest level is comprised of 'sub-atomic *strings* which vibrate');
- For only the illumined will 'enter in'—while the unenlightened will be eliminated (those continuing to insist upon theism with its transcendent God, will *disappear* from the earth).

As others (who along with the author) have noted, should Christians suddenly disappear (as would be the case should the *biblical rapture* happen in our day), those who profess they have 'awakened as one' will have a ready-made explanation for why the rest of humanity who weren't vibrating properly were teleported to a different reality.

How Many Types of Vampires Can We Believe In?

My son is a virtual expert on horror movies. As an aficionado of the macabre, he laments the acclaim given to the *Twilight* series of films—pointing out how little knowledge the author, Stephenie Meyer, really possesses about the history of vampirism. After all, whoever suggested that vampires twinkle when they encounter the rays of the sun? And why would wearing sunglasses cause them *not* to twinkle any longer? A true vampire catches fire and sizzles in the light of day—wearing sunglasses won't even help protect their vision. But playing fast and loose with vampire 'facts' isn't limited to this one interpretation of evil blood suckers. There are the 'True Blood' supernatural thrillers—one of the most creative and popular, if ghoulish series developed for HBO. This highly successful television series followed on the heels of a cinematic sequence of vampire stories starring Kate Beckinsale, *Underworld* (2003) and *Underworld Evolution* (2006). These were so popular that a third was produced and a fourth is slated for release in 2012.

A recent book in which the author participated[*] entitled *God's Ghostbusters* (2011, Defender Books, Tom Horn editor and contributor), provides several articles on the vampire craze as well as offering insights into what appears to be driving this supernatural 'rage'. Additionally, real vampires are discussed—at least as far as odd persons who crave blood and identify with the darkness implicit in vampirism. However, the most significant aspect of the movies and television shows, according to the authors who took up this subject in the book, is the allure of sex—specifically masculine and powerful sexy boy vampires having their way with beautiful, innocent young girls. It isn't just the supernatural that is appealing—*it is sex and the supernatural*—strange bedfellows to be sure.

The point: there is far more hoopla associated with the supernatural (even if much of it is silly or purely for entertainment), than ever before in America's cultural history. Our society today is overrun with the occult, ghost whisperers, ghost hunters, haunted houses,

---

[*] I provided two chapters on the subject of *remote viewing* which are expanded and enlarged in Book Two of *Power Quest*.

and paranormal inquiries of all kinds. Indeed, several of the biggest money making films over the past two years (2010 and 2011) are the movies, *Paranormal Activity I, II, and III.* The possible intrusion of demons in a suburban setting (not Victorian mansions with ethereal cobwebs naturally giving us the 'willies'), captivates audiences across the country. This fascination has become one of the pronounced features of our ethos today. When combined with Ufology, alien abduction, interest in extraterrestrials, and other unexplained phenomena (well-capsulized by the *X-Files* television series, one of my personal guilty pleasures), it is more patently evident than ever just how caught up Americans are in strange, spiritualistic story lines.

However, is this captivation just for 'kicks and giggles'? Or is there a deeper more meaningful explanation for why we are so intrigued and fascinated by these topics in our culture today?

Recently, in reaction to the release of the book *God's Ghostbusters*, an article appeared calling for the identification and training of thousands of teachers—to be focused on teaching the public about *Wicca*—aka witchcraft! Twenty years ago, this story wouldn't have appeared in any sort of serious media. But today, a story such as the following hardly raises eyebrows. We have become that desensitized to the commonplace interest in the bizarre, esoteric, and occult:

> (Salem, MA. October 15, 2011): Wicca is America's Fastest Growing religion, and it is anticipated by some Christian religious experts that it will become the third largest religion in the United States early in the 21st century, behind only Christianity and Islam. Just this week, a press release for the new book *God's Ghostbusters,* by Defender Publishing quoted editor Thomas Horn "In the United States alone, there are now more than two hundred thousand registered witches and as many as 8 million unregistered practitioners of 'the craft'."

> Witch School Co-Founder Ed Hubbard recognizes that the statements and numbers put out by Horn are similar to his own viewpoint. Hubbard offers "There is such a rapid spiritual reorientation

in America occurring that the need for thousands of Wiccan teachers over the course of the next decade will be required to meet the demand for basic teachings. Because of Wicca's liberating beliefs and useful skills, people want to understand and embrace it, and learn how to awaken their inner abilities."

Witch School believes that America is on the brink of awakening and discovering its inner magic, and this is changing belief systems around the world as well. How this change occurs depends on what people believe, and more people than ever are looking at Paganism and Wicca. Pagans have a different vision of everyday life where magic can occur in the workplace, alongside science and technology, among friends and co-workers, filling all those different places with a sense of awe and wonder. If Pagans are correct in their thinking, then they have a conduit to a whole other dimension that is outside of, and yet part of their already rich existence. They have a deep awareness of how much freedom individuals can truly have.

People who practice Wicca now have the ability to learn and share their faith in ways that have never before been conceived. They want to build their community in a free and open manner, legally protected under Constitutional law. Yet, Wiccans and Pagans remain fearful of the danger of their beliefs, knowing how discriminatory American culture can be. The desire to be open about their beliefs and share their knowledge and skills with other likeminded individuals is what continues to drive them. They know that to gain the acceptance of more people, they need educators to help spread that knowledge throughout the world.

Witch School has been working for the past 10 years to train teachers and mentors for the task that lies ahead. The online education system has made it easy to discover what Wicca has to offer, and has helped over 200,000 students learn more about this fascinating subject. You can discover more about Witch School at their website, WitchSchool.com.[22]

But entertaining a community of witches is hardly the most frightening thing happening in our society today. At least applying for membership in a coven remains a personal choice. Tragically, many are 'initiated' into the occult against their will. Despite the fact many experts doubt the veracity in claims of 'satanic ritual abuse' (SRA), thousands of victims of satanic rituals in America constitute far too many examples to constitute no more than urban legend. Well-documented by dozens if not hundreds of professionals in psychology, this troubling diagnosis (and the events which caused it) now seems no longer open to debate. It is a proven phenomenon testifying once again to the truth: Americans are deeply involved in the paranormal—even its darkest side. Perhaps coerced as a result of 'generational agendas', it is staggering how much activity transpires without the least bit of news or discussion in the media, popular awareness, or even in Christian churches, were one might suppose spiritual matters would be exposed and the truth spotlighted. But since disclosure is not forthcoming, I will open the door and shine a light on what has been happening. Prepare to be shocked.

Satanic Cults—Are They For Real?

One of the most conspicuous cults in American history, The Manson Family (founded by charismatic criminal, Charley Manson), introduced an innocent nation to the possibility of truly shocking behavior. What few realize is that Sharon Tate, wife of Roman Polanski, (murdered so gruesomely along with a number of her house guests), *was herself a member of a witch's coven with connections to Manson.* Peter Levenda points out that as Anton LaVey officially opened his Church of Satan on April 30, 1966 (the date being significant as it is the pagan feast of *Walpurgisnacht*—The Spring Festival, the second most important date on the pagan calendar):

> Sharon Tate was busy filming *The Fearless Vampire Killers* in London with director Roman Polanski, the man who would later become her husband. She had already filmed *13*, also known as *Eye of the Devil*, in London the previous year. Although she was perhaps better known to American audiences for her supporting role in *Valley of the Dolls*, her occult films gained her additional notoriety, especially after the Manson killings. It has been reliably report-

ed that during the filming of *13* she was initiated into a form of witchcraft created by the film's technical consultant, Alex [Alexander] Sanders. Sanders had developed an amalgam of Gardnerian witchcraft and ceremonial magic that was known as "Alexandrian," after its founder's name; Gardnerian witchcraft itself was the creation of Gerald Gardner, a one-time customs official in Malay and expert on the *kriss*—the wavy-bladed knife peculiar to Malay and Indonesia—who returned to Great Britain and became involved with Aleister Crowley. Crowley actually wrote many of Gardner's rituals after the latter became initiated into Crowley's OTO.[23]

When Polanski made *Rosemary's Baby*, he hired Anton LaVey to be his technical consultant. Both LaVey and Sanders were enamored with Crowley and both had connections to Manson's 'family'. Levenda cites the many linkages in various Hollywood films devoted to the occult, even including Marjorie Cameron who acted in one such

film (Cameron was the widow of Jack Parsons, founder of the Jet Propulsion Laboratory of Pasadena, CA—who we will discuss in depth in Book Two). The occult world is indeed a small one. Unfortunately for humanity, it is not small enough.

Satanic cults are not just the stuff of Hollywood. Today, there are a substantial number of books on the subject of 'trauma-based mind control' and satanic ritual abuse (SRA). These books are not manuscripts of sensationalists writing for an audience keen for 'thriller' horror stories. They are typically authored by psychotherapists, psychologists, and counselors who have been working with victims of these bizarre events for over three decades.

Figure 23 - Aleister Crowley

The most common ailment of these victims used to be called, multiple personality disorder (MPD), but today is now medically labeled, *dissociative identity disorder* (DID). The controversy surrounds whether such incredible behaviors (the presence of various personalities within a single patient, frequently with the 'host' or primary personality unaware of one or more of the 'alters') truly exist or whether it is caused by the physician who diagnoses it. *

The literature indicates the DID disorder is caused by stress or trauma, generally in childhood, resulting from severe abuse in which the child is subjected to unspeakable threats, often involving the demand that the female adolescent who was earlier impregnated by members of the cult (to which the young person is forcibly participating), kill her newly born offspring at the threat of her own death. Some studies suggest that cults intentionally 'break' the personality of the child, pushing them beyond what is socially seen as 'human' behavior (with many actions too disgusting to mention), to force 'attachment' to the cult. 'Attachment needs'—the desire to be accepted and loved by others—is a most basic element of the human personality. This need is used against the abused to cement their connection to the cult. Ironically, the child is taught that only members of the cult understand and are willing to protect the child. Exposure of the secrets of the cult will lead to severe punishment of the victim; thus, they are caught in a 'double-bind' believing that, as horrible as their experience in the cult is, there exist no sources of help on the outside.

The steps are itemized in the book, *Foundations of Psychiatric Mental Health Nursing: A Clinical Approach*, as follows:

---

* An illness caused by the treating physician is known as an *iatrogenic* adverse effect of therapy.

1. The child is harmed by a trusted caregiver and splits off the awareness and memory of the traumatic event to survive in the relationship.

2. The memories and feelings go into the subconscious and are experienced later in the form of a separate part of the self.

3. The process reoccurs at future traumatic events resulting in more parts of the self to develop, each containing different memories and performing different functions that are meant to keep the child safe and to allow them to form an attachment to the caregiver. Sometimes abusers attempt to do this deliberately, as in the case of the more morbid abusive group practices of various sects, or torture variations.

4. Dissociation becomes a coping mechanism for the individual when faced with further stressful situations. [24]

A recent book (published in 2011 documenting presentations at a conference of therapists and victims in 2009), *Ritual Abuse and Mind Control: The Manipulation of Attachment Needs*, offers a series of papers by experts sharing their experiences with victims of ritual abuse. Professor Brett Kahr, Centre for Child Mental Health, in London offers this endorsement of the work:

All books written by mental health professionals require intelligence, compassion, and sensitivity from their authors. But few demand courage.* The contributors to this impressive and chilling collection of essays deserve our deepest thanks for their bravery in exploring and exposing the most ugly underbelly of human psychology. In sensitive and measured prose, these cutting-edge colleagues have managed to help us understand that extreme abuse, mind control, torture, and other forms of multi-perpetrator assault do exist, and that to deny the personal testi-

---

* Courage is required since their colleagues in the psychological community intimidate those who openly treat victims labeling it as such, and from the cult members themselves who threaten therapists to 'leave the victims alone' and 'keep quiet' or they will be killed.

mony of survivors, as well [as] the growing body of clinical and forensic evidence, represents a horrific attack. The editors and authors of this collection share their moving psychotherapeutic work in a modest manner, helping all contemporary workers to develop a greater appreciation of the important work that demands our respect and our attention.

From the Introduction by Joseph Schwartz, the issue of denial of ritual abuse continues to be a challenge for practitioners: "What is the belief system behind the aggressive vociferous denials of ritual abuse torture? I believe that this is a refusal/ incapacity to see/ entertain just how brutal our social system has been and is… But in my experience, no amount of evidence can defeat a belief system. No matter what evidence is offered, there will always be vociferous and aggressive denial of the reality of ritual abuse torture or, as history of psychoanalysis shows, the reality of childhood sexual abuse, full stop." [25] Valerie Sinason asserts in her paper: "Indeed, the experience mental health practitioners go through when describing this work to skeptical colleagues provides us with a shadow of what survivors [victims who escape these cults] feel." [26] Sinason laments: "If it took me a year to talk about ritual abuse because initially I felt silenced, it took me ten years to talk about mind control." Although not specified, the latter subject was probably 'off-limits' to Sinason because it involved governmental participation in the act of torture and abuse, a subject which we will consider carefully in Book Two. There we will learn how the CIA, influenced by Nazi experts invited into our intelligence services after World War II, taught the 'ways and means' of mind control to our intelligence leaders who were all too eager to learn methods to strengthen their influence over operatives under their command. The CIA simply didn't want the assassin's conscience to get in the way. The *Bourne Identity* movie series provides a relevant and accurate picture of this phenomenon.

But back to the cultic aspects of mind control: Sinason offers this definition of ritual abuse…

A significant amount of all abuse involves ritualistic behavior, such as a specific date, time, position and repeated sequence of actions. Ritual Abuse, however, is the involvement of children, who cannot give consent, in physical, psychological, emotional, sexual and spiritual abuse which claims to relate the abuse to beliefs and settings of a religious, magical or supernatural kind. Total unquestioning obedience in thought, word or action is demanded of such a child, adolescent or adult under threat of punishment in this life and in an afterlife for themselves, their families, helpers or others. [27]

Evangelical Christian counselors and psychologists, who work with the victims of SRA, judiciously talk of how they help victims of ritual abuse. Often their activity includes exorcism of demonic entities, frequently introduced by the torturers into the personalities 'split' from the primary or host person.[28] The genuine 'alters' are not demons, but creations of the human personality mechanism. However, the alter personalities may also be infected with an entity (s) that is a distinct and separate personage from outside the victim. For evangelical practitioners who engage in this practice, it is an arduous and challenging task deserving of our admiration and support.

Their practice is quite distinct from the Roman Catholic Rite of Exorcism (so fancifully portrayed in movies)—exercising what orthodox believers assert is the authority given them by Christ over demonic forces.* Generally, demons are very responsive to commands by Christian (evangelical) exorcists to depart from their victims. Only in cases involving what amounts to 'higher authorities' (rulers and powers†) is there much of a fight put up by the spirit against the

---

* Luke 10:17, "The seventy returned with joy, saying, "Lord, even the demons are subject to us in Your name." (New American Standard Version)
† Ephesians 6:12, "For our struggle is not against flesh and blood, but against the rulers, against the powers, against the world forces of this darkness, against the spiritual forces of wickedness in the heavenly places."

exorcist. However, the dedication required to work with someone who is 'DID' (based on the author's discussions with a number of these therapists), is beyond comprehension. The casting out of a demon, in some cases, may not require much time. But identifying the involvement of a spiritual presence, other than an 'alter', is hardly instantaneous. And the healing process restoring a person suffering from DID certainly is not automatic just because the demon is removed. Such a 'stereotype'—no doubt familiar to some readers and evidenced by a few 'televangelists' of questionable integrity—is not what is witnessed today in the practices of bona fide therapists.

One such person is Russ Dizdar, who along with this author, participated in the creation of the book *God's Ghostbusters* (2011). In his submittal, Russ cites Holly Hector, a former hypnotherapist at Denver's Centennial Hospital, while working on the new satanic ritual abuse ward (part of the 'psych ward') who said that "there were by the early 90s, 2.4 million diagnosed cases of severe satanic ritual abuse that included trauma-based mind control (the splitting of the human personality to create alter or sub-personalities who could be programmed and demonized)." Russ goes on to say, "That has since been dwarfed by the acknowledgment of Dr. Colin A. Ross, [M.D.] and author of the book *Project Bluebird: [The Deliberate Creation of Multiple Personality by Psychiatrists]*. He believes that there may be to 10 million cases in the US and Canada. But adds the numbers in England, Australia, Ireland, and all of Europe and Russia... [may involve] a possible 40 million cases." Russ, along with dozens of others located in this country, England, and South Africa, some of which the author has studied, are actively engaged in helping the victims and 'survivors' of SRA. Dizdar comments: "When a psychologist tells a real SRA/MPD, that the memories of rituals are fake and a delusion, that demons are only a figment of the imagination and no one wants to control them, they offer helpless psychobabble and evidence the issue of SRA/MPD is beyond their expertise.

Even worse there are some psychologists who may be helping to silence sub-personalities and shut down the facts."[29] We will now consider an example from Russ' ministry.

His book, *The Black Awakening*, provides dozens of stories that are not only disturbing, but clearly an act of positive 'consciousness raising' for Christians—depicting the onslaught of what is literally the most diabolical aspect of the paranormal present in America in our age.

One of the most startling facts Dizdar asserts connects SRA to the Nazis of World War II. He says, "Case after case and victim after victim it all seems the same. The procedures to split, program and train *chosen ones* [satanic super soldiers—a subject we pick up in Book Two] have Nazi origins and the spirit behind the Nazis is still operating here in the US. Here in the US there are now over 4 million cases of SRA/MPD. Someone did this and the roots continue to go back to the black flame…Satan-serving Nazis."[30] [Emphasis in original] Dizdar tells of one woman, her father a Nazi, who came to his office with a friend. The woman was a victim of SRA and a 'multiple'. Her visit happened not long after her father died. As she was recounting the fact she was receiving calls with nothing but a dial tone (the caller would hang up—apparently attempting to frighten her), her personality switched from 'the host' to one of the 'multiples'—a voice originating from a very young personality within the woman. The voice began yelling:

> "You know. You know… you know about the men in white coats and the labs. You know about the military's involvement." Each time they would tell me things they got louder and louder. They just yelled and then spit at me. The women she brought with her sat amazed and perplexed. This dear woman feared that Nazi dad to the day he died. She was split, programmed, abused, and used by him and others. It was this Nazi man who personally took his two grandchildren to the military base that had the PSI OPS [psychological operations] unit and where MK ULTRA

mind control projects and the old Nazi doctor's worked in secrecy... here the Monarchs [members of a conspiracy to promote the development of 'super-soldiers' through SRA/DID] had deep roots. This too is a case that is still active.[31]

It is not my intent to go further down this dark path in Book One. But within this citation is foreshadowed the Nazi infiltration into the psychological experiments that was concealed within the military as part of the MK ULTRA project. In Book Two, we will examine the role that our intelligence services played in sparking the growth of trauma-based mind control as a means to create 'the Manchurian Candidate'—the development of assassins programmed against their will to do the 'dirty-work' (also known as 'wet work' amongst these practitioners) of our government. The extent and capability of these 'super soldiers' (as Russ calls them) is nothing short of astounding. Like the victims of satanic ritual abuse, the public simply has no idea how widespread and far-reaching are the results of this clandestine program, brought to light by the 1975 Church Committee in the U.S. Senate.[32]   To say the truth is startling is to do it a disservice. It is mind-boggling.

Conclusion—The Occult is 'Out in the Open'

This preceding selection of supernaturalism prevalent in America today is only a slight cross-section of its many instances. At the outset of Chapter Three, "The Witch Doctor Next Door", we provided an overview of another significant spiritualistic 'channel' through several popular authors who disclose their active use of hallucinogenic drugs to encounter the paranormal. As documented there, author Daniel Pinchbeck provides detailed personal accounts of his involvement in native rituals of South America and Africa, utilizing the indigenous drugs prepared by Shamans there, to facilitate the encounter with entities that provide insights into unseen realities, what the late Terrence McKenna called, "the invisible landscape."

Alternate historian Graham Hancock wrote his book, *Supernatural* (2007) to document his discovery of 'the teachers of mankind' who occupy our vision of reality once we imbibe such drugs as mescaline or other DMT-based substances. To these authors and others noted such as Aldous Huxley, Timothy Leary, (and even members of the Thule Society in early Nazism such as Eckart and Hitler), the super-natural is merely a short 'trip' away. With a little help from 'your friends' (to quote Ringo Star), the paranormal is not only nearby, it is a direct and inexpensive way to discover what the 'spiritual life' (in the world of the mystic) is all about.

What was once *hidden*—reminding the reader this is what 'occult' means—is now more than ever before, an open study exposing our popular culture's blatant belief in the supernatural. However, as we've shown, this is not a new adventure—it has always been a component of our American way of life. Today's version is more 'about me' and displays few if any of the 'social virtues'—common trappings of the paranormal ideologies of the nineteenth century.[33] But the core teachings are still very much the same. As Ecclesiastes said, *"There is nothing new under the sun."* (Ecclesiastes 1:9)

The upcoming and final chapter in Book One is the author's attempt to provide a context to understand the various ideologies of spiritu-alism in light of the more traditional supernaturalism of the Bible. I hope to provide a summary of the key aspects of *Christian cosmolo-gy*. This overview of how biblical Christianity understands the cos-mos will serve as a foundation to determine whether the various para-normal precepts of the 'power quest' have been exploited by individ-uals and groups within our government (and society in general) for reasons the God of the Bible would find not only ill-advised, but re-pugnant; indeed, in the final analysis, precepts worthy of judgment.

It is the contention of orthodox Christianity that not only are indi-viduals responsible to God for their actions; but also nations. They are held accountable for allowing offensive policies and practices to continue—which in our case have essentially grown worse, by many accounts, for six consecutive decades since the end of World War II.

What is so offensive to the God of the Bible? Many actions qualify, but to mention a few: (1) *governmentally*—power structures that keep the poor downtrodden with unjust courts which fail to protect the rights of individuals; power structures that institutionalize injustice (see Isaiah 61:1), and even, as we will discuss in depth in Book Two, sponsorship of actions that are forbidden by the Law of God, such as 'conjuring spirits' and practicing forms of divination (Leviticus 19:31, 21:6); (2) *societally*—sexual immorality, harming or killing animals or people, failing to respect the property rights of others, as well as failing to respect and protect the elderly and the young; (3) *individually*—taking part in societal ills above, plus misleading or misrepresenting the truth to anyone, especially falsifying your testimony concerning the actions of others. And of course, failure to worship God as the creator as well as loving God by treating others the way you want to be treated. These are the essentials as enumerated in the *Ten Commandments* (Exodus 20:1-17, Deuteronomy 5:4-20), in the *Golden Rule* as provided in the Mosaic Law (Leviticus 12:18, 19:34), and as asserted by Jesus Christ (Matthew 7:12, Luke 6:31).

Finally, is our nation at risk because we have offended the God of the Bible? Is it too late to chart a new course and set ourselves on a path of justice and righteousness? In Book Two, we will consider whether we have the opportunity to mend our ways. But first, to conclude Book One, we will study the nature (and supernature) of the cosmos, as the Bible (from the orthodox Jewish and Christian perspective) presents it. This will provide the grounding necessary to evaluate the actions and activities of our government, what I call, its *power quest*, when we examine these facts in Book Two.

NOTES

[1] In their newly published book, *The Master Game,* Robert Bauval and Graham Hancock provide an extended history of secret societies and their affect upon western culture. Not only do the authors discuss the structure and design of Washington DC as a reflection of Freemasonry, they offer extensive proof that Paris' central axis, the Champs Elysees, and the various monuments that adorn this 'axis mundi' (world axis) were revised after the French Revolution to likewise reflect the Egyptian pagan 'citadels' (Karnack and Luxor); and reflect the rising of the sun and the star Sirius on special days of the calendar, May 8 (supposedly, the Archangel Michael's appearance on various mountains in Europe) and August 6 (the supposed date of Christ's transfiguration), at 26° N and 26° S of the Equatorial point from the perspective of that French city (p.422-423). This angle was special because it aligned with the summer and winter solstice at Luxor at the time the temple was built there, taking into account the phenomenon known as 'precession' (the wobble of the earth's axis). They also supply details regarding how the 'layout' of central London (after the 1666 fire) and Vatican City central elliptical expanse (it's plaza) correspond to the designs of Rosicrucians and Freemasons.

[2] Bauval, Robert and Hancock, Graham, *The Master Game: Unmasking the Secret Rulers of the World*, New York: The Disinformation Company Ltd., 2011, p. 496.

[3] Quoted by Bauval and Hancock, ibid., p. 497, from David Ovason's book, *The Secret Architecture of Our Nation's Capital,* p. 76.

[4] Is this what the Bible means by 'the mystery of lawlessness'? "For this lawlessness is already at work secretly, and it will remain secret until the one who is holding it back steps out of the way." (II Thessalonians 2:7, New Living Translation) While debated amongst various orthodox Christian schools of interpretation, many regard the 'he who is now holding back' as the Spirit of Christ present in the body of Christ, i.e., true members of the church of Jesus Christ.

[5] *Social contract theory* is a segment of secular philosophy that most Americans would embrace, and in which few Christians if any would find fault. "Social contract theory, nearly as old as philosophy itself, is the view that persons' moral and/or political obligations are dependent upon a contract or agreement among them to form the society in which they live. Socrates uses something quite like a social contract argument to explain to Crito why he must remain in prison and accept the death penalty. However, social contract theory is rightly associated with modern moral and political theory and is given its first full exposition and defense by Thomas Hobbes. After Hobbes, John Locke and Jean-Jacques Rousseau are the best known

proponents of this enormously influential theory, which has been one of the most dominant theories within moral and political theory throughout the history of the modern West." See http://www.iep.utm.edu/soc-cont/.

[6] "Olcott utilized Western scientific reasoning in his synthesis and presentation of Buddhism... Notably, his efforts represent one of the earliest attempts to combine the scientific understanding and reasoning of the West with the Buddhist religion of the East. The interrelationship he saw between Buddhism and Science paralleled his Theosophical approach to show the scientific bases for supernatural phenomena such as auras, hypnosis, and Buddhist 'miracles.' See *en.wikipedia.org/wiki/Henry_Steel_Olcott.*

[7] Also known as 'New Thought'—the connection to Egyptian paganism is explicit. The neutral tone of Wikipedia is even set aside at the end of this summation of the movie made from the book:

> "*The Secret* website cites the Emerald Tablet, said to be written by Hermes Trismegistus (purportedly a 'secret teacher'), as '... one of the most important historical documents known to mankind'. Byrne posits that the earliest trace of 'the secret' occurred in the Emerald Tablet, followed much later by the Rosicrucians — a 'secret order that espoused many of the ideas of *The Secret.*' Mention is made of Victor Hugo and Ludwig van Beethoven's supposed membership in the order as well as Isaac Newton's purported work in translating the tablet. No solid evidence has been shown proving this; it is more speculation and fiction than anything else."

See en.wikipedia.org/wiki/The_Secret_(2006_film).

[8] David Wilcock, op. cit., p. 75. Wilcock suggests "it may very well be that we all have an energetic duplicate of our physical body that is constantly traveling outside ourselves, as in remote viewing, and reporting back what it sees to the pineal gland—through the silver cord. Ecclesiastes 12:6 seems to refer to this energetic cord: '*Remember him—before the silver cord is severed, or the golden bowl is broken.*'" (See p. 77). The Bible does speak of 'psychic' or clairvoyant powers... but it is not clear these powers are being manifested by the *individuals themselves.* Such persons may be capable of 'seeing' beyond their physical location through the Spirit of God who Christians believe 'lives' within them. In John's gospel we read of Nathaniel's proclamation that 'Jesus is the Messiah' simply because Jesus related how He 'saw him' the day before, where Nathaniel was sitting beneath the fig tree:

> When Jesus saw Nathanael approaching, he said of him, "Here is a true Israelite, in whom there is nothing false." "How do you know me?" Nathanael asked. Jesus answered, "I saw you while you were still under the fig tree before Philip called you." Then Nathanael declared, "Rabbi, you are the Son of God; you are the King of Israel." Jesus said, "You believe because I told you I saw you under the fig tree. You shall see greater things than that." He then added, "I tell you the truth, you

shall see heaven open, and the angels of God ascending and descending on the Son of Man. (John 1:47-51)

The fact that Jesus calls attention to entities outside of space-time may be significant as we will discuss in the next chapter.

[9] Ibid., p. 91.

[10] It is an intriguing fact that psychics often avoid eating meat believing that a vegetarian-only diet enhances their spiritual facilities. Could this be the reason that God allows (perhaps encourages) believers in Him to eat meat? It seems clear from many scriptures that the creation is declared good and we are to enjoy the creation. In Peter's vision in the book of Acts, chapter 10, we learn that God declared all meat 'clean' and no longer forbade avoiding meat of 'cloven-hoof' animals or shell fish. Of course, some regard the vision merely symbolic since the lesson was that non-Jews could now be included in the Church of Jesus Christ. (See cogwa.org/frequently-asked-questions/entry/did-peters-vision-in-acts-10-abolish-the-clean-and-unclean-laws for a discussion of this point of view).

[11] Ibid., p. 105.

[12] This book was instrumental in launching the Mayan awareness and the 2012 'movement'.

[13] Ibid., p. 111.

[14] Geryl believes that a retrograde motion of Venus in the constellation Pleiades, occurring at mid-day during the summer solstice of 2012, signals the end of the world as we know it. The apparent 'back up' in orbit of Venus, while in this area of the sky, happened 12,000 years ago according to Geryl. What is somewhat more difficult to defend about this prediction is that when this occurs, the sun will also be a mid-day, blocking this view of Venus moving backwards across the Pleiades. Figuratively, we might say, "We just can't see how this could be." That would literally be true as well.

[15] Simon, Tami, publisher, *The Mystery of 2012*, Sounds True, Boulder, Co., 2009, page xi.

[16] The fact is that her parents are fundamentalist Christians who were very strict in raising Perry. At 17, she left her parents to pursue her music career. Despite a tattoo of Jesus on her wrist, her outrageous lyrics and commitment to shock music suggest her commitment is not aligned with her parents.

[17] L.A. Marzulli, an expert on the UFO and alien abduction phenomenon, is astonished at Perry's song, discussing it at length in his new book, *The Cosmic Chess Match* (2011). See there. I knew colleagues would find this offensive to say the least. And I must agree with them wholeheartedly.

[18] Ibid., Ibid., pg. 13. Quoting from Gregg Braden, "Choice Point."

[19] Ibid., Ibid., pp. 27,28. Quoting from Peter Russell, "A Singularity in Time."

[20] Hamp, Douglas, *Corrupting the Image: Angels, Aliens, and the Antichrist Revealed*, Crane, Mo., Defender Publishing, p.198. Quoting Barbara Marciniak, *The Bringers of the Dawn*, Bear and Company, 1992.

[21] From www.awakeningasone.com, 'home' page, accessed 11-01-11.

[22] See http://www.prweb.com/releases/2011/10/prweb8879161.htm.

[23] Levenda, op. cit., p. 305.

[24] Carson VB; Shoemaker, NC & Varcarolis E., *Foundations of Psychiatric Mental Health Nursing: A Clinical Approach*, St. Louis: Saunders-Elsevier, pp. 263-267, cited in Wikipedia: en.wikipedia.org/wiki/ Dissociative_ identity_disorder#cite_note-41.

[25] Epstein, O.B, Schwartz, J., and Schwartz, R.W., editors, *Ritual Abuse and Mind Control: The Manipulation of Attachment Needs*, London: Karnac Books, 2011, from the introduction by Joseph Schwartz, p. xv.

[26] Ibid., Sinason, p. 4.

[27] Ibid., p. 11.

[28] This information comes from personal interviews with individuals engaged in this therapeutic activity.

[29] Russ Dizdar, *The Black Awakening: Rise of the Satanic Super Soldier and the Coming Chaos*, Canton, Ohio, A Preemption Book, 2009, p. 473.

[30] Ibid., p 200.

[31] Ibid., pp. 201-202. The voice speaking was probably not a demonic entity, but was the split-off personality. These multiples, according to therapists to whom I have spoken, have distinct personalities, often speak languages that the host personality may not be taught (which leads to some very interesting complexities about the nature of spiritual reality), and must be finally 'integrated' into the host personality by the therapist to facilitate a cure. Such work done by victims and therapists may take years.

[32] "The Church Committee is the common term referring to the United States Senate Select Committee to Study Governmental Operations with Respect to Intelligence Activities, a U.S. Senate committee chaired by Senator Frank Church (D-ID) in 1975. A precursor to the U.S. Senate Select Committee on Intelligence, the committee investigated intelligence gathering for illegality by the Central Intelligence Agency (CIA) and Federal Bureau of Investigation (FBI) after certain activities had been revealed by the Watergate affair." See http://en.wikipedia.org/wiki/Church_Committee.

[33] I should point out that this characteristic of demonstrating a strong social conscience was not just an attribute of cultic movements of the nineteenth century. Jim Jones' People's Temple, when it was located in San Francisco in the early 1970s, was strongly activist providing help to the poor. It

was, however, merely a means for Jones' ever-growing ego. Eventually, Jones moved his cult to Jonestown, Guyana where he finally coerced his followers to 'drink the Kool-Aid' in November, 1978, which was poisoned; thereby, leading to a mass suicide which ended the People's Temple and made Jones one of the world's most famous and villainized false Messiah's.

CHAPTER SEVEN:

TOWARD A CHRISTIAN COSMOLOGY AMIDST TODAY'S NEW-AGE WORLD

*Hearken unto me, O Jacob and Israel, my called; I am He; I am the first,
I also am the last. Mine hand also hath laid the foundation of the
Earth, and my right hand hath spanned the heavens: when I call unto
them, they stand up together... Come ye near unto me, hear yet this; I
have not spoken in secret from the beginning; from the time that it
was, there am I: and not the Lord God, and His Spirit, hath sent Me.*
(Isaiah 48: 12, 15, 16)

*The Lord is omnipresent. He resides everywhere at the same time. We
receive this amazing truth by faith in the fact that He created the
heavens and the earth. His position—outside the creation—means
that He superintended its origination and is present in its every detail.
More than that, because of His existence in a higher dimension, He
existed before their beginning and will exist after their end.
By definition, He exists beyond the borders of our
sharply defined zone of existence.*

Gary Stearman, *Time Travelers of the Bible* (2011)

The God Who Fills in the Gaps

Historically, religions in every part of the world advocate that those things which we cannot explain must be outside of nature—they must be assigned to a 'supernature'. For example, in times past, if an object moves on its own accord without any apparent physical force, a poltergeist (or some other supernatural entity) must be responsible. Other worldly phenomena are brought to bear to explain what happens in this world: God might be blamed for bad weather or poor crops; the devil might be blamed for death or an illness. When there is no natural explanation, we look beyond nature.

This approach appeared to work well for millennia until we discovered magnetism and learned invisible forces exist that still constitute natural forces—they too were 'components of nature'. Even more unseen forces became common knowledge, especially the flip-side of magnetism—*electricity*—and we discovered just how powerful its force could be. Once we harnessed electro-magnetism, the world became a completely different place.[1]

Today we substitute the word, *paranormal* for the term *supernatural*. But from the stand-point of what our culture generally believes to be true about our 'natural world', these terms are interchangeable. In fact, perhaps *abnormal* is a better word than paranormal. Just because we can't see it, doesn't mean it is supernatural. And yet, our propensity to dread the 'unusual' remains an ever-present reality in our personal psyche; it stems from our primal fear that malevolent forces are at play. We readily jump to the conclusion that something sinister could be the cause of what we witness when the 'paranormal' presents itself.

Throughout our history, the laws of nature continue to expand as our understanding of the cosmos grows. For some theologians in the nineteenth century (those within the framework of Christian liberalism), God was really nothing more than the explanation for those things we couldn't explain. He was, as it is known in theology, the 'God of the gaps'. Essentially this conception of God implied that any gap in our knowledge was where God must exist. If we can explain everything else without recourse to a 'God hypothesis', then God can only exist within the realm of what we can't explain.

As the reader can imagine, this put theism at a real disadvantage. Every time humanity learned something new, some piece of information that explained something 'naturally' without requiring God as the cause, the notion of God receded further into the distance. Indeed, God continued to withdraw from the 'real world' as science advanced. For those who believed God's existence depended on the 'unknowable', He became unnecessary. Two hundred years of 'enlightenment' eventually eliminated any place for the divine in the cosmos. Our 'modern' world believed that if science could explain everything without recourse to a 'supreme being', so much the worse for the notion of God's existence—we can live without Him.

However, this situation changed at the outset of the twentieth century. Surprisingly it was science that spilt the milk. Mystery once again crept into our awareness (and our depiction of the creation) with a colossal rethinking of the cosmos. We discovered *relativity* (Einstein) and *uncertainty* (Heisenberg) to be 'natural' aspects of our cosmos (what we now equate with s*pace-time*). With this new understanding, our intellectual hubris was diminished. Now we couldn't predict with certainty how matter would perform in certain experiments (at least at the sub-atomic level). We saw that Sir Isaac Newton's equations may still reign in the seen world—but not the unseen. Sometimes matter appeared to express itself as 'particles' and sometime as 'waves'. And even though time seemed to be a constant—something we could 'count on'—it turned out not to be certain either. We learned it was *relative* to the speed an object was moving.

These concepts were most unsettling. Would these newly disclosed nuances of reality resurrect the need for God as an explanation for what we couldn't explain? Was the God who 'fills in the gaps' back to help explain what we couldn't comprehend?

Time and Eternity are Distinct

In Chapter Two, we took up the challenging subject of the essence of nature—why some phenomena are not explained by the 'laws of physics' the way that Newton, and even Einstein, explicated them.

We entered into a discussion of *space-time* and specifically, that time itself is a *force*. *Time* possesses energy that, in the right circumstances, can be accessed directly. Additionally, we described it as the skeleton for all that exists within the empirical world. And with further deliberation, based on the research of a number of present day researchers who have made physics accessible to 'the rest of us', we explained that time may be the most fundamental building block of creation. Yes, objects are composed of *matter* (which can be converted to *energy* according to Einstein's famous equation $e=mc^2$); but matter/energy are actually 'knots' of time. At its lowest level, the empirical world, visible and invisible (but still directly measurable) is comprised of a single substance—what we call *time.*

At one level, for Christians at least (and I offer this opinion since this chapter concerns how we who call ourselves Christian interpret the cosmos), this statement should not be the least bit surprising. Christians (and orthodox Jews too) readily distinguish between *time* and *eternity*. We believe that God exists outside of time and that *He created time* as part of bringing the creation into being. Time is elemental to the created universe.

Consequently, the primary assertion of a 'contemporary' Judeo-Christian cosmology, is that **time is distinct from eternity.** If so, it follows we must assert that God dwells in eternity and He created time. Time may have more facets than what we suppose or believe to be true (or *have believed* to be true up to this point in our understanding).

Quoted in the epigraph, author Gary Stearman offers this insight which speaks the orthodox, historical Christian position: "[God's] position—outside the creation—means that He superintended its origination and is present in its every detail. More than that, because of His existence in a higher dimension, He existed before their be-

ginning and will exist after their end. By definition, He exists beyond the borders of our sharply defined zone of existence."[2]

This means that *time is not all there is. Eternity remains distinct
from time.* Eternity preceded time, continues while time (and therefore the creation) exists, and will be present after time no longer en-
dures. It logically follows that if God created the creation with a
substance called 'time', His existence lies outside of time itself.
And yet, since time has strange capacities that almost make it seem
like it could encapsulate eternity, we have to be very precise in our
descriptions—and articulate the nature of the cosmos very carefully.

To structure our study for the next several sections, we will refer to
David Wilcock's book which we've quoted before (*The Source
Field Investigations*). Wilcock, while not a scientist, is certainly a
brilliant student of science, the 'paranormal', and 'ancient wisdom'. I will cite his work frequently because his well-articulated
point of view represents today's New-Age (aka '2012 Movement'
perspective) extremely well. I will provide the Christian point of
view by referring directly to Scripture with only occasional references to Christian authors.

Make no mistake: David Wilcock is a superb writer. However, to
be clear, this author certainly disagrees with him on many counts,
most especially his conception of God—which, in essence, is synonymous with his notion of the 'Source Field'. Yet, through this
contrast Wilcock supplies for our consideration, we will be better
realize an understanding of Christian cosmology—which differs
substantially from his esoteric depiction of the cosmos. In other
words, despite his distinctly non-Christian interpretation of the universe, we will benefit a great deal from considering his insights and
the acumen of other experts whom he quotes. On to the task!

Has Light-speed Been Surpassed?

In Chapter Two, we discussed that time has a circular or spherical shape. This shape appears to contribute to the form of both tiny and gigantic 'things' alike—whether it be DNA on the one hand or galaxies on the other. Additionally, we learned time is considered a *dimension* of space. There are three common dimensions (height, depth, and width) which any good carpenter knows well. But there is a fourth (since Einstein opened our eyes), and it is time.

What we know now is that our experience of space is affected by time and vice versa. For example, if we were able to jump into a hypothetical spaceship that travels at near light-speed, we would discover that as we accelerate, our experience of time—relative to our colleagues at our starting point—would slow down dramatically. Time would nearly 'stand still' for us. Perhaps we set out to travel to Mars at this amazing pace. During our trip, to us it would seem like it only took a few seconds, while our now distant friends would have sensed it taking 5 or 6 minutes. What is more, if we both had clocks on 'our persons', the timepieces (be they analog, digital, or atomic) would register time exactly as we sensed it—a few seconds for us, and a few minutes for our friends. Then if we returned to that same space ship for our next mythical voyage and head to the nearest star, Alpha Centauri, our friends might assume they would never see us again— because it will take us almost ten years to fly there and back (4.7 parsecs[*], one-way, to be exact). While to us the experience may seem like only a few days (I'll leave it to the mathematicians to calculate the exact experience we would sense—the reader gets the idea), the actual elapsed time back on earth would be nearly a decade.

---

[*] A *parsec*, for non-Star Trek fans, is the distance light travels in one-year.

As described, time travel would be sensational way to stay young—but it isn't very kind to our friends. While we would grow older by a matter of weeks, our colleagues age ten years while we were away.

David Wilcock explains it this way:

> Einstein predicted that when you move through space, you're not simply moving through something that is empty and has no effect on you. Instead, as you move through space, you move through time as well. Ultimately, that means that time doesn't just happen on its own, as if by magic. Time is actually being powered by some form of energy, or what's called a fabric, that exists throughout all of space. The faster we move through space, the faster we move through time.[3]

But as amazing as the effects of traveling near the speed of light are, these effects pale in comparison to what we are now learning about the *speed of time*. In short, the speed of time is nearly infinite.

Indeed, perhaps the most novel notion about the essence of 'time' not covered so far, concerns the fact we can detect changes in certain 'states' of objects (such as their location) much faster than the speed of light would allow. For instance, the Russian scientist, Nikolai Kozyrev who we studied earlier in Chapter Two, could detect energy emissions from stars indicating where they would be (and actually now are) even though their starlight (what we see) lags way behind their actual present location (since they are many light years away from earth). Through a series of intricate measurements (too complicated to describe here), Kozyrev could see energy 'residue', if you will, from where the star once was (in the very distant past), where the light originating with the star indicates it now is (a more recent 'location' but-still-distant past), and where it actually is now (in the future since the starlight hasn't yet reached us). This discrepancy results from the difference in the speed of light from the much faster speed of the waves in the fabric of time. In other words, because the energy associated with 'time' has ripple effects that are thousands (if not millions) of times faster than the speed of light, we can detect where a star really is, not where its light suggests it is. To provide an example: if a star suddenly went supernovae (blew up), in theory we should be able to sense such a disruptive event almost instantly through its influence on the energy we can detect 'in the aether'... even though we might not see the brilliant light from the explosion with the naked eye or our best telescopes for a many years hence. As it turns out, at the core of this issue rests the potential to realize the elusive unified 'field theory' of 'particles' and 'waves'.

To arrive at this result, we need to rethink the number of dimensions in the universe. While the majority view suggests ten are necessary, six may be the better answer. Dr. Kozyrev was not the only physicist to propose the lesser number. Dr. Dewey Larson built a model of the Universe in the 1950s where 'time' has three dimensions, just as 'space' has three dimensions. In his model, the universe totals six dimensions. In essence, his proposed physics involved a 'reciprocal' relationship between space and time. He believed that these two fundamental facets of the universe were exact opposites. He proposed that we can think of the cosmos in two 'halves': (1) space-time and (2) time-space. In his thinking, drawing this distinction between the two implied the existence of a *parallel reality*.

Space-time presents the cosmos as *particle-like* (when we dwell on that side of the chasm), while time-space seen from our space-time vantage point appears to be wave-like. Should we leap to the other side of the chasm and find ourselves in time-space, we would discern it to be particle-like, while space-time would appear to consist of waves. This is most puzzling to be sure—but according to this alternative theory, when the details are examined it better characterizes the cosmos. David Wilcock explains:

> Simply put, all the energy that makes space in our reality is the same energy that powers time in the parallel reality. And all the

energy that makes space in the parallel reality is the energy that powers time in our reality. Although this seems totally impossible to visualize at first, the reason why it works is that this flowing exchange between space and time is constantly happening within every single atom and molecule of our visible Universe. That means both of these realities are stable locations we can visit—and they are totally interconnected with each other. Neither of these two realities can exist separately.[*] They are intimately and totally dependent upon each other for their own survival.[4]

While neither time nor space allow plunging too deeply into Larson's model here (pun not intended, but the reader must admit it is slightly charming), what we learn from Wilcock's continued explanation is this: if a person moves across the barrier (which turns out to be surprisingly common is our everyday world in selected circumstances)[5], it is possible to move through time. Once in *Time-space*, moving through space automatically means we move through time. Popping back into *space-time* would find ourselves with 'missing time' which is the anomalous experience reported by those who have found themselves accidentally going across the chasm. The famous experience of the 1974 National Airlines 727 jet landing late in Miami comes to mind—it disappeared off the radar for 10 minutes. But when it popped back on the radar, something unpredictable had occurred. 10 minutes had transpired 'on the ground' while no time at all elapsed on the airplane.[6]

But isn't time travel out of the question? One of the reasons we thought time-travel might be impossible was the fact that as we approach the speed of light, we take on mass. At the speed of light, we gain 'infinite mass'—at least that is what Einstein taught us. But

---

[*] Please note the dependency between the two 'sides' of the cosmos. If true, the creation would be separate from a non-contingent being, i.e., God. That is to say, a God who dwells in eternity would not depend upon His creation to exist—but the creation may depend upon His 'being there' to be sustained.

this supposed 'constant' is not correct according to these 'alternative' physicists. As we approach light speed, we lose mass.[7] Thus, one of the main 'hurdles' we thought must be overcome—to surpass the speed of light—turns out to be *a non-issue*. Thus, it is much easier to flip to the other reality than we could have imagined. We learn this to be so because cosmology isn't just about time and space—it concerns *motion* too.

Dr. Vladimir Ginzburg, another alternate physicist, explains:

> You may not be prepared to abandon immediately the century-old relativistic equations. But once you are ready to do so, you will discover many amazing things: Only when a particle is at rest, may [it] be considered as pure matter. As soon as the particle begins to move, its gravitational mass and electrical charge will start to decrease... so a part of [that] matter will be converted into a field. When the particle velocity V becomes equal to the ultimate spiral field velocity C [the speed of light], its gravitational mass and electric charge become equal to zero. At this point, matter will be completely converted into a "pure field."[8]

The essential commentary I would offer at this point: although this quality of the cosmos is fascinating and difficult to fathom, it actually says nothing regarding whether the 'cosmos' possesses a 'spiritual aspect' or not. Historically, upon learning about this phenomenon, Christians might jump up and proclaim, "There now, we told you that there is more to the creation than matter!" Used to be, we would see this mystery and assert that this proves God exists and the spiritual realm is now a demonstrated fact. But remember the moral of the story at the beginning of this chapter: taking this tact returns us to the fallacy in trying to prove God's existence by the existence of gaps in our knowledge or aspects of reality that seem to be spiritual (or incomprehensible) in nature. We must remember as soon as we thoroughly understand how this other facet of creation works (and how we can manipulate it), God will be retired once more from the discussion. When we can explain it naturally, we don't need the supernatural; we find no room for God.

Instead of going down this failed pathway, we should simply assume this enigma exists because God made the creation in this way. We may not have known about it before. And it certainly implies the creation is a very mysterious (and even strange or weird) place. But it doesn't pull God back into the debate to explain as a 'presence' within nature to explain why such a mystery exists. Neither does it prove that God is this mysterious 'other side'. True, the spiritualist may get goose bumps too supposing we've proven the 'divine' dimension of creation and therefore, the validity of pantheism. However, pantheism doesn't logically follow from the facts either. In reality, all we've proven is that the creation is very different than what we once thought. Why is this true? First, it fails to answer how creation came to be—the most essential question. Secondly, why this strange behavior exists is yet another question; and most likely, given enough time and research, science will explain it to our satisfaction removing the luster we celebrated when we first discovered this new and seemingly paranormal phenomenon.

Is Our Mind Made of Time Too?

Then there is the perplexing *matter of mind*, so to speak, with its ideas, visions, ruminations, anguish, and consciousness. Are these phenomenon a part of reality too? Or are they just inventions of our minds, existing only inside our heads? Or are they, as Scrooge exuberantly expressed when doubting the reality of Jacob Marley's ghost, "Just a piece of undigested potato"?

If our thoughts had no effect on our surroundings, it would certainly be held that mental images, feelings connected to mental states, willful hopes, emotional experiences—all would be nothing more than chemical reactions explicated by psychological goings on.

But what if they do affect the world around us? What if the mind really can bend a spoon, such as performed by the famous psychic Uri Geller? What if the spiritualist can make such things happen in the material world? What does that tell us about the connection between 'mind and matter'? In fact, is the famous phrase, 'mind over matter' actually a signal that the brain can control physical objects? Furthermore, if the mind can do such amazing things, does it prove that there exists some substance, some force which mental images, complex thoughts, and emotions are made of? Or our most precious possessions, our individual mental expressions, simply nothing more than a psychological glimmer?

Prospero proposes that life may 'matter' little, because it may only be but a dream in the 'divine mind'. We learn of his opinion from Shakespeare's *The Tempest, (Act 4, Scene 1, 148–158):*

> Our revels now are ended. These our actors,
> As I foretold you, were all spirits, and
> Are melted into air, into thin air:
> And like the baseless fabric of this vision,
> The cloud-capp'd tow'rs, the gorgeous palaces,
> The solemn temples, the great globe itself,
> Yea, all which it inherit, shall dissolve,
> And, like this insubstantial pageant faded,
> Leave not a rack behind. We are such stuff
> As dreams are made on; and our little life
> Is rounded with a sleep.

As we will soon enough see, some scientists are on the verge of proposing that our 'mind' (aka consciousness) is part of a larger mind (or meta-consciousness). Indeed, ancient wisdom and modern science may now be separated by little more than 'a choice of words and preferred metaphors' for communication purposes. Furthermore, according to those who subscribe to this theory, consciousness is just another creation of *time.* It is directly connected to time because mind is nothing more than a supple form of 'time'. The mind can 'move' matter because ultimately mind and matter are made from the same substance.

We have all heard stories of Buddhist mystics and their many feats. Frequently, the greatest example of the power of these monks, mostly inaccessible to the rest of the world (hidden away as they are in Temples and monasteries high in the Himalayas of Tibet and Nepal), is their ability to levitate their bodies simply through achieving a state of meditation. This was recently seen (in August, 2011) on a Discovery broadcast, *The Supernaturalist*, in which an American magician (Dan White) searched and found a subject with these skills in the 'foothills' of the Himalayas. For several minutes, we were treated to the meditating monk levitating several inches off the floor while the television camera and Mr. White walked around the monk and peered closely from several angles to see if any 'trick' could be detected. None was.

David Wilcock provides an even more amazing example of an Indian yogi named Tara Bey, who could suspend time in and around his body, placing himself into a state in which he could exist for days on end without moving or even breathing! His followers would seal the orifices of his ears, nose, and mouth with wax to keep insects 'out' (shutting out air in the process). David Wilcock supplies Bey's testimony and analysis:

> People, when confronted with the phenomena which I can produce, think it either some kind of conjuring, or else something entirely supernatural. In both cases they are wrong. They do not seem to grasp the fact that these things are perfectly scientific, obeying the laws of nature herself. It is true that I am using psychic laws which are little understood—but nevertheless, they are laws. Nothing that I do is arbitrary, supernatural, or against such laws.[9]

Wilcock provides an extensive study of the possible connection point between the individual mind and the collective mind. At the heart of the discussion is the mysterious little gland at the base of our brain—the *pineal gland.* In many cultures this gland is known as the 'third eye' and science seems to have proven that it sensitive to photons (light particles).[10] Biologists suggest that there are aspects of its structure resembling an eye.[11] Curiously most religious mystics describe it as a *pine cone.* The word itself is derived from the Latin word, *pinea* which means pinecone. And ironically, the pine cone appears in many spiritual monuments. Wilcock lists the many uses of the pinecone in religious symbolism:

- A Mexican god holds a pinecone and a fir tree in a sculpture;
- A staff of the Egyptian sun god Osiris from a museum in Turino, Italy, has two "kundalini serpents" that entwine together and face a pinecone on the top;
- The Assyrian/Babylonian winged god Tammuz is pictured holding a pinecone;
- The Greek god Dionysus carries a staff with a pinecone on top, symbolizing fertility;
- Bacchus, the Roman god of drunkenness and revelry, also carries a pinecone staff [Dionysus and Bacchus are the same god, simply named differently in the Greek and Roman cultures];
- The Catholic pope carries a staff with a pinecone directly above where his hand is positioned—and the staff then extends up into a stylized tree trunk [and to a crucifix];
- Many Roman Catholic candle holders, ornaments, sacred decorations and architectural samples feature the pinecone as a key design element;
- The largest pinecone sculpture in the world is prominently featured in Vatican Square—in the Court of the Pinecone.[12] [Bracketed comments added]

Wilcock even describes the god Quetzalcoatl, the "plumed serpent" at Teotihuacan, where you can easily see multiple images of pinecones carved alongside the serpents head, serving as a necklace! Finally, Wilcock provides pictures of several Greek coins portraying Apollo sitting on an *omphalos* stone, reputedly housed at the Oracle at Delphi, shaped to look like a pinecone.[13]   Clearly, *pagan mysticism believed the pineal gland was the key to the individual's connection with the divine.*   What is it about the pineal gland that deserves to be the locus of the human/divine or matter/spirit connection?   Wilcock quotes our friend from Chapter Four, Manly P. Hall—the famed historian of Freemasonry—describing the importance of the pineal gland, and its symbol the pinecone with these words from, *The Occult Anatomy of Man*:

> The Hindus teach that the pineal gland is the third eye, called the Eye of Dangma. It is called by the Buddhists the all-seeing eye, and is spoken of in Christianity [mystic Christianity, not orthodox] as the eye single... The pineal gland is supposed to secrete an oil, which is called resin, the life of the pine tree. This word [*resin*] is supposed to be involved in the origin of the Rosicrucians, who were working with the secretions of the pineal gland and seeking to open the eye single; for it is said in scripture; "The light of the body is the eye: if therefore thine eye be single they whole body shall be filled with light."...
>
> [The pineal gland] is a spiritual organ which is later destined to be what it once was, namely a connecting link between the human and the divine. [14] [Brackets in citation]

Wilcock notes the great rationalist, René Descartes, "believed that human beings were composed of two main ingredients—a body and soul—and the pineal gland was the junction point between them." [15] And we know from other sources we've discussed that certain chemicals from the brain are crucial to visions and encounters with entities 'on the other side' as described by Graham Hancock.[16] These substances include serotonin, melatonin, and especially dimethyltryptamine (DMT). The pineal gland is very active regulating these substances. The New Mexico University professor, Rick Strassman, has studied DMT extensively, writing a book about it, called *DMT: The Spirit Molecule* (2001). Strassman likewise, believes the pineal gland is crucial to the human 'vision' phenomenon.

Wilcock cites a number of other scientific facts, including an amazing discovery that the pineal gland contains...

> One hundred to three hundred microcrystals per cubic millimeter that [float] inside—largely composed of a common mineral called calcite. Each of these crystals were [sic] between two and twenty micrometers in length, basically hexagonal in shape, and were very similar to other crystals we find in the inner ear called otoconia. These inner-ear crystals are known to be *piezoelectric*— which mean they expand and contract in the presence of electromagnetic fields... Piezoelectric crystals can be used to tune in to radio stations without any electricity." [17] [Emphasis in original, brackets added]

'Hearing' crystals, as Wilcock describes, are used in microphones while other crystals related to these (that exist within the pineal gland) give off light in a process called *piezoluminescence*. The pineal gland appears to be richly supplied with both. It has natural receptors and emitters; as a result, it simulates a radio capable of receiving and sending electromagnetic signals. Is this gland the reason why we sense the invisible world of the mystics? Perhaps.

What is the Essence of True Spirituality?

We see there appears to be both chemical and material structures within the pineal gland which may in fact connect the mind to energy fields. Perhaps this gland, through its chemicals and its crystals, is the brain's junction box between space-time and time-space, *allowing our mind to perceive certain realities that otherwise would be invisible.* Can we be sure? Certainly not at this time. While these possibilities—although fantastic—do have some basis in fact; nevertheless, they should still be considered 'fringe science'.

However, conservative Christians needn't feel forced into skepticism or denial to protect their belief system in 'spiritual' reality and its primacy. For it is entirely possible that when God created our capacity to think, reason, and perceive, included in this created structure was an ability to make our minds sensitive to 'the other side' (to time-space) which is also part of His creation. This doesn't make spiritualists of those who believe we might have the capacity to sense such realities (and it doesn't mean those with such powers are possessed by a demon—although there is no shortage of descriptive examples of demonic activity in literature, television, and movies).

Our misconception arises when we conclude that this 'gland', with its mystical properties, is the doorway to *true* spirituality. To be specific, *whether or not we have or can develop the ability to manipulate this capability in no way implies being spiritual.* Biblical spirituality is much more than simply sensing invisible phenomena. It is a matter of ethical and moral attentiveness. It is the issue of *having faith in what cannot be seen*—it is *not merely the capability to see what others cannot.* We must distinguish between 'extra-sensory perception', 'spiritual intuition', and spiritually motivated behaviors.[18] The 'spiritual reality' we call heaven (or eternity) is not subsumed or comprised within space-time or time-space.

The Book of Hebrews teaches, *"Now faith is the substance of things hoped for, the evidence of things not seen... Through faith we understand that the worlds were framed by the word of God, so that things which are seen were not made of things which do appear"* (Hebrews 11:1, 3). The essence of biblical spirituality (as opposed to the spirituality of the theosophist, the Buddhist, and the gnostic) hangs on this very point. The spiritualist seems driven to reflect primarily on the self and proclaim the self, *God.* Depicting this pre-occupation with self, by asserting the 'self becomes God' when it is grows more conscious of 'the other side' is little more than self-indulgence and self-congratulation—it comprises the essence of *anti-biblical religion.*[*]

Joseph P. Farrell, who we have quoted frequently, has this comment to make about such 'religion' (e.g., Theosophy, Buddhism, and in this citation, *Gnosticism*) with one of his theological works when he makes the comment below (which, by the way, discloses Farrell's true roots—Christianity):

> Gnosticism not only invents terms, it invents its own literature, its own tradition, since ultimately these derive from the individual Gnostic's own experience. Thus, creativity itself is the mark both of the true Gnostic as well as of Gnostic systems in general. Man not only creates his own gods, but his own "religion" by which to worship them. The essence of Gnosticism is its elite and total concentration on self; it is, quintessentially, an invented religion. This is the ultimate spiritual basis behind **"sitz im lebenism"**, i.e. the view that all religion is of human invention...[19]

Perhaps it is true that 'mind' is just another form of matter, however discrete. This vantage point from my understanding of the biblical worldview, reflects a more biblically sound perspective than its opposite.[20] Indeed, consciousness may be a factor in all forms of life—it is arrogant for humanity to assume only it has a special quality of consciousness. Wilcock argues, based on several famous experiments performed forty-five years ago by Cleve Backster, plants even possess a distinct form of consciousness.[21]

For this reason, we cannot argue that merely possessing consciousness proves that spiritual reality exists. Likewise, I would contradict what the mystics proclaim, that gaining 'higher consciousness'

---

[*] Perhaps it is putting this self-aggrandizement in perspective by reciting the nursery rhyme: Little Jack Horner sat in a corner eating his Christmas pie. He put in his thumb and pulled out a plum and said "What a good boy am I"

makes one more spiritual. It may make one more sensitive to 'the other side'—but the other side contains entities both good and evil. We mustn't say that such sensitivity makes one 'closer to God'. Just because we can sense or even see 'entities' resident in another aspect of reality has little to say about the quality of spirituality we possess. And as I will argue later, the reality we call *God*—in the Bible's cosmology as upheld by orthodoxy—lies pervasively underneath (or within) the creation as well as entirely outside of it. *God is neither trapped within it, nor is He forced to exist completely separate from it.** Although paradoxical, this is the historical biblical position. Obviously, therein lays the principal distinction between theism and pantheism since it comprises the difference lying at the core of the definitions of both perspectives.

In summing up, I am reminded of one commentator who quipped during the Age of 'Rationalism' (in the days of Descartes, Spinoza, Hume, and Kant) regarding the 'mind versus matter' debate: Oh, *no matter—never mind!* However, before I offer any more tedious philosophic humor—we best move on to consider our conception of the Creator.

The Source Field as Creator

Wilcock equates the Source Field with *gravity;* but he does not do this consistently. Thus, given the *unity he describes between space, time, and gravity* it makes his *singular* identification less important (Wilcock posits *gravity* is 'the essence' of reality—whereas Farrell and others distinguish *time* to be so). Wilcock believes there is ultimately only one reality, one essence undergirding the 'source

---

* The same may not be said of His opposition whose existence may be 'locked into' creation and 'locked out of' eternity as a judgment against him.

field'. He asserts: "If there is a unified field—and most physicists are convinced there must be—it would automatically, by design, be responsible for creating all matter in the Universe. We're not just looking at an energy that drives the flow of time—we're looking at the Source of all space, time, matter, energy, and life in the Universe."[22] [Capitalization in the original] It is quite clear that by using 'caps' when labeling this essential fabric, Wilcock imputes a divine or god-like quality to this one element. This is not accidental or incidental—it is the heart of his thesis.

Wilcock provides further clarification regarding the manner of how the Source Field creates: "It does not appear that the Source Field created the Universe in a single, spontaneous Big Bang, in which all atoms then keep on running for infinity—with no new energy input. By design, the Source Field is actively responsible for keeping matter going—moment by moment."[23] He references Hal Puthoff (who we met before in the discussion on David Hudson's 'gold strike'), noted physicist who suggests that atoms "must be drawing off of an energy field in order to exist—just like a candle flame must burn oxygen and wax in order to stay lit."[24] Confirming the insights of Joseph P. Farrell and the vortex-like shape of 'time' (which is Farrell's synonym for this 'field'), Wilcock states:

> Since most single atoms are nice, round spheres, the Source Field will flow into atoms equally from all directions. The flow into the earth would obviously behave the same way. We would see a spherical current of Source Field energy flowing into it, moment by moment, to keep all the countless atoms and molecules that make up the earth humming along. The Source Field also needs to flow into all living creatures on earth. [25]

Prior to this point in his book, Wilcock demonstrated there are phenomena which can only be explained by some sort of 'field' that supplies energy to material reality, citing examples from a number of distinct scientific experiments and many different sources. He discusses 'pyramid power', Kirlian photography,[26] discoveries regarding the capacity for DNA to emit photons, energy from DNA that remains resident for up to 30 days even after the subject DNA has moved, light frequencies that heal or that cause sickness, and various other phenomenon suggesting the power of the Source Field. Based upon these many data points, Wilcock contends…

> We now have seen very strong evidence that all life forms on earth must continually absorb photons of light, and store them in their DNA in order to survive. The Source Field apparently creates these virtual photons when there is rotating, vortex movement within the field itself. For biological life, the most important frequency is 380 nanometers. If this frequency gets scrambled, our DNA can't absorb and store the light it needs—and we develop cancer.

In my review of his argument, I don't find fault with the data and preliminary analysis, although for many readers, such contentions as just mentioned above may seem outrageous. Where Wilcock and I come together is the belief that there are facets of reality that go well beyond the usual four dimensions (time being counted in this context as the 'fourth' dimension).[*] Where we disagree is whether this 'source field' comprises the full extent of all-that-is and whether the Source Field is necessarily predisposed to benefit humankind. Wilcock asserts this force field (of which our 'mind' is linked) comprises certain qualities that are predicates (attributes) of that reality heretofore labeled 'God'. He continues:

> You create a flowing current in the Source Field and it will still be there for a while—it doesn't immediately disappear. The pyramid structure appears to operate on the same basic principles—a solid-state machine, with no moving parts, that creates a stable, ongoing vortex in the Source Field simply due to its shape. The flowing

---

[*] It is clear that electromagnetism (along with gravity) are amongst the few invisible forces most skeptics will admit.

pyramid current doesn't seem to have any noticeable effect on the downward force of gravity, which is a much larger river of energy moving through the whole area—but the pyramid shape does create a dramatic increase in the coherence and structure of it surroundings, apparently by creating a measurable spin in the fluid like flow of gravity [or time]. This, in turn, generates greater crystallization and organization within physical matter—and dramatically improves the health of biological life.[27]

The latter assertion, regardless of whether we might judge it more an affirmation of faith than science—lacking as it does extensive independent accepted evidence to support it—can be subjected to a simple summary judgment (i.e., a quick rejection) based on the fact that *the source field clearly produces bad affects as well as good.* Of course, the '380 nanometers' Wilcock cites, isn't the only frequency of light the source field produces. Likewise, vortices can be dangerous—just consider the violence of tornadoes. As it concerns human subjects, the Source Field has the capacity to cause evil or good. Simply because human beings learn how to master it for good effects, doesn't impute divine quality of 'inherent goodness'—although Wilcock argues that since 'love' or good intentions have favorable results, the source field must prefer to be 'good' and maybe even should be equated to 'love' (instead of gravity or time). Being a bit romantic myself and believing that 'God is love' as John the Apostle wrote[*], I empathize with Wilcock's declaration. But whether or not we want the source field to be beneficent, which is what Wilcock hopes, has no bearing *on whether or not it actually is.* If we are looking for confidence in the triumph of good over evil, the 'Source Field', like any form of pantheism, holds little hope. It is neutral—it has the capacity for *good* and *evil*—and depicting it primarily as 'good' or 'evil' may be cheating. In other words, these

---

[*] 1 John 4:8, "Whoever does not love does not know God, for God is Love."(NIV)

qualities appear true or false in a relative way only; that is, *how the source field affects humans in a particular context of activity.*

Referencing the introduction, we noted how Nietzsche argued that morality has no metaphysical standing. Morality is an illusion. His argument is especially convincing as it relates to a pantheistic cosmology. George Lucas' 'Force' in *Star Wars* is another example. There is a good side and a dark side—but which one is really more essential? The fact that Luke triumphs over Darth Vader and the evil Emperor, may not have resulted from anything more than Vader, at the last minute, feeling guilty as a delinquent parent, failing to stand up for his son as the Emperor tortures him.

But putting Wilcock's argument on hold (which as the reader can see comes down to whether *evil* and *good* are actual realities or just our reactions to what happens in 'the Source Field'), we should first consider whether an 'ultra-dimensional' force field—whether we equate it with 'gravity' or 'time'—is supported within orthodox Christian theism. Some may be surprised to learn that… *it is*—but only to a point.

The Christian Concept of God

We begin by stating, **the God of the Bible is immanent[*] in His creation**. This concept is the second key aspect of a Christian cosmology: Through this doctrine, theologians through the centuries have sought to express the view that God exists throughout His creation (He is *omnipresent* or in everyday terms, everywhere His creation is); plus, He is *inherent* within it. The Encarta Dictionary describes 'inherent' as "part of the very nature of something, and

---

[*] Wikipedia defines immanence this way: "Immanence refers to philosophical and metaphysical theories of divine presence, in which the divine is seen to be manifested in or encompassing of the material world."

therefore permanently characteristic of it or necessarily involved in it." The Bible describes God as a sustaining force. If He was not ever-present, the creation would cease to exist.

Paul the Apostle, when speaking to the Athenians, compared the God of the Bible to their 'unknown God' quoting one of their poets when he says, *"For in him we live, and move, and have our being; as certain also of your own poets have said, 'For we are also his offspring."* (Acts 17:28) Colossians 1:17 says that *"through Him all things consist"* (King James Version) and is translated in the New Living Bible with these words: *"He existed before anything else, and He holds all creation together."* A similar statement is made at the opening of the book of Hebrews: *"The Son is the radiance of God's glory and the exact representation of his being, sustaining all things by his powerful word."* (Hebrews 1:3a, New Living Bible). Not only did God create the universe, He sustains it.

Psalm 139 expresses God's immanence, and its powerful poetry personally relates His omnipresence and His omniscience (infinite knowledge) to each of us. The biblical God has a plan for our lives. This involves far more than a 'cosmic mind' to which we may be a part and which may or may not be beneficent. Plus, this God goes well beyond a consciousness composed of human minds. The God of the Universe, infinite and powerful, knows who I am; He loves and cares for me. He doesn't have to love us—He is free to or not. But He chooses to do so, unconditionally. Consequently, He is worthy of our adoration:

- *"You hem me in—behind and before; you have laid your hand upon me." (verse 5)*

- *"Where can I go from your Spirit? Where can I flee from your presence? If I go up to the heavens, you are there; if I make my bed in the depths, you are there." (verses 7-8)*

- *"All the days ordained for me were written in your book before one of them came to be" (verse 16)*

- *"How precious to me are your thoughts, O God! How vast is the sum of them!" (verse 17)* [28]

The clear dividing line, which Christians must maintain, requires God to be both nearer to us than we can imagine (just as the Psalmist contemplates) and yet remain *transcendent*. This is the third key principle of our Christian cosmology: **God is distinct from His creation.** While the biblical God pervades His creation and His presence insures the creation continues to exist, He remains distinct from space-time and dwells in eternity. We cannot identify or equate God with the creation even if the creation is far more sophisticated, mysterious, and multi-faceted than we once thought. God stands within and apart—simultaneously—to the creation He has made.

We see this plainly presented in the Hebrew Scripture:

- *"Your throne was established long ago; **you are from all eternity**" (Psalm 93:2).*

- *"I was appointed from **eternity**, from the beginning, **before the world began**" (Proverbs 8:23).*

- *"He has made everything beautiful in its time. He has also set eternity in the hearts of men; yet they cannot fathom what God has done **from beginning to end**" (Ecclesiastes 3:11).* [Emphasis added, New International Version]

- *But as for you, Bethlehem Ephrathah, too little to be among the clans of Judah, From you One will go forth for Me to be ruler in Israel. His goings forth are from long ago, **From the days of eternity**. (Micah 5:2)* [New American Standard Version, emphasis added]

God's transcendence brings the next key principle to light in depicting the Christian cosmos. For God to be a person, He must be transcendent. In biblical theism, Christians affirm **God is a personal God.** If He did not remain transcendent, He would cease being *personal*. Hence, the Bible affirms the creation was made by a personal infinite being that created finite beings—*complete with their own personalities reflecting His image.* Personality is essential to the 'image of God'. Therefore, *personality itself is essential to what reality is.* The fact that Christians believe God exists in three persons within 'the Godhead', only reinforces the notion of personality more. As Francis Schaeffer proclaimed (paraphrasing): "Before the world came into being, love and communication existed between the three members of the Trinity. God did not have to create the world to express love or be love. Personality and love existed from eternity past and will continue forever."

Consequently, if we questioned God's personality as a constituent quality of His infinite being, the value of our individual personality is also jeopardized. As the existentialist contends, logically *the self* is meaningless apart from an infinite 'point of reference'. God is that point of reference. His attributes disclose the nature of what is.

While true that our consciousness provides useful equipment to survive in a dangerous world, the assertion is only a 'positivist' rationale (merely an observation) for why we have one. And if we prove new capacities are developed when we align our consciousness with a 'meta-consciousness', we can likewise underscore there exists another practical value in gaining this capability.

But we still lack an infinite point of reference to provide the context for why personality and individuality matter—because ultimately, who we are is subject to death. No matter whom we are, rich or poor, elite or humble, we don't survive. As C.S. Lewis wryly stated, "Death is 100% in all generations." *Death judges us harshly—its verdict confirms our existence is absurd* (most 'New Age' teachers apparently missed their philosophy classes back in the 1960s).

Meaning and purpose can be vainly supposed—but without God's endorsement, no true value is vouchsafed. That is why, even from the perspective of the *secular* philosopher, our personality—the importance of our individuality—cannot be substantiated apart from God. Who we are and what we become during our 'three-score and ten' (the normal life-span of 70 years—See Psalm 90:6-10) is authenticated only if (1) God exists to bestow meaning; and (2) our life and individuality live on after death (since when we die, our individuality dies right along with us).[*] For this very reason, the question of whether or not there is life after death and how it is 'lived' becomes another vital element of Christian cosmology. Therefore, we take up this crucial issue next.

The Christian Concept of Afterlife

The concept of reincarnation, common to the theosophical/new age/Hindu cosmology, attempts to rescue personality and individuality. But as a solution, it is not all that compelling. Reincarnation teaches that consciousness lives on because the person (now freed from their old body), returns to a new consciousness by becoming an entirely new person. But it takes little in the way of logic to recognize that whatever value could have been attributed to the prior life is subsumed in the next. The individual is lost; the personality dies. His or her value is therefore attributed, if any at all, to the next life.

It is primarily for this reason (although there are several others), that Judeo-Christian belief affirms *eternal life*—not the pagan notion of an impersonal immortal soul—but a personal resurrection of the body and the individual's identity returned to it. Furthermore, the Bible teaches that the body is raised incorruptible (never to die

---

[*] The notion of the life continuing in the form of spirit, effectively a ghost, is also a common attribute of the New Age cosmology. While we won't delve much into this issue, the Christian believes that the identity does live beyond the grave, but the soul/spirit is immediately transported to heaven or to an abode of the dead (technically, Sheol or Hades in the Bible) where it awaits the resurrection. Ghosts are believed to be demonic beings—*not departed human spirits.*

again) and is freed from striving (the purported accumulation of 'Karma'—as taught in the Hindu religion and included within New Age 'wisdom').

Furthermore, (and this is often not understood even by Christians), the New Testament teaches the 'new life' now includes the *glory of God* Himself. We are not just freed from guilt and the capacity or tendency to sin—we are now considered righteous and *glorious* in God's eyes.

- *Now if we are children, then we are heirs—heirs of God and co-heirs with Christ, if indeed we share in his sufferings in order that **we may also share in his glory (Romans 8:17)***

- *To them God has chosen to make known among the Gentiles the glorious riches of this mystery, which is Christ in you, **the hope of glory (Colossians 1:27)***

- *He called you to this through our gospel, that you might **share in the glory of our Lord Jesus Christ** (2 Thessalonians 2:14)*

- *Therefore I endure everything for the sake of the elect, that they too may obtain the salvation that is in Christ Jesus, **with eternal glory** (2 Timothy 2:1 0) [Emphasis added, New International Version]*

To summarize the difference between the biblical doctrine of the afterlife and the 'New Age' notion, I delineate below several key aspects of the afterlife implicit in the scriptures cited above:

- First, the personality or individual identity is secured in the Judeo-Christian view. It continues for eternity.

- Secondly, this identity will be returned to a physical body which is raised immortal. Death will no longer be experienced by the righteous individual.[*]

---

[*] How one is made righteous, of course, is a point of disagreement between Christians and Jews. For Jews, following the Law of God brings righteousness;

- Thirdly, for Christians (not necessarily true in Jewish belief), the new life is characterized by freedom from the tendency to sin and disobey the laws of God.

- Fourthly, distinctive to Christians, the new life that has been raised from the dead is equivalent to the life that was experienced by Jesus Christ after His resurrection. This life includes a glory formerly unique to the Godhead.

Entities from the 'Other Side'

But the moment we admit to invisible 'other beings' which God created besides humanity—namely angels and demons, we are challenged to assign them to one aspect of the cosmos or the other. In other words, if reality is split into 'two halves' (space-time and time-space), where do we assign those entities that appear to us in visions, dreams, apparitions, hallucinogenic 'teaching sessions' (as depicted by Hancock in his book, *Supernatural*), and sometimes visibly to the 'naked eye'? If we admit they exist, which reality do they call home?

If we acknowledge that God dwells distinct from creation (from space-time and time-space), making His 'home' in *eternity*, what does that imply about these other beings? If we acknowledge their existence (and logically or illogically, pantheists in the New Age seem willing to agree they do exist), where do they reside? Are they restricted to space-time or can they exist in eternity as well?

In regards to angels, it is implied more than stated as there are hierarchies or distinctions in level of authority and purpose. We know according to the Bible and Jewish teaching, one type of angel is the

for Christians, accepting the merits of the death of Christ to atone for our sins is the means by which we are made righteous in God's eyes.

seraphim ('burning ones'—used in Isaiah as attendees to the throne of God); a second type is the *cherubim* ('mighty ones', listed dozens of times in the Old Testament). Generally, there are *angels* (messengers mentioned throughout the Bible, also called 'The sons of God' in the Book of Job), and *archangels* (referenced in I Thessalonians 4:16, where the archangel shall announce the return of Christ and in Jude 1:9, where Michael is called an archangel). These *messengers* (which is what the word *angellos* means), can move back and forth between heaven and earth. This appears to confirm that they dwell in eternity as well as serving as God's agents who work in the creation at the behest of God. For instance, we know that when God appears to Abraham, he is accompanied by two angels, who journey beyond where Abraham resided to escort Lot and his family to safety before Sodom and Gomorrah is destroyed.

Paul the Apostle states that not only do angels and demons exist, but these forces exist within a hierarchy. In Ephesians 6:12 we read, *"For we wrestle not against flesh and blood, but against principalities, against powers, against the rulers of the darkness of this world, against spiritual wickedness in high [places]"*. Each power 'type' implies a different level of authority (principalities, powers, rulers). Based upon actual experiences described to me by those who work in what is, to the outsider at least, the dark (but necessary) field of exorcism, the amount of 'fight' varies greatly.[29] The higher the level, the more difficult it is to remove the 'power' from the personality of the victim.[30] In the spiritual realm, power, protocol, and authority are understood and honored—even by the rebellious spirits we call demons.

Christianity cannot answer the question of the 'origin' of evil with the precession we might like. There remains considerable mystery. Gary Stearman, who we quoted earlier, points this out with these words, "Before the creation of the heavens and the earth, we must assume that there was only the realm of the eternal. Then Satan fell. His sin produced a monumental rift in the Kingdom of Heaven. We are told very little about the actual effect of his act of iniquity. But we do know that he corrupted about a third of the angelic host that had formerly been dedicated to the service of God."[31] It is generally thought, through the ages, that Satan was in fact an archangel, possessing great beauty and power. The passages that describe such an evil personage in Isaiah 14 and Ezekiel 28 are typically referenced in this regard, and the name Lucifer, which actually refers to the 'morning star' and a bearer of light, are derived from these passages.

Recently, a friend of this author, David Lowe in his new book, *Deconstructing Lucifer*, argues while there is no question Satan exists, is rightly called the Devil, and is properly understood as the adversary of God—affixing the name Lucifer to him is mistaken based on an understanding of the original Hebrew and subsequent translations into Greek and Latin, even though this has been a common conclusion of Christian theologians down through the centuries.

Satan appears in the book of Job with 'the Sons of God' who appear before the throne of Jehovah. But is he an angel? The phrase, *son of God*, appears to relate to any being who is a direct creation of God, such as Adam, Jesus Christ, and the angels who were created directly by God (not as a result of angels begetting angels). This is common to Christian affirmations and creeds. But, while Satan may be a son of God in this sense, it does not logically follow that Satan is an angel or that his 'proper name' is Lucifer. Can I necessarily agree in totality with Lowe's argument? Not fully at this time. However, his argument is worthy of careful consideration.[32]

On the other hand, Gary Stearman offers an astonishing assessment that is also highly relevant to our study. He proposes that the status of Satan changed dramatically when he tempted Adam and Eve leading them astray from believing in God's word, challenging His commandment not to seek immortality and power aside from God's plan for them (which is my interpretation of the meaning of the Tree of Life and eating of its fruit). Stearman suggests that Satan may have been barred from heaven; as such, eternity was no longer open to him. Instead, Satan became trapped within the cosmos—within space-time (and time-space). "Once privileged to traverse the vaults of eternity, he was sentenced to the time line of the solar system. In other words, time was his punishment. Once, without limitation, he was free to serve the Lord throughout the expanses of the heavens. But his sin enclosed him within the restriction of the Lord's redemptive timeline."[33] Meanwhile, "During the present period, Satan is functioning as the 'prince of the power of the air' (Ephesians 2:2). He ranges across the domain of the atmospheric heavens, seeking to corrupt and enslave those who find their fatal attraction in the world system. He masquerades as an 'angel of light' (2 Corinthians 11:14) and functions as a 'roaring lion'" (1 Peter 5:8).[34]

I would offer another possible model to interpret the 'residence' of these evil powers. What if Satan is prince of time-space? We noted above that he is considered 'prince and power of the air'. Could the word *air* infer the *aether*? These English words are virtually exact equivalents of their counterparts in the original Greek of the New Testament. The line of thought would proceed this way: Humankind was created to operate in both space-time and time-Space. After the fall, humankind was restricted to reside in space-time as a means of protecting it from 'the evil one'. Eden itself may have been a doorway to both sides of the cosmos and was protected by two angels (seraphim) to keep humanity out. Prior to humanity's creation, the Triune God and his angels resided in eternity. Christian cosmology suggests that one-third of the angels left their heavenly estate and 'fell' with Satan. This may have occurred long before the creation of Eden and the subsequent creation of humankind. From the Bible and selected books lying outside the canon of Scripture, such as the Book of Enoch, we learn that 200 of God's angels, aka, the 'watchers' came to earth and took human wives. This is referenced very tersely in Genesis 6:4. Christian scholars down through the centuries taught that the offspring of these angels and 'daughters of Eve' were the Nephilim—the mighty ones of old.[35] After their death, the Nephilim became demons. These 'spirits' are responsible for the evil activities attributed to demonic entities, these being the most prevalent 'evil forces' on earth. Other fallen angels, those who did not father hybrid offspring, continue to reside (and like Satan) are locked out of eternity existing 'in the atmosphere' (or aether) of the creation. They occasionally appear in space-time, but generally only when they are 'conjured' by humans. Otherwise, they reside 'on the other side'. For our protection, God placed a chasm between space-time and time-space. In Jesus' parables involving demons, he infers these forces 'seek a hospitable abode', wandering in dry places (see Matthew 12:43-45). Inhabiting a human personality allows them to reenter space-time, apparently a much more desirable 'state' than existing solely in time-space.

Of course, these reflections are conjecture. I offer it up for others to consider who find the 'model' useful and biblically acceptable. However, I would propose this interpretation of Christian cosmology in respect to 'the other side' and such sinister forces is supported by the conclusions drawn from our study. I cannot be dogmatic about it. I offer it as a possible way to 'integrate' the notions of time-space with the cosmology expressed in the Bible and in particular, how orthodox Christians understand the cosmos.

Conclusion—God and His Creation

While Buddhism teaches that the Buddha 'state' is achieved by recognizing *all is one* and *our self-consciousness is an illusion,* New Age thinking combines the meditative aspects of the Orient with the individualism of the West encouraging super-spiritual experience which achieves personal power in the supernatural realm.

Therefore, the thinking of theosophy and more recently, the New Age, reflects much more than 'Buddhism revisited'.

The unique aspect of this worldview, this *Weltanschauung*, is how it modifies the traditional pantheistic *monism* of Eastern religions with an emphasis *on individual experience—specifically the encounter with the supernatural*. As emphasized before, it also seeks to express its views with scientific language to appeal to the western mindset. Science is leveraged to encourage belief in a 'god' within nature when expounding the 'new physics'; this tact seems useful for it conveys that what we mean by God can be explained by our new understanding of a 'force-field' (Wilcock's Source Field) that permeates all of reality.

At the outset, we discussed the 'fantastic reality' of Pauwels and Bergier. Next we explained the mysterious concept of nature by considering its 'vortical, spinning nature' and its universal presence—best reduced to the most elemental of elements—'time'—albeit much more elaborate than how Einstein and Heisenberg depicted it. As we continued explicating the 'aether' which pervades all-that-is, further qualities were added which amplified its mystery and contributed to its affects in ways unsupported by mainstream science until the last sixty years or so. We crested with David Wilcock's enthusiastic explanation for this 'Source Field'—and although he most often equated it with gravity, he seemed most intent on identifying a singular reality, whatever label ('time'; 'space-time/time-space'), we choose to assign it. What is important—unlocking the purpose of the Source Field for Wilcock—is its identification as the key to human meaning.

New Age thinking, aka the cosmology of 2012, advances *beyond pantheism*. Despite self-aggrandizement by offering an 'erudite' worldview—meshing 'scientific thinking' with 'super-sensible awareness'—at its core, the 2012 creed remains *occult* paganism.

The more recent and much more thoughtful treatment of a cosmology that incorporates the 'new science' still keeps its distance from traditional theism. It espouses a multi-layered expression of nature, as we discussed in Chapter Two and in this chapter. This updated view is more sophisticated, more scientific, and certainly more mystical. Nevertheless, it still does not make room for the God of the Bible. It meshes the divine as defined by the pantheists into the 'other side' of space-time (time-space as it is considered a 'reciprocal' to space-time). It is for these reason that despite the more 'spiritual' quality of the cosmology championed by its proponents, it lacks the opportunity to distinguish *personality* from the cosmos. Personality is not based upon an infinite point of reference if it is to be more than an artifact of creation. Indeed, even in this more magical nature of the latest take on physics, there is no place reserved for God to exist anywhere except in nature—however nuanced or articulated. And if God cannot transcend his creation, by the Judeo-Christian definition, He cannot be God.

In fact, it is this very issue of transcendence (that at their core metaphysical bases), divides Judaism and Christianity. Judaism believes that God is so 'other' from His creation, it is impossible and unthinkable that He could be incarnated in human flesh as Christians express through *their central affirmation of faith:* Jesus Christ is 'fully God' as well as 'fully human'. The New Testament is quite emphatic—Jesus Christ is God. As the evangelist John said quoting Jesus in response to Philip's request to "show us the Father, "*Anyone who has seen me has seen the Father. How can you say, 'Show us the Father'?"* (John 14:9, New International Version). But in Judaism, the Messiah, while anointed of God, is not thought of as 'divine'—and certainly not synonymous with God. God could never be born of a woman.

Despite this cosmological 'constant' proposed by Judaism, at Christmastime, over 2,000 years ago, we who are Christians believe in what was thought impossible by Jesus contemporaries and by Jews today. Something that could never happen in the cosmos created by their God—Yahweh—*did happen*: God became a human being, lived fully as a human, and submitted his body to death redeeming humankind and the creation, reconciling the world to Himself (i.e., making things right once again). This is the essence of the *evangel*—the gospel—*the good news.*

Paul provides His testimony:

So from now on we regard no one from a worldly point of view. Though we once regarded Christ in this way, we do so no longer.

Therefore, if anyone is in Christ, he is a new creation; the old has gone, the new has come!

All this is from God, who reconciled us to Himself through Christ and gave us the ministry of reconciliation;

That God was reconciling the world to Himself in Christ, not counting men's sins against them. And He has committed to us the message of reconciliation.

We are therefore Christ's ambassadors, as though God were making His appeal through us. We implore you on Christ's behalf: Be reconciled to God.

God made Him who had no sin to be sin for us, so that in Him we might become the righteousness of God.

(II Corinthians 5:15-21, New International Version).

And of course, it is the incarnation of God into the man Jesus, that is, in the final analysis, the most distinctive element of Christianity for it brings together many of the other core assertions of what the Bible teaches regarding the cosmos. John says it famously well in the prologue to his gospel:

In the beginning was the Word, and the Word was with God, and the Word was God.

He was with God in the beginning.

Through Him all things were made; without Him nothing was made that has been made.

In Him was life, and that life was the light of men.

The light shines in the darkness, but the darkness has not understood it...

He was in the world, and though the world was made through Him, the world did not recognize Him.

He came to that which was His own, but His own did not receive Him.

Yet to all who received Him, to those who believed in His name, He gave the right to become children of God—children born not of natural descent, nor of human decision or a husband's will, but born of God.

The Word became flesh and made His dwelling [tabernacled] among us.

(John 1:1-5, 10-14, New International Version).

With this invitation to the reader to adopt the biblical cosmology (and Jesus Christ, the Bible's protagonist), Book One is concluded.

NOTES

[1] At the Chicago World's Fair in 1893, Nikola Tesla and George Westinghouse provided electrical lighting at a special exhibit there—switching on a revolution, so to speak in illumination.

[2] Stearman, Gary, *Time Travelers of the Bible: How Hebrew Prophets Shattered the Barriers of Time-Space*, Crane, Mo: Defender Books, 2011, p. 171.

[3] Ibid., p. 225.

[4] Wilcock, *The Source Field Investigations*, op. cit., p. 271.

[5] Wilcock describes the effects of tornadoes, waterfalls, and several other situations where there is enough added speed to the molecular activi-

ty in space-time, that space-time springs a leak and pushes molecules over into time-space.

[6] Cited by Wilcock on p. 274, referencing the account from the book, *The Bermuda Triangle*, written by Charles Berlitz.

[7] Ibid., p. 277.

[8] Ibid., p. 278, quoting Vladimir B. Ginzberg, "About the Paper" from his web site, Spiral Field Theory Website, 2000. http://web.archive.org/web/20010217014501/http://www.helicola.com/about.html.

[9] Wilcock, *The Source Field Investigations*, op. cit., p. 264.

[10] Wilcock, citing A. F. Weichmann, in the professional science journal, *Experimental Eye Research*, 1986, p. 57.

[11] Wilcock, citing Richard Cox from USC's *Health and Medicine Journal*, pp. 56-57.

[12] Wilcock, op. cit., p. 42.

[13] Ibid., p. 47.

[14] Ibid., p. 53, quoting Manly P. Hall, *The Occult Anatomy of Man*, Los Angeles: Hall Pub. Co; 2nd ed. (1924), pp. 10-12.

[15] Ibid., p. 55.

[16] Reference is to Hancock's book, Supernatural (2007).

[17] Ibid., p. 59.

[18] When Elisha the prophet prays to God, requesting that his servant be able to see the massive army of angels fighting on their behalf (which Elisha could see and his servant obviously couldn't), this doesn't necessarily mean that his servant was 'unspiritual'—it may just have meant that Elisha had sensitivities to 'the other side' while the servant didn't. The two abilities—the first, to be tuned into God's will and purpose, is different than the second, the ability to sense the beings that were present in the adjacent, parallel reality. *"And Elisha prayed, and said, LORD, I pray thee, open his eyes, that he may see. And the LORD opened the eyes of the young man; and he saw: and, behold, the mountain [was] full of horses and chariots of fire round about Elisha."* (2 Kings 6:17)

[19] From Joseph P. Farrell, Scripture, Tradition; Gnosticism, Criticism. An excerpt from *God, History and Dialectic*.

[20] This is not to say that 'spirit' is less real than 'matter'—the substance of eternity, whatever that may be—is more real. But realities existing in time-space may not be purely 'spirit'—they may be but *matter* in a different form.

[21] Wilcock opens his book discussing the *Backster Effect*, which was documented by Cleve Backster in 1966, after leaving the CIA. See Discussion beginning on p. 13. Backster connected plants to polygraphs and could

see electrical impulses from the plants when they were threatened—simply from an emotional state raised by the human 'threatening' them. We read,

> The very moment the imagery of burning that leaf entered my mind, the polygraph recording pen moved rapidly to the top of the chart! No words were spoken, no touching the planet, no lighting of matches, just my clear intention to burn the leaf. The plant recording showed dramatic excitation. To me this was a powerful, high-quality observation... I must state that, on February 2, 1966, at 13 minutes, 55 seconds into that chart recording, my whole consciousness changes. I then thought, "Gee, it's as though this plant read my mind!

Quoted by Wilcock, p. 15, from Backster, Cleve, *Primary Perception: Biocommunication with Plants, Living Foods and Human Cells.* Anza, CA: White Rose Millennium Press, 2003, p. 25. http://www.primaryperception.com.

[22] Ibid., p. 243.

[23] Ibid., p. 243.

[24] Ibid. p. 243.

[25] Ibid., p. 243.

[26] Kirlian photography, named after Semyon Kirlian, was a phenomenon that placed images on photographic material from a living object, even when a portion of the object was removed from the plate capturing the image. In the 1939 discovery, a leaf was cut and the tip discarded. But the full image of the leaf still shown on the image of a subsequent photograph suggesting that photons emitted from the leaf (or some other energy) remained present despite the tip of the leaf being removed.

[27] Ibid., p. 246.

[28] These citations are from the New International Version of the Bible.

[29] As I have indicated in other comments, exorcism, by itself, is not essentially the primary means to achieve the end—which is the health of the human psyche and the reconciliation of a person beset with mental health problems. It is one weapon in the arsenal of the spiritual counselor, but it is not the only tool and is not likely the primary tool. The healing process, such as described briefly regarding those who are victims of satanic ritual abuse and dissociative identity disorder requires significant painstaking care and counsel with the professional who performs the counseling.

[30] The field of exorcism has received more credibility due to the scholarly work of Scott Peck, author of the popular book, *The Road Less Traveled.* Peck confessed to be a Christian in later works and provided studies on the subject of evil and exorcism. I provide the following synopsis of his work in Wikipedia as a small point to lend credibility to the discussion for those who assume exorcism is superstition and the work of frauds:

M. Scott Peck, an American psychiatrist, wrote two books on the subject, *People of the Lie: The Hope For Healing Human Evil*, and *Glimpses of the Devil: A Psychiatrist's Personal Accounts of Possession, Exorcism, and Redemption*.

Peck describes in some detail several cases involving his patients. In *People of the Lie: The Hope For Healing Human Evil* he gives some identifying characteristics for evil persons whom he classifies as having a character disorder. In *Glimpses of the Devil, A Psychiatrist's Personal Accounts of Possession, Exorcism, and Redemption* Peck goes into significant detail describing how he became interested in exorcism in order to debunk the "myth" of possession by evil spirits–only to be convinced otherwise after encountering two cases which did not fit into any category known to psychology or psychiatry. Peck came to the conclusion that possession was a rare phenomenon related to evil. Possessed people are not actually evil; they are doing battle with the forces of evil. His observations on these cases are listed in the Diagnostic and Statistical Manual of Mental Disorders (IV) of the American Psychiatric Association.

[31] Stearman, op. cit., p. 177.

[32] I have personally provided David with extensive feedback on his argument which he articulated with great care and professionalism. I esteem his treatment of scripture and recommend his works highly to the reader.

[33] Ibid., p. 179.

[34] Ibid., p. 187.

[35] See Douglas Hamp's *Corrupting the Image* (Defender 2011), for an extended treatment of the patristic teaching regarding this subject.

BIBLIOGRAPHY

Andrews, Samuel J., *Christianity and Anti-Christianity in Their Final Conflict*, Chicago, IL, The Bible Institute Colportage Association, 1937, 358 pages.

Baker, Russ, *Family of Secrets: The Bush Dynasty, America's Invisible Government, and the Hidden History of the Last Fifty Years*, Bloomsbury Press, New York, 2009, 379 pages.

Baigent, Michael and Leigh, Richard, *The Temple and the Lodge*, Arcade Publishing, New York, 1989, 306 pages.

Bauval, Robert and Gilbert, Adrian, *The Orion Mystery: Unlocking the Secrets of the Pyramids*, New York, Three Rivers Press, 1994, 325 pages.

Braden, Gregg, *Fractal Time: The Secret of 2012 and a New World Age*, Hay House, Inc., Carlsbad, CA., 2009, 253 pages.

Braden, Russell, Pinchbeck, Jenkins, et al., *The Mystery of 2012*, Sounds True, Boulder, CO., 2009, 465 pages.

Bradley, Michael, *The Secrets of the Freemasons*, Barnes & Noble, New York, 2006, 208 pages.

Butler, Alan and Dafoe, Stephen, *The Knights Templar Revealed*, Barnes & Noble, New York 1999, 233 pages.

Byrne, Rhonda, *The Secret*, Atria Books, New York, 198 pages.

Chesterton, G.K., *Orthodoxy*, Image Books, Doubleday, 1959, 170 pages.

Church, J.R., *Guardians of the Grail: And the Men Who Rule the World*, Prophecy Publications, Oklahoma City, OK., 1989, 318 pages.

Collins, Andrew, *Beneath the Pyramids: Egypt's Greatest Secret Uncovered*, Virginia Beach, VA, A.R.E. Press, 2009, 262 Pages.

Dawkins, Richard, *The God Delusion,* First Mariner Books, New York, 2008, 463 pages.

Dizdar, Russ, *The Black Awakening: Rise of the Satanic Super Soldiers and the Coming Chaos,* Canton, OH., 2009, 661 pages.

Ehrman, Bart D., *Truth and Fiction in The Da Vinci Code,* New York, Oxford University Press, 2004, 207 pages.

Ellis, Joseph J., *American Creation: Triumphs and Tragedies at the Founding of the Republic,* Alfred A. Knopf, New York, 2007, 283 pages.

Epstein, Orit Badouk, Schwartz, Joseph, and Schwartz, Rachel Wingfield, *Ritual Abuse and Mind Control: The Manipulation of Attachment Needs,* London, UK, Karnac Books, 2011, 183 pages.

Estulin, Daniel, *The Bilderberg Group: The True Story of,* Walterville, OR., Trineday, 2005, 398 pages.

Farrell, Joseph P., *The SS Brotherhood of the Bell: The Nazis' Incredible Secret Technology,* Kempton, IL., 2006, 459 pages.

-----------, *Genes, Giants, Monsters and Men: The Surviving Elites of the Cosmic War and their Hidden Agenda,* Port Townsend, WA., Feral House, 2011, 239 pages.

-----------, *The Philosophers' Stone: Alchemy and the Secret Research for Exotic Matter,* Port Townsend, WA., Feral House, 2009, 350 pages.

Ferguson, Marilyn, *The Aquarian Conspiracy: Personal and Social Transformation in the 1980s,* J.P. Tarcher, Los Angeles, 1980, 448 pages.

Flew, Anthony, *There Is A God,* Harper One, New York, 2007, 222 pages.

Flynn, David, *Temple at the Center of Time: Newton's Bible Codex Deciphered and the Year 2012,* Official Disclosure, A Division of Anomalous Publishing House, (Crane, Mo.), 2008, 296 pages.

Garrison, Jim, *America as Empire: Global Leader or Rogue Power?* San Francisco, Berrett-Koehler Publishers, Inc., 224 pages.

Geryl, Patrick, *The World Cataclysm in 2012: The Maya Countdown to the End of Our World*, Adventures Unlimited Press, Kempton, Illinois, 2005, 273 pages.

Hale, Christopher, *Himmler's Crusade*, Edison, NJ, Castle Books, 2006, 422 pages.

Hall, Manly P., *The Secret Destiny of America*, New York, Tarcher/ Penguin Books, first published, 1944, 262 pages.

Hamp, Douglas, *Corrupting the Image: Angles, Aliens, and the Antichrist Revealed*, Crane, MO., Defender Books, 348 pages.

Hancock, Graham, *Supernatural: Meetings with the Ancient Teachers of Mankind,* New York, The Disinformation Company, 2007, 468 pages.

Hancock, Graham and Bauval, Robert, *The Master Game: Unmasking the Secret Rulers of the World*, The Disinformation Company, 2007, 636 pages.

Hoagland, Richard C. and Bara, Mike, *Dark Mission: The Secret History of NASA*, Feral House, Port Townsend, WA., 2009, 616 pages.

Heron, Patrick, *The Nephilim and the Pyramid of the Apocalypse,* Citadel Press, Kensington Publishing, New York, 2004, 241 pages.

Hitchcock, Mark, *2012: The Bible and the End of the World*, Harvest House Publishers, Eugene, OR., 2009, 184 pages.

-------------, *Who is the Antichrist: Answering the Question Everyone Is Asking*, Harvest House Publishers, Eugene, OR., 198 pages.

-------------, *The Late Great United States: What Bible Prophecy Reveals About America's Last Days*, Multnomah Books, Colorado Springs, CO., 2009, 191 pages.

Horn, Thomas R., *Nephilim Stargates: The Year 2012 and the Return of the Watchers*, Anomalous Publishing House, (Crane, MO.), 2007, 232 pages.

------------, *Apollyon Rising: 2012*, Anomalous Publishing, Crane, MO., 2009, 352 pages.

Horn, Dr. Thomas, Editor, *Pandemonium's Engine, Satan's Imminent and Final Assault on the Creation of God*, Defender Books, Crane, MO., 2011, 372 pages.

------------, *God's Ghostbusters*, Defender Books, Crane, MO., 2011, 480 pages.

Horowitz, Mitch, *Occult America*, New York, Bantam Books, 2009, 290 pages.

Howarth, Stephen, *The Knights Templar*, Barnes & Noble, New York, 1982, 321 pages.

Hunley, Raymond C. Ph.D., *Will the World End in 2012?* Thomas Nelson, Nashville, TN., 2010.

Hunt, Dave, *A Woman Rides the Beast: The Roman Catholic Church and the Last Days*, Harvest House Publishers, Eugene, OR., 549 pages.

James, Terry, *The American Apocalypse: Is the United States in Bible Prophecy?* Harvest House Publishers, Eugene OR., 292 pages.

Jenkins, John Major, *Maya Cosmogenesis 2012*, Bear & Company Publishing, Rochester, Vermont, 1998, 425 pages.

Jeremiah, Dr. David, *The Coming Economic Armageddon: What Bible Prophecy Warns about the New Global Economy*, Faithwords, New York, 2010, 293 pages.

Jones, Marie D., *2013: The End of Days or a New Beginning?* New Page Books, Franklin Lakes, NJ., 2008, 286 pages.

Joseph, Frank, *Atlantis and 2012*, Rochester, VT., Bear & Company Books, 2010, 246 pages.

Jung, C.G., *Flying Saucers: A Modern Myth of Things Seen in the Skies*, MJF Books, New York, 1978, 138 pages.

Knight, Christopher, and Butler, Alan, *Before the Pyramids: Cracking Archeology's Greatest Mystery*, Watkins Publishing, London, 2009, 271 pages.

Kreisberg, Glenn, Editor, *Lost Knowledge of the Ancients: A Graham Hancock Reader*, Bear and Company, Rochester, Vermont, 2010, 241 pages.

Lapin, Rabbi Daniel, *America's Real War: An Orthodox Rabbi Insists that Judeo-Christian Values are Vital for Our Nation's Survival*, Multnomah Publishers, Sisters, OR., 1999, 377 pages.

Lawrence, Joseph E., *Apocalypse 2012: An Investigation into Civilization's End*, Broadway Books (New York), 2007, 2008, 262 pages.

Levenda, Peter, *Sinister Forces: A Grimoire of American Political Witchcraft, Book One: The Nine*, Walterville, OR., Trineday, 2005, 371 pages.

Livio, Mario, *The Golden Ratio: The Story of Phi, the World's Most Astonishing Number*, Broadway Books, New York, 2002, 294 pages.

Lowe, David W., *Earthquake Resurrection: Supernatural Catalyst for the Coming Global Catastrophe*, Wichita, KN., 2005, 323 pages.

----------------, *Then His Voice Shook the Earth, Mount Sinai, The Trumpet of God, and the Resurrection of the Dead in Christ*, Seismos Publishing, Wichita, KN., 165 pages.

----------------, *Deconstructing Lucifer: Reexamining the Ancient Origins of the Fallen Angel of Light*, Seismos Publishing, Wichita, KN., 2011, 241 pages.

Lutzer, Erwin W., *Hitler's Cross: The Revealing Story of How the Cross of Christ was Used as a Symbol of the Nazi Agenda*, Chicago, IL., Moody Press, 1995, 216 pages.

Marrs, Jim, *Rule by Secrecy*, Harper Collins, New York, 2000, 467 pages.

------------, *PSI Spies: The True Story of America's Psychic Warfare Program*, New Page Books, Franklin Lakes, NJ., 2007, 319 pages.

------------, *The Rise of the Fourth Reich: The Secret Societies that Threaten to Take Over America*, HarperCollins Publishers, New York, 2008, 435 pages.

------------, *The Trillion Dollar Conspiracy: How the New World Order, Man-made Diseases, and Zombie Banks are Destroying America*, HarperCollins, New York, NY., 2010, 452 pages.

Marzulli, L.A., *Politics, Prophecy, and the Supernatural: The Coming Great Deception and the Luciferian Endgame*, Anomalous Publishing, Crane, Mo., 2007, 248 pages.

------------, *The Cosmic Chess Match*, Malibu, CA., Spiral of Life, 2011, 336 pages.

Monteith, Dr. Stanley, *Brotherhood of Darkness*, Radio Liberty, Soquel, CA., 2000, 160 pages.

Nietzsche, Friedrich, *The Antichrist: A Criticism of Christianity*, New York, Barnes and Noble Publishing, 2006, Originally Published in 1896, 77 pages.

------------, *Thus Spoke Zarathustra*, Barnes and Nobles Classics, New York, NY., 2005 (First published in 1883), 315 pages.

Nostradamus, *The Complete Prophecies of Nostradamus*, A & D Publishing, Radford, VA, 2007, 151 pages.

Newton, Sir Isaac, *Revised History of Ancient Kingdoms: A Complete Chronology*, Larry and Marion Pierce, Editors, Master Books, Green Forest, AR., Revised Edition, 2009, 205 pages.

Ravenscroft, Trevor, *The Spear of Destiny*, Samuel Weiser Inc., York Beach, Maine, 1st American Edition, 1973, 362 pages.

Ravenscroft, Trevor and Wallace-Murphy, Tim, *The Mark of the Beast: The Continuing Story of the Spear of Destiny*, Weiser Books, Boston, MA., 1990, 245 pages.

Redfern, Nick, *The NASA Conspiracies: The Truth Behind the Moon Landings, Censored Photos, and the Face on Mars*, New Page Books, Pompton Plains, NJ., 2011, 237 pages.

Pauwels, Louis and Bergier, Jacques, *The Morning of the Magicians: Secret Societies, Conspiracies, and Vanished Civilizations*, Destiny Books, Rochester, Vermont, 1960, 414 pages.

Perloff, James, *The Shadows of Power: The Council on Foreign Relations and the American Decline*, Western Islands Publishers, Appleton, WI., 1988, 272 pages.

Picknett, Lynn and Prince, Clive, *The Stargate Conspiracy: Revealing the Truth behind Extraterrestrial Contact, Military Intelligence and the Mysteries Of Ancient Egypt*, Berkley Books, New York, 1999, 425 pages.

Pinchbeck, *Daniel, 2012: The Return of Quetzalcoatl*, New York, Penguin Group, 2007, 411 pages.

--------------, *Breaking Open the Head: A Psychedelic Journey into the Heart of Contemporary Shamanism*, Broadway Books, New York, 2002, 322 pages.

Sanger, Mel, *2012: The Year of Project Enoch?* Rema Marketing, London, 2009, 253 pages.

Shorto, Russell, *Descartes' Bones: A Skeletal History of the Conflict Between Faith and Reason*, Vintage Books / Random House, New York, 2008, 299 pages.

Stearman, Gary, *Time Travelers of the Bible: How Hebrew Prophets Shattered the Barriers of Time-Space*, Crane, MO., Defender Books, 2011, 539 pages.

Stenger, Victor J., *God: The Failed Hypothesis, How Science Shows That God Does Not Exist*, Prometheus Books, Amherst, NY., 2007, 294 pages.

Stevens, Henry, *Dark Star: The Hidden History of German Secret Bases, Flying Disks and U-Boats,* Adventures Unlimited, Kempton, IL., 366 pages.

Thomas, I.D.E., *The Omega Conspiracy: Satan's Last Assault on God's Kingdom,* Anomalous Publishing, Crane, MO., 2008, 195 pages.

Vision Revisited, *The Antichrist Identity,* Prime Republic Ltd., London, 2008, 179 pages.

Vowell, Sarah, *The Wordy Shipmates,* New York, River Bend Books, 2004, 254 pages.

von Däniken, Erich, *Chariots of the Gods,* Berkeley Books (Penguin Putnam), New York, 1999, 200 pages.

Wilcock, David, *The Source Field Investigations: The Hidden Science and Lost Civilizations behind the 2012 Prophecies,* Dutton / Penguin Group, New York, 2011, 536 pages.

Woodward, S. Douglas, *Are We Living in the Last Days? The Apocalypse Debate in the 21st Century,* Woodinville, WA., Faith-Happens, Inc., 2009, 312 pages.

----------, *Decoding Doomsday: The 2012 Prophecies, the Apocalypse and the Perilous Days Ahead,* Crane, Mo., 2010, 380 pages.

----------, *Black Sun, Blood Moon: Can We Escape the Cataclysms of the Last Days?* Crane, MO., 2011, 212 pages.

INDEX

rhodium, 82
Richard Dawkins, 63
Richard Leigh, 149, 170
Richard Wagner, 10, 53, 55
Rick Strassman, 249
Ringo Star, 228
Rite of Exorcism, 224
Ritual Abuse and Mind Control:
    The Manipulation of Attachment
    Needs, 222
Ritual and Dogma of High Magic,
    118
Rob Skiba, xxi
Robert Bauval, 230
Robert Boyle, 39
Robert Frost, 51
Robert Jackson, 173
Robert Schuller, 134
Robert Wentworth Little, 39
Robert Youngson, 74
Robespierre, 136
Rockefeller, 178
Rockefeller Foundation, 187
Rockefellers, 30
Rodrigo Borgia, 10
Roger Boscovitch, 67, 72
Roman Catholic, 224
Roman Polanski, 219
Romanov Court, 53
Rome, 3, 8, 178, 193, 200
Rosemary's Baby, 220
Rosicrucian, 146
Rosicrucian Society, 39, 59
Rosicrucianism, 206
Rosicrucians, 144, 145, 148, 198,
    230, 249
Rothschilds, 30
Royal Academy, 41
Royal Society, 39, 68, 145, 151, 198
Rudolf Bultmann, 61
Rudolf Glauer, 47
Rudolf Hess, 182, 186

Rudolf Steiner, 40, 46, 55, 100
Rupert Murdoch, 132
Russ Baker, 34
Russ Dizdar, xxi, 225, 226
Russia, 174
Salem, Massachusetts, 105
Samuel Mathers, 40
San Antonio World's Fair, 197
Sanat Kumara, 125
Sarah Vowell, 138
Satan, 30, 156, 264, 266
Satan disguises himself as an angel
    of light, 156
satanic ritual abuse, 219, 220, 225,
    227
satanic super soldiers, 226
Satanism, 110
Satanist, 108
Saw Rohmer, Peck, 40
scaffolding filling an immense
    cathedral, 76
scaffolding in the cathedral, 77
Scorpio, 106
Scotland, 39
Scott Peck, 273
Scrooge, 245
Seal of the Senate, 177
Seal of the United States Courts,
    177
séances, 109
Second Reich, 57
Secret Doctrine, 45, 48, 123, 154
secret societies, 42
Secret Societies, 162, 196
Secretary of War Edwin M.
    Stanton, 115
Semyon Kirlian, 273
Senator Frank Church, 233
seraphim, 266
Seth, 155
Seven Sisters, 210
Shakespeare, 152

ABOUT THE AUTHOR

Over the past three years, S. Douglas Woodward ("Doug") has authored four books on the topics of biblical prophecy, the history of millenarianism, and apologetics. He has contributed to two other books published by Defender Books: *Pandemonium's Engine* (2011) and *God's Ghostbusters* (2011). He is a frequent guest on radio and television shows dealing with these topics.

His 'day job' is as an independent consultant serving emerging companies. Over the past twelve years, Doug has served as CEO, COO, and CFO of numerous software and Internet companies. Prior to his tenure in entrepreneurial efforts, he worked as an executive for Honeywell, Oracle, Microsoft, and as a Partner at Ernst & Young LLP. His technical background is in enterprise business strategy, software development and most recently in venture financing and business strategy.

Doug grew up in Oklahoma City, going to high school there and college at nearby Norman. At 15, Doug was struck with a serious form of adolescent cancer, *Rhabdomyorsarcoma*, which forced him to lose his left leg as a means to treat the disease. At the time of his illness (1969), recovery was likely in only 10% of the cases diagnosed. The experience had a dramatic impact upon Doug's spiritual life, linking him with dozens of family members, friends, ministers, nurses and doctors who showed great compassion and provided him with remarkable support.

Doug attended the University of Oklahoma where he received an Honors Degree in *Letters* (Bachelor of Arts), graduating Cum Laude. Upon graduation, for three years Doug served as a Youth Minister and Associate Pastor in the Methodist and Reformed Churches for before experimenting with the computer industry as a possible career choice. He grew to love it and has spent thirty-five years in various capacities there. He has written various articles and spoken at many conferences and seminars on topics related to information technology throughout his career. Through the years, Doug has also served in various capacities in Methodist, Presbyterian, and Reformed Churches. Most recently, Doug served as Elder in the Presbyterian Church.

Doug lives with his wife Donna and together they are celebrating thirty-seven years of marriage. They have two adult children, Corinne, and Nicholas, and several dogs treated far too well.

BLACK SUN, BLOOD MOON

"Woodward addresses prophetic topics with the precision of a scholar and the concern of a committed believer."

In this book, Woodward digs deep into traditional prophetic subject matter, including the real meaning of many crucial Bible passages and many fascinating subjects, including:

- *Escaping the Cataclysms of the Apocalypse,*
- *The Nature of the Afterlife,*
- *The Bible and Immortality,*
- *The Identity of the Antichrist,*
- *Predicting the Date When All These Things Happen*
- *The Creation Account and its Implications on the End of the World,*
- *the Book of Enoch,*
- *the Nephilim*
- *and many other timely topics.*

At the heart of the book is Woodward's call for personal preparation and the expression of a confident hope in the Bible's promises for those living during 'the end of days.'
We can escape the cataclysms to come and find hope while we are keeping watch!

$14.95   WWW.BLACKSUNBLOODMOONBOOK.COM

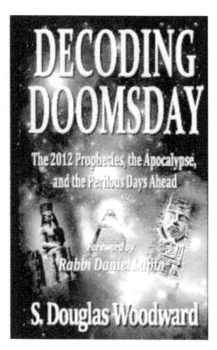

ARE WE LIVING IN THE LAST DAYS?
THE APOCALYPSE DEBATE IN THE 21ST CENTURY

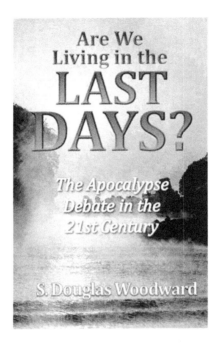

Are We Living in the Last Days? In this study, Woodward argues that how we interpret the Bible, our hermeneutic, determines what we believe about prophecy in the Bible. The author examines the three dominant Protestant methods for interpreting the Bible (Mainline Denomination Liberalism, Covenantal Theology and Dispensational Theology) and their respective positions on new and classic topics of the Apocalypse to shed light on their meaning today. In exploring the prophetic subjects, many other pertinent issues are tackled including the Gnostic gospels, the dangers of literalism, how Liberalism and Evangelicalism differ on the meaning of truth in the Bible, and why some theologians dismiss the future value of Bible Prophecy.

$19.95 WWW.FAITH-HAPPENS.COM

Made in the USA
Monee, IL
22 March 2021